About To UnEat an Elephant

What happens in childhood never stays in childhood

*It shouldn't be too hard
to gather everyone together*

*Unless someone at the table
can no longer swallow the family secrets*

*How far can a daughter challenge
her father before the entire family implodes?*

After a childhood of isolation, Cherilyn won her independence when she left the woods and her father's belt behind. As she embarks on a journey of self-discovery, she finds it complicated to live like "normal" people.

She misses her family. Her biggest dream is to gather them around a table to celebrate life. The knowledge, people, and places she's experienced have inspired her to live more authentically, but sometimes that means breaking the family rules.

When her siblings join her in the real world, Cherilyn hopes they can support each other. But survivors of family secrets each have their own way of dealing with the past. It seems their differences might divide them when they need each other the most.

This is the true story of a young woman trying to preserve relationships with her family while seeking the freedom to become her true self.

To Uneat an Elephant is the sequel to **Chasing Eden**.

Reviews

"To Uneat an Elephant," the stand-alone sequel to "Chasing Eden," is both poignant and captivating. It was very difficult to put it down! " -Susan

"Riveting. I couldn't stop reading. With haunting honesty and vulnerability, Cherilyn Clough pens well-chosen words, metaphors, an analogy to bring us on her journey from childhood insecurity to brave hopefulness and healing freedom." -Janis Wyman Mayfield

"The author's writing style in "To Uneat an Elephant" is intimate and inviting, akin to sharing heartfelt stories with a close friend over a comforting cup of coffee. The raw and authentic portrayal of the protagonist's struggles and triumphs creates a deep connection with the reader." -Brooke Bigelow

"To Uneat an Elephant" has everything I love about the memoir genre: the ability to enter into another person's experience and realize that the human condition is as unique and complex as each of us. Cherilyn has beautifully written about how a youth spent in the midst of the tangle of neglect, parental mental illness, fear, and love can emerge into adulthood and emerge as a beautiful and complicated life." -Sarah Cooper

"I felt like I was right in the story, Cherilyn's writings have impacted me in a profound way and strengthened my understanding of what others might be going through." -Merry Herrman

There's a moment in this book where Cherilyn loses her temper at her brother's girlfriend for describing their family as "dysfunctional." As anyone who read Clough's previous memoir, "Chasing Eden," already knows, "dysfunctional" is a very apt descriptor that maybe doesn't go far enough to describe the way in which Clough and her siblings were raised by their ultra-fundamentalist parents. Her reaction to that word in the context of the story she's telling alerts the reader not that the brother's girlfriend is wrong in her assessment but rather reminds us of how deeply enmeshed such family dynamics can be. Throughout this memoir, Cherilyn struggles to build an adult life apart from her family, but still feels tied to them by bonds of love, worry, fear, and duty. -Trudy Morgan-Cole

"When I read Cherilyn's books, I want them to go on forever!" -Esther Recinos

"Cherilyn Christen Clough's "To Uneat an Elephant" deftly examines the trials and triumphs of finding and protecting your freedom from oppressive religious institutions enforced within your own family. Clough avoids retreading the same territory from her first memoir, "Chasing Eden," and instead shows us exactly how difficult and rewarding it is to become free indeed." -Bonnie McLean, PhD

"It's not every sequel that can stand alone on its own merit. I waited eagerly for this installment of Cherilyn's story after reading the account of her childhood in a fundamentalist Christian family. I was certainly curious as to how dependent the second installment would be. I can say that it takes a skilled writer to dive into the telling of young adulthood with enough details to inform a reader who might be starting with volume 2. Cherilyn delivers." -Shelley Curtis Weaver

"Clough's ability to weave together such a rich tapestry of her life's experiences is truly commendable. The portrayal of relationships and emotions felt authentic and relatable, drawing me into the story and making me reflect on my own life's journey." -Graeme Johnston

"I love Cherilyn's writing style, her authenticity, and courage in the telling of her story. I just downloaded the Kindle version this afternoon and barely tolerated any interruptions before finishing it." -Laura Nelson

"To UnEat An Elephant" continues the author's story as she moves into adulthood, striving to form an authentic identity, a process that seemed inevitably to be in conflict with parents who are locked into their fearful view of the world. In this volume, the author shares how extreme parental loyalty to certain religious beliefs created such dysfunction and family trauma." =Andrew Dystra

"To Uneat an Elephant" is a riveting and thought-provoking read, infused with true drama that keeps readers engaged until the very end."-Cynthia Zirkwitz, Retired Domestic Abuse Counselor

To Uneat an Elephant
A Memoir

Cherilyn Christen Clough

Little Red Press

Copyright ©2024 Cherilyn Christen Clough
All rights reserved.

No portion of this book may be reproduced in any form without written permission from the publisher or author except as permitted by U.S. copyright law.

Print ISBN: 978-0-9960332-9-9
E-Book ISBN: 978-1-955663-99-1

Cover Art and Design by Emmalee Shallenberger

Disclaimer

This book is a memoir. It reflects the author's recollections. For the sake of space, I've had to combine and condense events, but the stories are true. Names and characteristics have been changed, and dialogue has been recreated. I have done my best to be as honest as possible. I've also been corrected on some points. My sister once claimed that a guy I described as handsome was actually quite homely, but I've allowed such disparities to remain because this is a book about my memories and not hers.

To Lisa Boyl-Davis
My cheerleader,
if it weren't for you,
neither this book,
nor my first memoir
would ever have been written.
Thank you for listening to my stories.
And here's to
all the chosen sisters
who become family by default.

For Jake,
You noticed the elephant first.
You were the brave one
who dared to speak your truth.
For that
I will always love you.

*There's a phrase,
"the elephant in the living room,"
which purports to describe
what it's like to live with
a drug addict,
an alcoholic, an abuser.
People outside such relationships
will sometimes ask,
"How could you let such a business
go on for so many years?
Didn't you see the elephant
in the living room?"
And it's so hard for anyone living
in a more normal situation
to understand the answer
that comes closest to the truth;
"I'm sorry, but
it was there when I moved in.
I didn't know it was an elephant;
I thought it was
part of the furniture."
-Stephen King*

Contents

1 Walking on Sunshine — 1
2 These Dreams — 11
3 What a Feeling — 19
4 Holding Out for a Hero — 29
5 Alone — 37
6 Honesty — 49
7 Footloose — 63
8 Girls Just Want To Have Fun — 73
9 Drive — 81
10 Sweet Child O'Mine — 91
11 Livin' On a Prayer — 99
12 That's What Friends Are For — 107
13 All Out of Love — 121
14 Can't Fight This Feeling — 131
15 Down Under — 143
16 Time After Time — 153
17 Hard Habit to Break — 163

18 A Groovy Kind of Love	171
19 Everybody Wants to Rule the World	183
20 Glory of Love	195
21 Papa Don't Preach	203
22 Nothing's Gonna Stop Us Now	217
23 That's What Love Is For	233
24 Stay For Awhile	243
25 I Just Called to Say I Love You	261
26 I Want to Know What Love Is	271
27 It's All Coming Back to Me Now	279
28 Don't Stop Believin'	289
29 What About Love	301
30 My Life	315
31 Greatest Love of All	325
32 What's Love Got to Do with It	333
33 Straight from the Heart	341
34 You're the Inspiration	349
35 Epilogue–I'm Still Standing	359
Acknowledgements	365
Thank You	367
About the Author	369
Also by	371

1 Walking on Sunshine

*Because you are alive,
everything is possible.*
-Thich Nhat Hanh

When I woke at Ruth and Earl's that morning, I enjoyed a hot shower, looked in the mirror, and winced. Across my shoulder was a red mark. I thought I'd avoided Daddy's belt, but I'd been in such a hurry to pack that I hadn't noticed the welt. I'd worn similar marks before, but this time, I smiled at my foggy reflection because I had finally won my freedom.

The Persuader, as my parents had christened the belt, had hovered over me for twenty years like a dark cloud. I never woke without being aware of its constant threat. And when I fell asleep, I never forgot the way it stung my legs.

The first time Daddy spanked me, I was one week old. He said he had to do it because I was acting spoiled and crying for attention. He claimed it was necessary for my salvation—if I learned to submit to him, I could better submit to God. He repeated this story throughout my childhood to remind me that he was in charge of my salvation.

Everything changed on Mother's Day 1983 when I ran from the Persuader for the last time. A friend had found me a place to stay with strangers, and Daddy finally allowed me to leave because I was almost twenty.

On my first day of freedom, I decided to do something Daddy would never do—get a job. All my life, I'd wanted to live like normal people. From what I could tell, employment was the dividing line between my family and normal people.

When I arrived in College Place, Washington, it was a relief to discover my host was in a wheelchair. I figured I could outrun him if he got any ideas about hurting me, but it didn't take long to realize Earl was a kind soul who would never touch me.

Earl told me that Harris Pine Mills was hiring. The neighbor boy said the pay was better than most jobs on campus. I knew nothing about working in a furniture factory, but it seemed a good place to start since I had no money.

When I stepped out into the sunshine that morning, the Persuader fell from my shoulders like an impotent, outgrown snakeskin. No more walking on eggshells. No more leaping to finish chores. No more wincing as I braced for its sting. I'd enjoyed blue skies, the scent of flowers, and bird songs before, but on my first day of freedom, the sun shone brighter, the lilacs smelled sweeter, and the robins sang louder. My feet danced over the cracks in the sidewalk to know that I was free from Daddy's control.

Ruth suggested I wear my best clothes for the interview, but she hadn't looked in the black garbage bag I'd brought for a suitcase. There was one dress for church and two worn-out blouses. I chose the pink one, which was so faded that it almost looked white. I was so excited to start my new life that I didn't care what anyone thought about my appearance.

College Place was a small town in southeastern Washington State. It surrounded Walla Walla College, a Seventh-day Adventist liberal arts school. The streets had quaint houses, manicured lawns, and friendly dogs. I didn't mind walking a mile to the factory. I wanted to see how other people lived. I was so excited that my heart felt like it was racing down the street ahead of my body. I imagined that every stranger, whether on foot or in a passing car, was a potential friend. Two girls close to my age and dressed in stylish clothing passed me on the opposite sidewalk. They called out, "Good morning," and I smiled and waved in return.

The morning shift had already begun when I arrived at the plant. As I stepped into the large metal building, I was hit with the familiar scent of pine. It smelled just like the Montana woods, and a wave of homesickness washed over me for a moment. But I got over it when I thought of the cabin with no running water and the huge gaps in the walls.

I passed a young woman with red hair wearing a pink shirt and goggles. Her saw screamed as it tore through the wood. A cute guy wearing a hard hat flashed me a smile. He was stacking small chunks of wood and setting them on a conveyor belt where they passed under a sign that read, "Caution: Hot Glue."

Curious, I stood in the middle of the factory, mesmerized by spinning saws and rotating belts. Everything was so loud I wanted to plug my ears. Wondering where to turn, I heard a high-pitched horn honking and turned to find a forklift coming straight at me. The driver slammed on the brakes, and a pallet of wood stacked several feet high slid off the lift and scattered across the floor at my feet.

"Shit! Get out of the road before you get killed!"

As he spit out the words, I could feel the blood rushing to my face. At the sound of laughter, I turned to find several pairs of eyes on me. I wished the smooth concrete floor could open up and swallow me.

"Where's the office?"

The driver tipped his head and pulled out a yellow earplug.

"What?"

He motioned toward the front of the building and jumped off the forklift to begin collecting his scattered load.

Above the screeching saws and rattling equipment, I heard a voice shouting.

"If you're looking for the office, it's up here."

A young woman in a turquoise pantsuit, high heels, and red lipstick waved from the front of the building. She looked like a movie star. A large sign over her head said "Office," and under that, a smaller sign read, "8 days without an accident."

She smiled and offered her hand as I awkwardly followed her through the door.

"I'm Debbie. Can I help you?"

"I need a job."

"Fill out this form, and we'll put you to work."

The words "put you to work" inspired me to hum while I completed the paperwork. I couldn't wait to write to Momma about my first real job. She had worked at Loma Linda Foods when she was in college. I tried to imagine the relief on her face when she opened my letter and found money for groceries.

I had to leave most of the lines blank because I had no work history except babysitting and hauling wood for an old farmer back in Montana. I also didn't have any references. I returned the form to Debbie, who quickly glanced at it and handed it back.

"You forgot your social security number."

Joy evaporated, and panic set in when I realized what I'd done. How could I be so stupid? I forgot I needed a social security number to get a job.

I gave the paper back. "I don't have one."

"You can get one at the Social Security office in Walla Walla."

Feeling dizzy, I tried to slow my breathing and hide my emotions, but Debbie noticed my distress.

"Oh hey, don't worry, we'll hold the job for you. Here, have some chocolate." She held out a jar filled with mini candy bars.

I took one candy, but I knew chocolate couldn't help me. My dilemma was much worse than not having those nine digits. My parents had been trying to protect me by not getting me a social security number. As long as I never got one, I'd be safe. They believed it was only a matter of time before the wrong man got elected for president, and social security numbers could be used as the "mark of the beast."

According to Daddy, the only way to escape the "Time of Trouble" was to live outside of the system. This meant living off-grid where the government had no control over us. The further we moved into the wilderness, the harder it would be for anyone to find us. But now, I'd run pell-mell into the wicked world with all of its hazards.

Debbie leaned over to observe my face. "Are you okay?"

I tried to hold back the tears because I didn't want to look silly, but the truth spilled out. "I don't want the mark of the beast."

At first she looked puzzled, then slowly, a smile of understanding came across her face. "Look, everyone here has a number. I have one. The college president has one, and even the pastors have one. No one can get a job without one. If a social security number is the mark of the beast, then everyone you see on campus will be lost, and I doubt that will happen."

Daddy would call her deceived, but I wanted to believe her. I had to believe her. My future depended on this being true, so I took a deep breath and let the chocolate melt on my tongue.

She encouraged me as I left the room, "You'll be fine. Just get your number so you can start your new job."

If only it were that easy.

Ruth took time off from her nursing job to drive me to the Social Security office the next day. A woman with a beehive hairdo and a pickled expression shook her head.

"Most people get a social security number at birth."

My face flushed with shame as I handed her the birth certificate Momma had given me.

She twisted her lips. "This is not a certified copy. You'll need to send to California for an official one."

I returned to Harris Pine the next day to let Debbie know I was on the slow track to getting a job. She reassured me I'd have one as soon as I returned with that number.

Eager to get on with my new life, I explored the Walla Walla College campus. I filled out forms at the administration building and met with my advisor, Mr. Dickinson. He was a tall, friendly man who asked nosy questions.

"Where are you from?"

"Montana."

"Did you go to Mount Ellis Academy?"

"No, I was homeschooled."

"What does your father do for a living?"

"He's an auto broker."

"What makes you want to take communications?"

"I like writing."

He smiled as he glanced at the form in his hand to remind himself of my name, and then he said, "Well, Christen, I think you've come to the right place."

"Cherilyn."

He tilted his ear toward me, "What?"

"My name is Cherilyn—Christen is my last name."

He chuckled, "People often go by their last names around here. You'll get used to it."

I liked my advisor, but I left his office with a knot in my gut. I felt like a fake. My family was living in Montana when I left them, but I'd grown up in Washington. My dad called himself an auto broker, but he rebuilt and sold insurance totals for a living. The worst omission was saying I was homeschooled when I'd never taken one class. I passed the math section on the GED test by one point to get accepted into college, but I felt too ashamed to tell my advisor such vital information. The only honest thing I'd said was that I liked writing.

For twenty years, I'd been keeping my family's secrets, and even though I'd moved miles away, I still had reasons to continue the practice. My parents told me they might end up in jail if we kids were caught not attending school. My youngest sister, Abby, was still school-age, and I couldn't take a chance on the authorities arresting my parents.

Leaving my advisor, I went downstairs to the financial aid department. A grumpy man looked over my form and returned it, saying it couldn't be processed without my social security number. I reassured him I'd have it within a week.

A week later, Ruth baked a chocolate cake to celebrate the arrival of my proper birth certificate. We'd returned to the Social Security office that day, and I was now the skeptical owner of a new number. I set the little piece of paper on the table and stared at it with fear and trembling. While I described my fears, Ruth and Earl exchanged glances.

With a mischievous smile, Ruth said, "We've had our numbers for years. Do we look like we have the mark of the beast?"

Earl's face beamed as he examined my new acquisition. "This number is the ticket to your future, young lady!"

Their positive vibes helped me sleep peacefully that night.

The next day, I returned to Harris Pine Mills and got hired for $4.25 an hour. I also received my first on-the-job training. For orientation, my supervisor had me try several stations throughout the factory. I came home covered in sawdust from head to toe. Ruth and Earl patiently waited while I took a shower so we could all eat supper together. I loved them for that.

Earl asked about my new job while I devoured my supper.

"The people are friendly, and the job seems easy enough." I was so glad to have a steady paycheck that I was willing to overlook the itchy sawdust.

Ruth knocked on my bedroom door as I prepared for bed that night.

"Here's your mail."

I hoped to hear from Momma, but it was just a letter from the Financial Aid Department. I'd given them my social security number earlier that day. I figured it was just a notice that passed in the mail, but I discovered they wanted something more. They needed a copy of my father's income tax form to process my file.

Long after Ruth and Earl went to sleep, I sat on the floor, rocking against a stack of blankets as quietly as possible. I was trying to figure out what to do. I thought I was finally beyond Daddy's control—that what he did and thought wouldn't affect me anymore—but I was wrong.

There was no way I could produce the necessary document because Daddy hadn't paid taxes since I was born. This was one of the secrets Momma had warned me to never speak about. If the government found out, Daddy could get arrested. And if Daddy went to prison, what would Momma do?

2 These Dreams

*Our truest life is when
we are in dreams awake.
-Henry David Thoreau*

My heart was beating with excitement as I opened the front door to see my family for the first time in six months. My siblings smiled politely with their best behavior as they entered Ruth and Earl's dining room and sat down at the table.

The scent of the yellow roses Ruth brought in from the garden that morning mingled with the aroma of lentil loaf and fresh dilly bread. I chose the blue and yellow placemats because those were Momma's favorite colors.

Despite Momma's dream to be like the Waltons on TV, gathering around the table was a rare occasion for my family. When I was young, Momma took pride in setting a beautiful table, but we'd eaten off paper plates around a wood stove for much of my life. Years of moving and living off-grid in cabins without running water had taken their toll.

As Momma's first-born daughter and right-hand helper, her dream had become mine. I imagined we'd be okay if we ate around a table like the happy families on TV. With Ruth's help, we were going to enjoy a nice meal together, and I wanted everything to be perfect.

Earl rolled his chair to the stereo, slipping a cassette tape into the player. The strains of "Will the Circle be Unbroken?" moved my feet under the table while the Heritage Singers sang softly in the background.

Mara, Jake, and Abby munched on carrot sticks and dilly bread while they listened to Daddy and Earl exchange tales from their logging days. Ruth and Momma quietly traded recipes at the other end of the table. I was relieved to see my parents finding things in common with my hosts, but I was too nervous to eat, so I sat back to bask in the familiar faces. These were the five people I loved most in the entire world. They were the only people I could be myself with, and it felt good to see them.

I felt slightly anxious when Momma took a slice of Ruth's lentil loaf. On special occasions, Momma cooked with dairy, but my parents were strict vegetarians who refused to have an egg in the house because they believed eggs cause cancer. I sighed with relief to see her swallowing without any signs of distress. Perhaps she couldn't taste the egg.

My shoulders grew tense when Earl started asking Daddy questions, but even that seemed to go well. When he asked about my siblings' education, his tone was kind, but Earl didn't realize how much Daddy hated people meddling in his business. He wouldn't tolerate it from the government, and he didn't count any man as a friend who spoke to him about money or how he raised his family.

"Do you have plans for your other children to attend college?"

The room grew silent. Jake and Mara glanced from one adult to another while Abby searched my face for clues that everything was okay. Momma set down her fork while Ruth naively took another bite—not realizing her guests had quit eating.

Daddy glanced at Momma, raised his eyebrows, and cleared his throat. I'd seen this signal to pay attention throughout my childhood.

"The way we raise our family is none of your business." He pushed his chair back and stood up. "Come on, kids, we're leaving."

Acid rose to my throat. This was not how I expected our beautiful meal to end. Hoping I could stall Daddy and change his mind, I raised my voice.

"Wait! I have a present for Momma. Let me find it."

I tried to make eye contact with Momma, but she lowered her eyes and followed Daddy out the door. Mara, Jake, and Abby trailed behind, leaving their half-eaten plates of food on the table.

I rushed out the door while my family got into the van, "Daddy! You came so far—please, just stay a little longer!" I tried to hide the tremor in my voice.

He ignored my pleas as he turned the key in the ignition and backed out of the driveway. I ran after the van until a pinch in my side forced me to stop. When it disappeared around the corner,

I fell to my knees on hot asphalt, with my lungs screaming for oxygen and tears wetting my cheeks. I opened my mouth to wail, but my throat was so dry that nothing came out. Gasping for air, I opened my eyes and sat up in bed.

The mirror on the dresser reflected the full moon outside the open window. The babbling creek in the backyard reminded me that I was in Ruth and Earl's guest room. It was just a dream, but it had awakened a lifetime of unsettled feelings.

I jumped out of bed and grabbed my flashlight. Opening the closet door, I shuffled through a cardboard box until I pulled out four packages of butter mints. Tearing a bag open, I stuffed the pink, yellow, and green pastels into my mouth. I couldn't tell which color I was eating in the dark, but they all tasted alike.

My friend Carla had canceled her wedding and left me with the bridal shower supplies. I told her not to worry—it was better than getting stuck with a husband she didn't want—but I didn't tell her I kept the mints.

Moving to College Place had been a dream come true, but while my new life was beginning to take shape, my family was constantly on my mind. The memory of Mother's Day left me feeling sick. We'd been moving into a mice-infested cabin without running water or power, and I hated moving. I hated living off-grid, and I hated that we couldn't do something nice to celebrate Momma. She deserved better. I'd been invited to live with strangers near the college, but I hadn't prepared to leave right away. When Daddy chased me with the belt, I impulsively chose to leave overnight.

The mints melted like cotton candy on my tongue. I only planned to eat a few, but before I knew it, I'd ripped open a second bag and crammed those into my mouth.

After growing up in isolation without any close friends, my family was everything to me. Winter was coming, and I felt guilty living in a comfortable house with modern conveniences while my family struggled in a rustic cabin. I lay awake at night wondering if my siblings were warm enough or if Momma had enough money for food. Were they still at the cabin, or had Daddy taken them to Seattle this time? There wasn't a phone at the cabin, and nobody answered my letters, so it was hard to know.

I pulled out the third bag of mints but hesitated to eat them. I should have known it was a dream. Daddy would never visit me at Ruth and Earl's. He never liked to discuss how he made a living. The fact that Earl was an accountant only made him seem in cahoots with the government, but there was a time when Daddy and Earl had a lot in common. They'd both worked in the woods, felling trees, until accidents ended their logging careers.

Earl's life changed when a tree fell on his legs. Daddy rolled a backhoe and walked away from it, but the damaged equipment caused his business partner to sue him. They each had a wife and two children at the time of their accidents, but they took different roads afterward.

Earl learned to maneuver in a wheelchair, then studied to become an accountant while Ruth got a degree in nursing. They worked hard to send their children to Christian schools from grade school to college. By the time I came to live with them, their children were grown with children of their own.

Daddy's path was more complicated. He'd dropped out of high school at fifteen to work in the woods. After he got his GED, he went to Pacific Union College, where he met Momma. He was studying to become a pastor when I was born but went back to logging after the birth of my sister, Mara.

I decided to break open the third bag of mints and found myself feeling shaky and nauseous, but I couldn't stop swallowing candy after candy.

Daddy never liked working for anyone but himself. After his accident, he got fired or quit every job he had. As the son of a Danish immigrant, he was always looking for new ways to make fast money.

To complicate our lives further, Daddy didn't believe in women working outside the home, so Momma couldn't get a job even if we were desperate for food. His need for control and his inability to keep a job obstructed our lives at every turn.

Daddy couldn't afford to send us to a private Adventist school, and my parents worried we'd be exposed to drugs and evolution in public school, so my formal education ended in sixth grade. I taught my younger siblings to read, but they had less of an education than I had. When people asked where we went to school, my parents told us to lie and say we were homeschooled even though we didn't have one textbook.

As I grew into my teen years, my family became a sort of prison where my parents controlled every aspect of my life. They controlled what I ate and wore and became suspicious of me when I made friends outside the family.

We moved every six to nine months—often in houses, but sometimes we were homeless, living in motels, campgrounds, or off-grid cabins. Moving made it challenging to make friends, especially since my parents never let me out of their sight. When I did find a friend and asked to spend time with them, Momma said, "We can't have anyone over until all the boxes are unpacked."

One day, I realized the boxes were always in a state of packing or unpacking. In alarm, I shouted, "But the boxes will never be unpacked."

"I'm sorry, honey. Someday, maybe we'll live like normal people."

"But Daddy will never settle down long enough for us to be normal."

Momma sighed because she hated moving as much as I did. "For now, we need to put our lives on hold."

As the years went by, my dreams of having friends, learning to drive, and getting a high school education faded while I waited. Daddy said Jesus would come before I grew up, but four months before my twentieth birthday, I realized Jesus wasn't coming, and it was time to leave.

Most of my college peers couldn't relate to the way I'd been raised, and their families were a mystery to me. When other girls moved into the dorm, I stood in the shadows, watching with fascination as their parents helped them. I wondered what it would be like to have a mom who took me shopping for a banquet dress. Or a dad to carry stacks of boxes to a dorm room before taking me out to dinner. I was grateful for Ruth and Earl. They were kind and helpful, but I still craved being normal, and I always missed my abnormal family.

Too sick to eat more mints, I slid the last bag into the box and quietly shut the closet door. What was wrong with me? Grabbing my pillow, I stuffed it over my mouth and screamed, then collapsed onto the bed. I hoped the pillow would stifle my sobs so I wouldn't wake Ruth and Earl, who were sleeping in the next room.

A church lady once told me that no one is normal. She said to get normal out of my head and accept what was, but she had no clue about my life. Since childhood, I knew other kids had things I didn't. Normal kids lived in a house with a real bed instead of sleeping on the floor. Normal kids took showers at home—not at the state park. Normal kids didn't move every six months. Normal kids didn't live in fear of the belt. And most importantly, normal kids went to school and had friends.

I'd dreamed of being normal my entire life, but I'd almost given up hope until Ruth and Earl invited me to live with them. As far as I could tell, they'd been living like normal their entire lives. If I could just get the secret formula for normal and carry it back to my family, there might be hope for all of us. Daddy and Momma thought I came to Walla Walla College to find a husband. Ruth and Earl thought I had come to get a degree. But I alone knew the truth—I came to find out how normal people live.

3 What a Feeling

*Everything you can
imagine is real.*
-Pablo Picasso

It didn't take long to acquire the skills for my new job. After learning how to sort, stack, and glue wood, I'd graduated to the cleat saw. My arms ached as I pushed board after board through the screeching machine. The blade often kicked sawdust back into my face, making me sneeze, but I was grateful for goggles to protect my eyes. The noisy furniture factory, full of whirring, pounding, and roaring machines, sounded far away, muffled by my earplugs. It was a monotonous job, but the danger was real. In my first week, a coworker cut off the tip of his finger. The memory of his blood pooling on the concrete floor kept me alert.

I glanced at the big clock in front of the plant. Was it only nine-thirty? It seemed like I'd been working for hours. It was

Friday. I was excited because my shift ended at noon, and Ruth had agreed to take me shopping. Millwork was dirty and dangerous but holding that paycheck in my hand made it all worthwhile.

The bell rang for the mid-morning break. I flipped the switch on my machine, removed my gloves and goggles, and pulled the earplugs from my ears. The entire mill had gone silent by the time I lifted my baseball cap with a flourish and shook the sawdust from my long, feathered hair. I knew Billy, who worked across the aisle from me, was watching. He always applauded when I let my hair down. He was cute, but he had a girlfriend. I gave him a friendly smile before stepping out into the sunshine.

My fall-to-gravity haircut had been a gift from a friend back in Trout Creek, and it was my saving grace in this new collegiate world. After a childhood of curly hair, while everyone else wore straight, I'd finally come into my own in the eighties. My clothes might be shabby, but big, messy hair was the latest style, and I had lots of it.

I sat on the bench, took the tweezers out of my pocket, and was pulling a sliver from my finger when Debbie joined me.

"How's it going?"

"I'm grateful for a paycheck, but I leave wearing enough sawdust to cage a hamster every night."

She rolled her eyes. "Would you like to try packing the kits? It's mostly counting pieces of wood, but there's less sawdust on that side of the plant."

I shook my head. "Counting legs and screws for furniture sounds more boring than running a saw."

Colleen, from kit-pack, joined us. "It might be safer, but I still get slivers."

I glanced up at my coworkers. Debbie was the only one wearing a dress and heels. The rest of us wore old clothes, heavy boots, and baseball caps. "I'd like to find a job where I can serve people and not take a shower at the end of my shift."

Colleen nodded. "I go home and dress up. I get tired of dressing like a man."

I squinted at the stubborn sliver. "I used to beg my dad to let me wear blue jeans, but he says it's an abomination for a woman to dress like a man. Now look at me, and I still don't own a pair of jeans."

Another girl named Carol slid closer to me. "I grew up like that and bought jeans with my first paycheck."

Debbie pulled a handful of lipstick samples from her purse and set them on the bench. "I sell Mary Kay, so if any of you gals want a makeover, I can give you a free one."

I wanted to take Debbie up on the offer. I ached to be like these other young women, but I'd been taught a good Christian woman's beauty should only come from within. Daddy had threatened to belt me for wearing tinted lip balm. Momma even called her own mother vain for wearing makeup to church.

The other girls had agreed to meet for a makeup party by the time the bell rang. One lone lipstick sample remained on the bench. Debbie looked at me as if waiting for me to pick it up, but I turned my head and pretended to study the bumblebee in the hanging planter above us.

Debbie took one last sip of her pop, scooped up the lipstick sample, and lowered her voice. "I hear the cafeteria's hiring. They don't pay as well, but it's a people job, and you wouldn't need to shower after work."

I thanked her and headed back to my station. The itchy sawdust seemed more tolerable when I remembered it was payday.

When I got off shift, Debbie stood by the plant door in her cute dress and flawless makeup, holding a clipboard. I wondered what I had in common with someone so polished and popular, but her smile was genuine as she handed me a paycheck and crossed my name off the list.

I passed the Walla Walla College Cafeteria on my way back to Ruth and Earl's and stopped to stare at the tall glass windows. I wondered what it would be like to work there. A line of students entered the building for lunch. It was the center of campus since everyone had to eat. It only offered vegetarian meals, which was fine by me. Those who wanted to eat meat could drive into town. The City of Walla Walla was like any other medium-sized city, with downtown strip malls and plenty of restaurants.

It didn't surprise me that my polyester pants and faded blouse brought a few stares. The students I passed on the sidewalk wore designer clothes. New student orientation was coming up, and I hoped this shopping trip would help me find more stylish clothes.

I rushed through the front door, ran to the bathroom to strip off my itchy clothes, and jumped in the shower. Ruth looked as excited as I felt when I came out clean and dressed.

When I got my first paycheck, I'd asked Ruth for a stamp and envelope to send a letter to Momma. I didn't say what I was doing, but Earl suspected it.

With raised eyebrows, Earl spoke to me in a fatherly tone. "Make sure you save some money for yourself, young lady. You've worked hard for it, don't give it all away."

I knew he meant well, but I figured Earl didn't know my family. He didn't understand how hard Daddy struggled to make ends meet or how much Momma worked to stretch every dollar for food. If I could help them by sending a little cash, I would.

This time, Earl encouraged me to spend my money. "You're only young once. Find something you like and have fun."

Ruth drove to the only mall in Walla Walla at the time. It was so small we went through every store within a couple of hours. We were near the men's section when I smelled the scent of fear mixed with leather. Men's belts in every shade of brown and black caught me off guard. It was an eerie wall of Persuaders. I knew they were meant to hold up slacks, but I felt overcome with the urge to run and hide.

Even though I was far from Daddy, my neck was tense, and my heart began to race. My vision narrowed into a dark tunnel while I fought the urge to dash into a bank of winter coats and hide like a hunted animal. I tried to understand what my body was saying. I stumbled out the door into the mall, where I collapsed on a bench and struggled to catch my breath.

Ruth stood over me with a furrowed brow. "What happened? Are you okay?" Her voice was gentle and kind.

I nodded, but I couldn't understand what was wrong with me. Shopping was something I'd rarely done with my family. Those threatening belts reminded me that life was full of consequences. I felt guilty buying new clothes while my sisters wore rags. What would become of us?

My eyes searched the window displays for an escape. When they fell on a mannequin wearing Calvin Klein jeans, I knew what to do. The only way to fight fear was to face it. I wanted to do something so defiant that the act might bring on the fate I dreaded. Wearing jeans was like flipping the bird to the Persuader and anyone who dared to use it.

Ruth didn't care if I bought jeans. She wore them herself. I slipped into a pair of the forbidden blues and turned around in the three-way mirror to admire my figure. Perfect.

As we left the mall, we stopped for ice cream. A woman passed us with a white poodle begging Ruth for her cone. In the sunlight, I noticed a faint line on Ruth's neck. Was she wearing makeup? I hadn't noticed that before. Whenever neighbor girls wore makeup, Momma called them Jezebels. Jezebel was a wicked queen in the Bible who put on makeup and then fell out the window to be devoured by wild dogs. Watching Ruth pet the poodle, I decided she didn't look any more like a Jezebel than the poodle looked like a wild dog.

Ruth was as good as anyone I met. I could hear her patient voice helping Earl get dressed each morning. She didn't seem to resent that the strapping young man she'd fallen in love with would never walk again. Despite her hard work, she always found ways to serve others.

"Ruth, what do you think about wearing makeup?"

She chuckled. "I once heard a preacher say, 'If the barn needs painting, go ahead and paint it.'"

As I swallowed the last of my chocolate cone, I made a decision. If a wonderful woman like Ruth wore jeans and makeup, I could, too.

A week later, Debbie smoothed my cheek with a makeup sponge. "I figured you might enjoy a makeover."

"Because I look like a country bumpkin?"

She smiled. "There are more country girls around here than you know."

She highlighted my eyes with a brush and then handed me a mirror.

"What do you think?"

I was surprised at the stranger looking back at me. "Do I look like normal people?"

"Aren't you normal?"

"I don't know. Sometimes, it seems like everyone has the secret code but me. Other people know what to wear, what to say, and how to act, while I feel like a freak."

She added a little more blush to my cheeks. "Sometimes you just gotta fake it 'til you make it."

Debbie's advice applied to everything about my new life. I was working hard to be like other people. I didn't want to be that girl who came from the woods wearing granny clothes with pitch stains on her hands and messy, untamed curls. I didn't like people knowing how many times I'd moved, or that I'd been homeless, or had never gone to high school. Most of all, I didn't want anyone to know I'd been beaten with a belt.

It wasn't long before I wore makeup whenever I left the house. If Ruth and Earl noticed, they never said a word. I even wore it to work, which was silly since it gave the sawdust a place to stick.

I took my new look to the cafeteria and got hired on the spot. I was nervous about my new job. It would require asking strangers what they wanted to eat and serving food on their plates. And to be honest, I felt a twinge of sadness to leave Harris Pine Mills. Debbie had been my first friend in this new world, but if she was right about the social security number, maybe she was right about faking it, too.

The first night I worked at the cafeteria, my hands shook as I carefully set food on the plates. The students were hungry and impatient. It was my job to ask what they wanted, but I felt tongue-tied. Beautiful young women dressed in colorful sweaters and cute jeans glared at me as they turned their noses up at the food. Guys in athletic clothes proclaiming their favorite team asked for a second scoop of mashed potatoes.

There were lots of couples. Then came a lone theology major carrying a Bible. He was followed by two engineering majors with their noses in books. They barely looked at me or the food, grunting and pointing when I asked what they wanted. It was hard to concentrate with my boss standing behind me, urging me to go faster. One girl yelled at me for accidentally putting peas on her plate. Others rolled their eyes when I spilled the gravy into the pan of macaroni and cheese.

I was afraid I'd get fired. I wasn't used to talking to people my age and felt insecure. Toward the end of my shift, I remembered what

Debbie said about faking it. I decided to pretend like I was the cheerful girl in the McDonald's commercials on TV. It worked. The people coming through the line had no idea who I was or where I'd been. As far as they were concerned, I was just a friendly girl serving them supper.

A few weeks later, I walked across campus in my Calvin Klein jeans and a red sweater. I tossed my feathered hair as my eyes searched the buildings around me. I had an eerie feeling someone was watching.

When I looked up and saw a guy staring at me from an ivy-framed window on the third floor of the administration building, my heart froze. Momma had warned me that even on a Christian campus, men could hurt me. My breath caught, and I started to look for someone to walk beside, whether I knew them or not. When his attention turned toward another young woman, I resumed my carefree walk. He was probably looking for potential dates. Realizing that he saw me as just another girl on campus gave me a thrill. I was finally beginning to fit in with my peers, and it was the most incredible feeling in the world. Then I had an idea. Normal girls went on dates. If I could pass as normal, I might even get a date.

4 Holding Out for a Hero

*Be yourself;
everyone else
is already taken.
-Oscar Wilde*

Daddy never approved of me going to Walla Walla College. He thought the theology department taught "cheap grace," encouraging people to live sinful lives. His main concern was that I might marry a man who didn't share his religious views. I thanked God that Ruth and Earl were giving me a chance to follow my dreams instead of Daddy's.

Walla Walla College was nicknamed "Western Wedding College," but I wasn't ready for a husband. For twenty years, I'd been told what to wear, what to eat, and what to believe. The thought of a husband telling me what to do made me sick.

Most of my peers had been dating since high school. Socializing was like riding a bicycle for them. They knew what to say and how to act, but I'd never been on a date. Buying designer jeans and a layered haircut wasn't hard, but I couldn't just order a date from the cafeteria menu. I was eager to see if I could fit in with normal people, but I had to wait for someone to ask me out.

Charlie asked me out first, but he failed to mention that his only form of transportation was a motorcycle. Momma called them death traps. Earl was excited about my date—or at least the bike. He and Charlie talked about the ride for several minutes while I tried to think of a way to avoid it. I remained calm outside while Momma's worst-case scenarios played sirens in my head.

Following Charlie out to the bike, I took the helmet from his hands and awkwardly crawled onto the back. I shut my eyes in a desperate prayer for help. My eyes remained closed while I waited for Charlie to take off, but nothing happened. Maybe he sensed how terrified I was and had decided to let me off.

I opened my eyes just as Charlie started the bike and tore off like we were in a race. I clung to his back while he shouted for me to lean to the left or right with each turn. We spun past Whitman College and Fort Walla Walla Museum, then up into the foothills, where Charlie pointed to the Blue Mountains. I couldn't focus on anything he was saying because my mind was full of pictures of bodies and blood splattered across the asphalt. He finally stopped for a milkshake at the Iceberg Drive-In, but fear of death kept me from enjoying my huckleberry shake.

Charlie seemed as relieved as I was when he dropped me off. Like nosy grandparents, Ruth and Earl were waiting in the living room, eager to hear how it went. I appreciated their concern, but I could barely articulate how stressful those two hours had been, so I bid them goodnight and collapsed onto my bed. In the morning, I wrote Momma to tell her how my first date had almost killed me.

Jeff asked me to a movie while I was working in the cafeteria line. I took my time to answer as I scooped his mashed potatoes carefully and put the gravy in a well, hoping to make his plate look as appetizing as possible.

I liked him. I wanted to say yes, but I'd never been to a theater. Daddy said theaters were evil places where holy angels had to wait outside. The thought of losing my heavenly protection scared me.

"I'm sorry, I don't go to movies." I could see the disappointment in his eyes.

The next evening, when Jeff came through the supper line, his eyes wouldn't meet mine. I wanted him to know I was interested. He was wearing a picture of a UFO on his t-shirt from a movie I had never seen, but with my most endearing McDonald's girl smile, I said, "My dad saw a UFO once."

He took the plate from my hands and stared incredulously. "You won't go to movies, but you believe in UFOs? You're crazy."

I heard people snickering in the line behind him. I didn't want people thinking I was crazy or I'd never get a date. Mortified, I scooped up french fries and burritos as fast as possible to keep people moving through the line. While I cleaned up after my shift, the boss complimented my speedy work. That's how I became the fastest server.

I had a crush on Wes when I was sixteen, but our fundamentalist parents didn't believe in dating at the time, so we had to hang out with all of our siblings and never touch each other. It was nice when he looked me up in College Place and took me for a couple of drives. I was able to write to Momma that his green eyes were as dreamy as ever. When I wrote to my family, it was like sending letters to outer space because no one answered. Then Wes's sister came to town and told me that Wes was taking Mara for drives in Montana. I couldn't believe he had the nerve to try dating us both. I didn't blame Mara. She had less dating experience than I had, but why didn't Mara or Momma write to me and let me know?

When Wes returned the following week, I met him at the door.

"I won't allow any guy to come between me and my sister."

He stood in the doorway, begging me to forgive him. It was hard to stay strong while his beautiful green eyes filled with tears, but I shut the door in his face anyway.

All the cute guys loved motorcycles and airplanes. Momma hated airplanes even more than motorcycles. When she met Daddy, he was finishing his pilot's license, but she convinced him to quit. So when Todd invited me to go up in a two-seater, I was conflicted. I was nervous because Momma was scared. At the same time, I was curious to know what Daddy loved about flying. I decided to take a chance. It was such a tiny plane that it felt like we were riding in a soup can above the clouds. I held my breath the entire trip. When I got back on the ground, I decided I'd need a tranquilizer if I went up in such a small plane again. That ended my relationship with Todd.

Dating sucked, but it was my own fault—I was not a fun date. I was afraid of motorcycles, airplanes, restaurants, and movies.

The safest dating opportunities were going for walks or going to church. I had a few dates to the Friday evening service, but it was hard to get to know someone sitting beside them in silence for an hour.

Working at the cafeteria gave me the confidence to talk with strangers, but I wasn't sure what to say when alone with a man. Part of the problem was the family secrets. It was easier to say I was homeschooled than to explain why I had no high school education. When my conscience pricked me for lying, I added that my parents forgot to buy the books. People laughed, but I wasn't joking. I didn't want people to know that I wasn't normal because then I might lose hope of ever becoming normal. I figured the only solution was to keep faking it until I could make it.

I caught a ride to Montana for Christmas that year. It was a relief to find my family living in an old farmhouse close to town with running water and electricity. Momma made the kitchen cozy with the same blue curtains she unpacked from a box and hung every time we moved. Those blue curtains signified home more than any place.

I was annoyed when Daddy told church people that I was majoring in social life, but in a way, he was right. I had a lot to make up for after being separated from my peers for most of my life.

Sitting around a table with the people I loved and enjoying a meal together made me happy. Bringing presents for everyone was fun, and my heart was filled with joy as I returned to school.

I'd only been back a week when Ruth and Earl sat me down to talk with long faces. Earl's sister was dying, and they needed the room I was staying in to take care of her. I was grateful for their hospitality, but my heart sank as I wondered where to find a new place to live.

That night, I pulled the pillows off of the bed and sat on the floor, rocking for hours. Where could I go? I never told Ruth and Earl that I couldn't get financial aid for another year and a half. It wouldn't matter now. I was already going through college at a turtle's pace. Taking two classes a quarter sucked up my income. There was no way I could work enough to pay for classes and rent a place, too.

Meanwhile, I'd agreed to go on a date with Bones. Earl immediately became suspicious when he heard the name. As soon as I got into his car, Bones caught me by surprise by sticking his tongue inside my mouth.

I gagged. No one had kissed me like that before.

I tried to find a way to stall him.

"Let's talk."

"Don't you know there are other ways of talking?"

"Like what?"

"Let's go to the park, and I'll show you."

I had never been to the park with a man. We were not out of the driveway yet, and I was already getting a creepy feeling about Bones. I noticed the living room drapes were still open, or were they opening wider? Earl usually closed them. I could hardly hide the smile on my face when I realized Earl was watching us.

Bones stared at my chest while I turned toward the door handle.

"Does it really matter where we go?"

"Yes, it does. And I'm more interested in talking than kissing."

I grabbed the handle, swung the door open, and raced into the house. By the time I joined Earl at the window, Bones was gone.

Ruth stuck her head out of the kitchen from where she was baking. "That was a short date."

I told them what Bones said, and Ruth walked over to the window and shook her rolling pin fiercely. "You better watch out, Bones, or I'll teach you some other ways of talking."

Earl and I laughed until we had tears rolling down our faces. What a relief to be safe in the comfort of their home—until I remembered I'd soon be on my own. Then my eyes filled with the other kind of tears.

"Thank you. I don't know what I'll do without you guys."

Ruth grabbed a tissue. "Now you're gonna make me cry."

Earl motioned for me to sit down on the sofa. "You were busy getting ready for your date, so we were waiting until you got home to let you know that we found another place for you to stay."

Relief flooded my heart as I thanked them for everything they'd done for me.

Before I moved out, Earl lectured me about money. "You have expenses, so don't be sending your hard-earned money to your parents."

I promised to be careful, but Earl didn't understand my family. We'd been through so much together that we could never be like a regular family. Most families took food and shelter for granted, but my family never had. I could never feel good about sleeping in a bed as long as my siblings had to sleep on the floor. And I could never enjoy a meal without wondering what Momma was trying to scrape together for supper.

Ruth drove me to my new place. The black garbage bag I'd used for a suitcase had been replaced with an apple box of clothes and textbooks. Before she drove off, Ruth left me with some motherly advice.

"Enjoy the simplicity because the more boxes you fill up, the more complicated life will get."

I'd lived with Ruth and Earl for eight months, but I still wasn't sure how to live like a normal person.

5 Alone

Nothing makes us so lonely
as our secrets.
-Paul Tournier

When I crawled up the narrow stairs to my new attic room, I found a handmade quilt on the bed and dried flowers adorning a vase on the bookcase. A small wooden desk sat in front of the window. It was a cozy room, perfectly arranged for a student. After hanging my clothes in the narrow closet, I went downstairs for supper.

My new hosts, Bill and Mabel, were a friendly retired couple. They asked about my family and classes and then surprised me by announcing they were going south for the winter. The thought of staying in their big house alone sent a chill down my spine, but I was grateful to have a roof over my head.

Bill encouraged me to complete the financial aid paperwork. I smiled and nodded, swallowing the acid in my throat as I tried to eat the fried potatoes, a slice of tomato, and some cottage cheese Mabel set on my plate. I hated secrets, but I couldn't tell them why I had no financial aid. I was afraid Daddy would go to jail if I told anyone about him not paying taxes.

Mabel offered to stock the kitchen with any groceries I requested. I asked for vegetable soup and vegetarian hot dogs in a can. Those were the comfort foods I'd grown up eating with my family around the fire. Somehow, I felt closer to them when I ate these foods.

After my hosts went south, I kept all the doors locked even in the daytime, took extra shifts at the cafeteria, and studied at the library to avoid being alone at night. I didn't have many friends and wished Momma would write, but by then, I realized writing letters wasn't her thing.

Each day, as I walked back between the college and the house, I listened to Amy Grant's album *Straight Ahead* on my Walkman. Amy was a friend I could relate to, even though we'd never met. When I felt afraid at night, I played the Angel song on repeat. That album strengthened my faith in God despite Daddy's warning that syncopation was from the devil.

The weeks flew by, and before I knew it, spring had arrived, with pink cherry blossoms filling the sidewalk. Mabel and Bill returned, and life felt less lonely.

One evening, I was walking up the hill when someone shouted my name. I was surprised to see it was Bobby McGhee. He was a big man on campus, while I was a nobody. He was driving a station wagon with the roof cut off. It resembled a pickup. Behind the driver's seat was an armchair facing backward. A man was sitting on the chair, like a king on a throne. He had a quilt wrapped around his shoulders. As I drew closer, I recognized my favorite teacher at Hope Institute, Mr. McGhee.

Mr. McGhee jumped out of the back, shouting, "There's my girl," and threw his arms around me.

It had been five years since we'd seen each other. I felt like the prodigal daughter returning home.

"Where's your family living now?"

"Last I heard, they went back to Seattle, but they don't write much." I failed to mention they were living at a state park.

"What's your major?"

"Social work, but I have to work a lot, so I'm only taking classes part-time."

I felt embarrassed to admit I was so far behind the other people my age, but Mr. McGhee wasn't judgmental.

Just as he did when I was sixteen, Mr. McGhee wiped his eyes with his handkerchief and said, "Remember, you can do anything you set your mind to do, young lady." Then he jumped back on his throne, and they sped off. I watched as the father and son tore down the road with the Beach Boys blaring to let everybody know how much fun they were having. My heart was warm, but I also felt a wave of homesickness. I wondered how Bobby McGhee got so lucky. My dad would never visit me and have fun like that. And he would never listen to the Beach Boys.

Since my parents didn't visit me, I felt compelled to go to them. At the end of the school year, I caught a ride to Seattle. They were living at a State Park. Daddy had bought a travel trailer with a bed for my parents while my siblings slept in tents. Jake had a pup tent, and I joined my sisters in a larger one. We cooked on the trailer's stove and ate meals around the campfire like we'd always done.

I enjoyed hanging out with my family. For a time, my heart seemed full. It was hard to remember that I'd spent the year at college. Some days, it felt like I'd never separated from them. I needed to earn money for school, but I discovered getting a job with an address at a state park was nearly impossible. I made some money car detailing for Daddy and Uncle Joe, but it wasn't much. I decided to head back to college early to make money at the cafeteria.

When I returned to Walla Walla, I was grateful for hot running water, power, and a comfortable bed. When Bill and Mabel asked what I thought about my family's place in Seattle, I told them it was okay. I failed to mention they were living at a state park.

That autumn, I switched to the breakfast shift at the cafeteria. One morning, as I punched my card at the time clock, I heard a deep voice say, "Good morning, Cheri."

Lucas usually prepared the salads, but this time, he was scrambling eggs with a wrinkled nose. "Do you like eggs? I've never seen you eat them."

A wave of concern washed over me. Was Lucas stalking me? Why would he notice that I never ate eggs?

"I don't know what an egg tastes like—my parents never had them in the house."

"Well, I don't like immature chicken embryos either."

His dignified smile intrigued me. He was tall with blond hair, blue eyes, and a wide smile. He looked Norwegian. Momma had always told me to find a good Scandinavian man. Daddy was Danish, but I could settle for a Norwegian if he were as cute as Lucas. I soon discovered he hated eggs and drank soy milk like I did. Perhaps this was a sign.

Lucas was from a small town in the Midwest, but he'd already studied and traveled across Europe for a year, which explained why he said good morning in a different language every day of the week.

Since I hadn't eaten at a table for much of my life, I didn't eat in the dining room because I was nervous about eating in front of people. I was afraid my manners would fail me. People had already pointed out that I held my fork wrong. It seemed easier to take my food in a takeout container and eat in private.

One day, as I left the cafeteria, I heard Lucas calling my name.

"You always eat alone—why don't you join us?"

It was hard to resist his friendly face, so I followed him to a back room, where the kitchen workers gathered around the cook's table. The main cooks were Jessie and Mary, two middle-aged women from Idaho who made the trip to Walla Walla every week. They looked after the students with motherly affection and called us their kids.

Sitting around that table was like being in a family. It was what I'd been craving—to look into people's faces and enjoy a meal. No one seemed to notice how I held my fork or whether I spoke with food in my mouth—although I did try to watch my manners in front of Lucas. It wasn't long before we ate breakfast together several times a week.

Lucas was different from the other guys because he asked my opinion. He'd planned to be a doctor since childhood and liked to discuss the latest scientific news. He often entertained us with his travel stories. I shuddered at the thought of getting on a plane, but Lucas described his exhilaration whenever the aircraft lifted off the ground. He was proof that people could fly to Europe and survive to tell about it.

One day, Lucas asked if I'd walk two miles to Whitman College to watch a movie with him.

"I don't go to movies."

"Why not? Would you go to a video party at someone's house?"

I had to admit that I would.

"Then what's the difference? It's just the venue. Besides, the movies at Whitman are art house films. It's almost like watching a movie for class."

I could feel my heart speed up as his blue eyes searched mine for a response. I'd never wanted to be normal more in my entire life. If Lucas was normal, then I would risk my life to become normal.

"Sure, I'll walk to Whitman with you."

That's how I became willing to leave my angel outside the door to watch a movie. It was a bizarre seventies flick called *Harold and Maude*, about a kid who drove a hearse and fell in love with an older woman.

As we walked back to College Place, Lucas explained how he planned to attend medical school on a tight budget and rarely drove his car to save money. Some people might think he was cheap, but coming from a low-income family myself, I understood. Even though it was past midnight, and the streets of Walla Walla were dark, I felt safe. Lucas was the first guy I'd gone out with that I could trust.

We continued working together for months. We sang in the choir and sometimes hung out with his sister and her boyfriend. I hadn't planned to go when the men's dorm had an open house, but Lucas insisted I visit his room. As a reward, he made me a mixtape of Journey and Chicago, which included the song "Oh, Sherrie" by Steve Perry. No guy had given me a mixtape before, and I wasn't sure what it meant, but I liked it.

By the end of my second year, I was comfortable eating at the table, watching movies, and going for long walks with Lucas. He never kissed me, but I enjoyed his intelligent and witty conversation.

Even though we weren't officially dating, I'd lost interest in the other guys on campus. I'd started out looking for a boyfriend so I could fit in, but Lucas was more than a date or ticket to becoming normal—he was a compassionate, funny, and intelligent human being. For the first time, I wondered if I might be falling in love.

One day, Lucas invited me to the park. His face grew serious as he motioned for me to sit beside him on one of the double-swinging benches.

When I heard the words, "I like you, but...," the shrieks of ravens in the trees drowned out the rest of his words while the bright green of the trees faded into gray.

"I'm transferring to Loma Linda University."

I had heard about the Adventist Medical School in California all my life. It had a reputation for cutting-edge and lifesaving techniques, but I couldn't imagine Walla Walla College without Lucas.

Desperate for him to stay, I confessed that I liked him, and then I regretted it before the words were even out of my mouth.

Lucas looked uncomfortable, and I began to wish I was sitting on a different swing. Why had I been so foolish as to share my heart?

His voice was gentle and kind. He didn't seem repulsed by my declaration of love.

"Cheri, we don't know each other that well." He paused and sighed. "I'm still getting to know myself."

I had a good cry in the privacy of my room. Staring at the ceiling, I realized Lucas was right. I'd been so busy trying to fit in that I wasn't myself. I was so guarded about my family secrets that Lucas had never gotten to know the real me. I never told him I'd been beaten, homeless, or missed out on a high school education. I was afraid I'd lose him if I told him those things, but in the end, I lost him anyway. Or maybe I never had him in the first place. It hurt to think I was alone and would probably always be alone.

Dating might be fun for other people, but it was painful for me. It was easy to get a date, but moving on to a relationship was complicated. I was studying social sciences to understand people's motivations. Why couldn't Daddy keep a job? Why was Momma willing to let Daddy make all the decisions? Why was it so easy for Lucas to move on and never look back? Most of all, I wondered what was wrong with me, that I could never be myself. Was it even possible for me to be normal?

I'd grown up on the bottom rungs of Maslow's hierarchy. I'd spent my life searching for food and shelter while most of my peers were in the middle rungs with stable homes and relationships. I decided that my relationships would continue to fail unless I could move up that ladder.

As I neared the end of my second year in college, my battery was running low. I missed my family more than ever. My siblings knew what we'd been through together. I needed a recharge with the only people who understood me.

After my last test, I walked to the college store and put quarters in the phone. Work and classes had kept me busy, and I hadn't spoken to Momma for several weeks. I'd given up writing letters because no one wrote back, and it was hard to keep track when they kept moving. Momma always kept in touch with Grandma, so I dialed my grandparents' number.

Grandma sounded excited to hear my voice, but her inflections dropped when I asked if she'd heard from Momma. She sounded worried—as if she had bad news.

"Oh yeah, they came by here. When was that, Don?"

I strained to hear what Grandpa was saying in the background as I put more quarters into the slot. My grandparents seemed to be arguing over a date. Then Grandma spoke directly into the phone again.

"Well, Grandpa remembers it differently, but either way, they've gone to Alaska."

"Alaska? What are they doing up there?" Silently, I wondered how Daddy, who couldn't even afford rent, found the funds to move the family to Alaska.

"Grandpa says your dad found a job in a body shop."

My heart sank. I'd never known Daddy to keep a job. And Momma had never wanted to move back to Alaska since we left when I was two. I would never have believed it if anyone, but Grandma had told me this news. I sighed. It was disappointing to find out they'd moved two thousand miles away. Grandma gave me their number, and I wrote it down.

After we hung up, I decided to put more quarters in the slot and call my parents before they moved again.

As soon as Daddy answered, I asked, "What are you doing in Alaska?"

"It's beautiful up here! Hey, why don't you join us for the summer? I'll send you a ticket."

"On a plane? How'd you get Momma to fly?"

"We drove up the Alcan, but a one-way ticket is pretty cheap."

"One-way? Daddy, I can't move to Alaska. I'm finally getting financial aid next year—I don't want to drop out of school. Plus, I need a summer job."

"Get a job up here. We'll take you back in September."

Traveling and seeing new places was something Lucas would do. Perhaps I needed more adventure in my life.

I boarded my first commercial flight with a racing heart and a silver Chinchilla Persian. Satinee was born the month before my nineteenth birthday while we lived in the cabin. I'd begged to keep her and left her with my family when I went to Walla Walla. When they moved to Alaska, they'd left her at Grandma's, but Grandma had more cats than she could handle. Since my flight was leaving from Portland, it was easy to pick her up. Daddy paid extra for a pet carry-on, and so Satinee flew to Alaska with me.

The plane wasn't full, so instead of placing the cat carrier under my seat, I strapped it on the seat next to mine.

I nervously waited for the thrill of lift-off that Lucas described, but I only felt the flutter of swallows in my gut. I tried to ignore Momma's worst-case scenarios about commercial flights crashing during take-off or landing. Once I knew we were in the air, I breathed a sigh of relief that I might live for at least three more hours.

I pulled my diary out of my carry-on and began to leaf through it. The woman on the other side of the cat carrier wore bright red lipstick with a Madonna bow in her hair and a silver cross dangling from her neck as she leaned over to peer at Satinee.

"I always wanted to be rich and afford a cat like that."

"Oh, I'm not rich—my family just breeds Persians."

"Okay, then I wish I had a rich family with Persian cats." She chuckled, adjusted her seat, and leaned back to shut her eyes.

I was annoyed by her assumptions, but I could hardly blame her. Owning a Persian cat while requiring financial aid was just another contradiction in my life that was hard to explain.

While my seatmate slept, I carefully scribbled down a list of everything I'd learned in my social work classes. I couldn't wait to share these concepts with my family. An hour later, I set my pen down and sighed, As I stared at the stars, I realized I was heading to Alaska with more baggage than I could fit inside my suitcase.

6 Honesty

*The greatest burden
a child must bear
is the unlived life
of its parents
-Carl Jung*

When the plane landed in Anchorage, I was relieved to see signs of civilization and hopeful that I could find a job in such a large city.

My heart danced as I stepped off the plywood ramp and searched the crowd for familiar faces. The naturally curly hair I shared with my siblings made them look windblown, but it was good to see their smiles. These were my people and the only true friends I'd had throughout my life. Despite meeting in new places, whenever we got together, I immediately felt at home.

Sixteen-year-old Abby grabbed the cat carrier. She had always loved animals and was eager to reconnect with Satinee.

Seventeen-year-old Jake flooded me with tales about his adventures riding the motorbike he'd found at the house where they were staying. I glanced over his shoulder to see Momma roll her eyes and shake her head in resignation. I could only imagine the battles they'd had.

As we got into the double-cab pickup, twenty-year-old Mara slid in next to me and whispered that she would come to Walla Walla in the fall. I was glad to hear her news. As the second oldest, she'd ridden shotgun beside me throughout our childhood, and she deserved freedom as much as I did.

Exhausted from the flight, I glanced at my watch. It was ten o'clock, and the sun was still shining.

"When does the sun go down?"

Daddy laughed. "Sometime after midnight, but it'll come back up around three."

"How do you guys get any sleep?"

"Black garbage bags. Momma taped them over all the windows." Abby spoke like she'd lived in Alaska her entire life.

I yawned. "How long before we sleep?"

Daddy cleared his throat. "Well, it depends on whether you want to sleep on the drive or wait 'til we get home."

"How far is "home?"

"It's three hours to Glennallen."

"What? Three hours?" I glanced at Anchorage through the back window and collapsed onto my seat. "So much for civilization."

"Oh, come on, people don't come to Alaska for civilization—they come for the adventure." Daddy's excited tone made me nervous.

"I'm too tired for adventure. I just wanna sleep."

"You might want to stay awake. We're driving through some beautiful scenery."

Staring at endless trees and boulders soon became monotonous. I rolled my coat into a makeshift pillow, leaned against the window, and fell asleep.

I don't know how long I slept, but my head bouncing against the glass jarred me awake.

"Did we just hit a deer?"

"Frost heave," Daddy's tone was a matter of fact.

Turns out there were almost as many frost heaves as trees and boulders. I had no choice but to stay awake as we bounced and ricocheted along a swerving road next to a river.

The poor cat began to wail like she was dying. She was probably scared and just wanted a peaceful place to rest. I couldn't blame her.

When I woke the next morning, I jumped up to peel the black garbage bag off the window to get the lay of the land. I found a bleak, gray sky with scrub brush, rocks, and evergreens as far as the eye could see. There was a massive mountain in the distance, but I saw no cars, buildings, or any place to find a job.

"Where's the town?"

Mara laughed. "We're at the edge of the wilderness, and most of the local businesses cater to hunting expeditions."

"I need a job."

I dressed and ran down the stairs to find Daddy making pancakes for breakfast.

"Good morning. Are you hungry?"

"I need a job. You didn't tell me there weren't any jobs here."

"Hang on. We're planning to move to Fairbanks in a few weeks."

"A few weeks? By then, half the summer will be over."

"Oh, come on, don't act so spoiled."

I felt a tightness in the pit of my stomach. Even though I'd been away for two years, my shoulders tensed whenever Daddy raised his voice—years of running from the Persuader made it hard to relax around him.

I grabbed my coat and laced up my shoes for a walk.

"I'd be careful out there."

I ignored his warning and let the door slam behind me, but I only took a few steps before running into a moose.

It was my first time seeing one up close, but I didn't waste any time when I realized two calves were following her. I flew back into the house and slammed the door just as Mara came downstairs.

"Oh, I see you've met the neighbors."

"How do you walk with a moose hanging around?"

"Well, the good news is the moose aren't always here, and the bad news is the mosquitoes never leave."

Mara was right. I never saw the moose again, but every time I stepped outside the door, a massive cloud of mosquitoes surrounded me. When Momma, Mara, and I went for a walk later that day, we each had our own dark cloud hovering over us. Even Jake, tearing around on the motorbike, couldn't escape them.

Daddy kept his word—within two weeks, we packed up and drove five hours north to Fairbanks. A couple of hours into the drive, I noticed the trees were getting shorter and shorter.

"What's with all these skinny, short trees?"

"Permafrost." Daddy didn't need to explain more. I'd read a magazine article once about permafrost stunting trees.

The miles of stunted forest reminded me of a miniature Christmas display—minus the lights and angels.

This road also wound back and forth over frost heaves. As we hit one dip and bounced over the next, it felt like we were riding on a rollercoaster. Daddy suddenly brought the pickup to a screeching halt. I stretched my neck to peer around his shoulder to see a moose crossing the road.

"This wild country might be fascinating and beautiful, but what would've happened if we hit the moose?"

"Stop worrying. We didn't."

I was probably getting on Daddy's nerves as much as he was getting on mine. It made me sad because I loved him. At the same time, I couldn't help but notice we were miles from any emergency services. What had I gotten myself into? A few miles down the road, we stopped for another moose—this with a calf. I stopped counting moose sightings and began praying we'd survive the trip to Fairbanks.

It was a relief to discover that Fairbanks was a proper town with stores and restaurants. Daddy found a place for us to stay near Chena Hot Springs in another stunted forest. The cabin was cozy and larger than most cabins we'd lived in. The best part was that it had hot water and power.

Taco Time was hiring, and I had no trouble getting a job at the drive-up window. The manager was my age, and everyone else was under twenty. We spent our shifts tossing tacos through the window and dancing to Michael Jackson. I no longer had to pretend I was a fast-food girl—now I was that girl.

I was waiting for Momma to pick me up one afternoon when a friendly woman approached me and asked if I'd like to make some extra money.

She explained that the cost of shipping freight to Alaska was passed on to the consumer, making goods expensive. Avon paid part of the freight, making Avon products a good deal. She couldn't find enough Avon representatives to keep up with the demand, so she was offering a sign-on bonus if I was willing to try it. I was skeptical, but I signed up while keeping my Taco Time shifts.

It turns out she was right. Alaskan women were buying most of their cosmetics through Avon. The Avon job turned out to be more lucrative than working for Taco Time, and I soon had more orders than I could handle.

I suggested Mara get her social security number and sell Avon, too. After all our arguments when I was younger, I was prepared for a fight. But Momma stoically drove us to the Social Security office while I went inside with Mara. I was even more surprised that Daddy never mentioned the Mark of the Beast. Were these the same parents that raised me?

The officer accepted Mara's copy of her birth certificate without any questions, and we began making Avon rounds together.

The cabin was filled with Avon boxes for the rest of the summer. Mara and I walked mile after mile, knocking on doors, collecting orders, sorting out shipments, and delivering makeup, lotions, and perfumes. Neither of us had a driver's license, so Momma had to drive us everywhere.

Every night, I enjoyed Momma's cooking. It was simple fare like homemade bread and vegetable stew, but it was delicious. My heart filled with gratitude for everything she did. I understood why Daddy thought a woman's place was in the home, but Momma's days of raising kids were coming to an end. I wondered what she'd do when we were gone.

I fell into a familiar rhythm with my family. It was almost like I'd never left—except I had, and I'd learned things that couldn't be unlearned. Since my parents had changed their stance on social security numbers, I hoped they might change their minds about rock music and makeup. I tried to share what I'd learned in my classes every day.

When Mara and I started wearing makeup to demonstrate the products, I was surprised Momma didn't say anything. Daddy seemed too busy working at the auto repair shop to notice that my lips kept changing color.

One day, we were making up the Avon orders when I told Mara about my assertive theory class. "Feelings are never wrong, and we all have a right to how we feel."

"That's not exactly true. You're still responsible for what you do with your feelings." Momma added her two cents to all of my lessons.

Another time, as we were making our rounds, I told Mara about the different types of relationships. "There's authoritarian—with one person in control. Then there's complementarian—where both partners have separate roles. And my favorite is egalitarian—where both partners are equal."

"A complementarian marriage is just as equal as an egalitarian one." Momma kept her eyes on the road.

"How can you say that? You've never had a job since you got married."

"Having a job is not all you might think. Daddy doesn't make me do anything I don't want to do. Our roles might be separate, but we're equal."

I thought about all the times Daddy had decided to move and disrupt Momma's plans to set up a home. She couldn't see it, or she wouldn't admit it, and I didn't like her ignoring the truth. I stared out the window at the miniature trees and sighed quietly. I felt like I needed to return to college before I became stunted like Momma and those trees.

College didn't start until the end of September, but when I woke up to snow at the beginning of the month, I was anxious to leave. It turned out that leaving was more complicated than hopping on a plane. Before we could go, Daddy had to sell a car to pay for the trip. Then, we needed to pack up the camp trailer with enough food and supplies to survive our journey down the Alaska-Canada highway.

While the rest of us prepared to move, Abby was working as a nanny for some of Momma's college friends. With Daddy's track record of burning bridges, leaving her alone in Alaska seemed a little risky. I hoped someone would come back to get her.

When I compared Abby's life to mine at sixteen, I found it surprising how much my parents let her do. Her employers even provided her with a book so she could study for the GED. I realized her teenage years were much different than mine, but I was glad for her. Even the Persuader seemed to have retired—which made the summer more pleasant for all of us. Why couldn't it have always been this way?

We finally loaded the double cab pickup and hooked the trailer to it. I was glad we'd have a safe place to sleep to protect us from wildlife along the way. Daddy said it should take about two weeks to drive down the Alcan and drop Mara and me off at Walla Walla, but I worried he might have underestimated how long it would take.

We were traveling along a stretch of gravel road when Daddy noticed a stream of sparks flying out behind us. One of the trailer tires had blown, and the wheel was striking gravel. Fortunately, we had a spare and were soon on our way.

As we crossed the Alaska border, I breathed a sigh of relief but exhaled too soon. Somewhere in the Yukon, we heard a loud grating noise. Something was wrong with the pickup. Daddy pulled into a primitive campground, opened the hood, and discovered the carrier bearing was going out.

"We can't drive it anywhere until it's fixed."

I looked around at the wilderness that seemed to be swallowing up our vehicles and any hope of returning to school on time.

"I should've stayed in Walla Walla."

Daddy slammed the hood down with vengeance.

"Oh, for Pete's sake, Cheri, grow up."

Momma shook her head. "I think that assertive theory class ruined you. Try to be grateful that we didn't get in an accident."

It was thirty miles to Whitehorse. Daddy had no choice but to put on a heavy coat and stand by the side of the highway, holding out his thumb. We all held our breath and waited. Eventually, a truck picked him up, then we prayed for his safety.

He said he might be gone overnight, but he'd have no way of communicating with us.

Momma worried something bad might happen to him. And then what would happen to us? All we could do was pray and wait.

Daddy returned the next day.

"The auto parts store had to order the part, so we'll be stranded for at least a week."

I was furious.

"A week? School starts in just over a week Now, I know I'm going to be late for sure."

"There's nothing I can do. We have enough food to get by if we ration it, and we can buy more when we get to town. I just hope the part comes before we run out of propane and firewood."

"I knew I should have stayed in Walla Walla."

"Oh, come on, you've had a great summer."

"I hate that you never plan."

"We can't control everything."

I looked around at the campground, which had nothing but an outhouse and a water pump.

"There's not even a place to take a shower."

"You can always heat some water over the campfire and wash up. Have you forgotten how to do that?"

"How could I forget? I have an elephant's memory, and I remember everything. I remember how you wouldn't let me go to high school."

Daddy's face grew red.

"Oh, come on, when are you going to stop living in the past?"

"When I stop paying for your choices every day of my life."

"You need to learn how to forgive and forget."

He stepped out of the trailer and slammed the door. I could hear him chopping wood.

Mara and Jake remained silent while Momma shook her head.

"You aren't as smart as you think you are, young lady."

"You know what makes me mad? We've lived on the bottom rungs of Maslow's hierarchy our entire lives. And it's because we're always moving while normal people stay in one place."

I stormed out of the trailer and climbed into the pickup to sit with Satinee and the dog.

After a while, Momma came out and got into the cab with me.

"I understand your frustration about getting back to school late, but I'm afraid your comments will only make Daddy feel like a failure. We need him to stay strong to get us out of here."

I put my arm across Momma's shoulder.

"I'm sorry. I don't judge you for not working—I'm grateful you're my mom."

She smiled mysteriously. "I wonder what would happen if I took over your Avon territory when you leave."

It was the first time I'd heard Momma discuss getting a job, but with Abby working as a nanny and Mara joining me in College Place, she'd only have Jake at home. It was time for her to do something for herself.

I didn't enjoy spending a week in the wilderness while I was supposed to be at school. It wasn't fun. We had to ration everything and watch out for moose and grizzlies every time we went to the outhouse. I was grateful for a hard-sided trailer to protect us from the wildlife and the cold winds, but the beautiful scenery and time with my family were lost due to my anxiety about starting school late.

By the time the part came in, I was resigned to being late, but Daddy did his best to get me back to school as soon as possible. Even though it was dark when he finished fixing the truck, we soon hit the road, and Daddy drove all night. In the morning, my friends would be standing in line for registration, but I was still days away.

It felt good to be rolling down the road again. I slipped Billy Joel's Greatest Hits into my Walkman and began to rock my way down the Alcan. As I stared at the stars through the window, the Milky Way seemed brighter, and the trees were taller than I'd seen them all summer.

7 Footloose

Freedom is not worth having if it does not include the freedom to make mistakes.
-Mahatma Gandhi

Shivering in the December air, I stepped across an icy puddle to reach Mara's door. She lived in a converted garage across the street from the mill. It boasted a large picture window where the door used to be, outlined with colored Christmas lights that seemed to promise warmth inside.

My sister opened the door with an excited smile. "Jake should be here any minute."

I entered Mara's apartment to find white walls with the thinnest layer of gold carpet covering a concrete floor. A dilapidated refrigerator stood beside a small stove and a tiny sink in one corner. There was no furniture to sit on, but two foam camping pads and a few blankets sat in another corner. Across from the bedding was a drafty bathroom with a narrow shower and toilet. It was the bleakest apartment I'd ever seen, but an indoor toilet and electric lights made it a step up from many places we'd lived.

In contrast to Mara's apartment, I found it challenging to live in the dorm. My roommate was noisy, and people stopped by our room at all hours. My work and classes left little time to visit with anyone. I hoped Christmas break would allow me time to catch up with my siblings. We'd barely seen each other since we returned to the lower forty-eight.

Mara had always shown me other ways of doing things. When I first arrived in College Place, Ruth and Earl gave me room and board with the expectation that I would attend Walla Walla College. I never questioned their plan despite my lack of financial aid.

Thanks to Daddy's non-existent tax forms, Mara couldn't get financial aid either, but my friend Debbie kept her promise to save my sister a full-time job at Harris Pine Mills. Unlike me, Mara wisely put her education on hold and went to work full-time.

Despite living in a dump of an apartment, Mara had accomplished more in a few months than I had in two years. She got contacts, passed her driver's test, and had her wisdom teeth out. We didn't have health insurance while growing up. As a student, I considered it a luxury, but Mara showed me that working full-time could make insurance possible.

Mara's latest purchase was an old rattletrap of a car. It was a bright green eyesore, but it enabled her to use the laundromat and buy groceries—if she could keep it running. It gave me hope to see Mara beginning to live like normal people.

We hadn't seen Jake since September. He was supposed to go back to Alaska with our parents, but Grandma's heart attack changed their plans. Daddy flew to Fairbanks alone while Momma and Jake stayed in Portland to help Grandma.

Jake called me just before Christmas. He would be eighteen in a few months, and he wanted to be in charge of his own life.

"If I return to Alaska, I'll be stuck there until I can raise enough money to return. Can you help me find a ride to Walla Walla?"

A pang of concern struck my stomach as I thought of Momma's feelings. She didn't like any of her kids fleeing the nest, but Jake was her only son and the apple of her eye. I could also tell by the tone of Jake's voice that he was determined. If I didn't help him, he'd find a way to Walla Walla anyway, so I called a friend visiting in Portland who agreed to give my brother a ride.

While we waited for Jake to arrive, Mara set her boombox on the windowsill and turned the radio dial to the top forty station. "Man in Motion" from *St. Elmo's Fire* filled the dingy walls and put us in a festive mood. The theme of young people finding themselves resonated with us. A new era was beginning. We Christen kids were ready to enjoy our independence. We couldn't wait to show Jake what a joy it was to be free from Daddy's belt and rules.

As soon as we heard the knock, we rushed to open the door to find our little brother standing even taller than we remembered.

After we hugged Jake, I noticed my friend Monte was still standing in the driveway with the colored lights flickering across his face.

He looked lonely. It was almost Christmas, so I motioned for him to join us. He wasted no time stepping through the door and tossing his overcoat on the floor next to the other jackets.

"I was telling your brother he should go for an engineering degree. I'm taking some classes, and he seems to have a natural interest in it."

Mara's eye caught mine, and I knew she was thinking the same thing. Our brother was smart, but Monte didn't realize that Jake had no education beyond the third grade. I wondered how hard it might be to earn an engineering degree with such a limited education. Mara and I remained silent about our concerns because we never discussed our lack of education in front of people outside of the family.

Munching on sandwiches, potato chips, and cookies, we caught up on the family news. Abby had left her job as a nanny to move in with Daddy. Grandma was doing better. And despite Momma's anxiety about flying, she was planning to head back to Alaska to join Daddy.

When Jefferson Starship came on the radio with "We Built This City," I noticed Monte bobbing his head, and I couldn't keep my feet still. Mara turned up the volume, and before we knew it, we were dancing. The colored lights strobed across our faces while we swayed to the music.

I'm not sure how long we danced, but songs like "We Are the World" reminded us that we were no longer isolated, but part of the world community. We would be visible from now on and never hide in the shed again. We set aside Momma's fears and Daddy's depression. We stopped worrying about the Time of Trouble and embraced rock and roll. Most exhilarating of all, we danced on the grave of the Persuader. We were free, and everything was possible. The only thing that would have made that party better was the presence of our sister, Abby.

Monte found a deck of Rook cards in his glove compartment, and we sat down on the floor to play. Many Adventists frowned on using regular playing cards, but Rook was an approved game. Whenever a song inspired us, we all jumped up to dance some more. We were the grown-ups now, and none of us believed caffeine was a sin, so we refueled on the once-forbidden Dr. Pepper and partied until four in the morning. I'd never had so much fun losing sleep.

Mara's next-door neighbor was out scraping the ice off his car when Mara rolled out a sleeping pad for Jake, and Monte gave me a ride back to the dorm. By then, the caffeine had faded, and I could barely keep my eyes open.

As I got out of the car, Monte shouted. "Thanks for the fun night. Your family is so cool."

My heart swelled with pride as I went back to my room. I loved my siblings and looked forward to more parties in the future. I hoped to find a guy like Monte who would like my siblings as much as I did.

The addition of other people to our circle soon ruined our camaraderie. Monte had been safe because he had a fiancée and wasn't planning to join our family, but the trouble started when Jake met Carrie.

Carrie was a survivor. She had grown up with an abusive and very religious stepfather who beat her and slammed her so hard against the door frame one day that he knocked out her two front teeth. She was taken away to have her teeth fixed and had a police escort to collect her belongings from the family home. Her mother took her stepdad's side and offered no sympathy for her daughter. Carrie was alone at eighteen, without anyone to care for her. She was fortunate to find an elderly woman who offered her a room to sleep in.

I understood why Jake and Carrie connected. I liked Carrie. She seemed a lot like us. Some people thought she even looked like one of Jake's sisters. We all had brown eyes and brown curly hair. She was kind and thoughtful, and she seemed to belong with us.

A few days later, when Jake stayed out all night, Mara worried since he was only seventeen. When Jake admitted that he'd spent the night with Carrie, Mara got angry. I understood her concern, but I couldn't blame Jake for wanting to sleep in an actual bed with his girlfriend.

I agreed that Jake should find a job before he got a girlfriend, but he didn't want anyone to tell him what to do. He'd be eighteen in a few months and had no intentions of obeying his older sisters. After a heated argument, Jake and Carrie disappeared.

It was disturbing that we'd agreed to watch over our little brother, and now he was missing. I asked Mara what I should tell Momma at my Friday night check-in.

"She'll be upset to find out that we don't even know where Jake went."

Mara rolled her eyes. "Then don't call Momma. I never call her."

That was the difference between us. When I left the family, I couldn't go a week without writing a letter or calling Momma, but Mara did things differently.

While we were discussing Jake's disappearance, someone knocked on Mara's door. A man from Harris Pine, who always gave me weird vibes, asked Mara if she'd like to go for a walk with him. After he left, I glanced out the window to make sure he was gone.

"Honestly, Mara, walking with Trent seems almost as dumb as Jake running off with Carrie."

She rolled her eyes. "Don't be ridiculous. It's just a walk."

"Would you go for a walk with Ted Bundy?"

"No, but he's not Ted Bundy."

"I have a weird feeling about him. Doesn't it seem creepy to walk in the dark with some man you don't know?"

"I've seen him around the mill. You're just jealous."

"No. I'm not jealous. He's older than us and doesn't even own a car."

"You dislike him because he doesn't have a car? That's half the guys on campus."

"Well, he's plenty old enough to hold down a job and get a car—if he tried.

"I remember you walked to Whitman College with that guy you liked—what was his name? Lucas?"

"That was different. Lucas had a car—he just didn't want to drive it."

"Had a car and didn't drive it. I got a car so I could drive it. Now, who was dating a dummy?"

We argued as sisters do.

Mara placed her hands on both hips. "And you stole my quarters."

"What? I didn't steal them. I just borrowed them. You have a whole jar. I just took a few to do my laundry."

"Well, it's still stealing!"

"Oh, come on, that's how our family's always done things. Daddy and Uncle Joe have traded money back and forth as long as I can remember, and no one calls it stealing. Whoever has money shares it with everybody else."

"Well, I don't want to live that way. It reminds me of Daddy stealing our money in Montana."

I felt my face growing hot. "I'm sorry, Mara. I never thought about it that way. I don't want to be like that."

Mara was just getting started.

"And there's a reason I never call Momma and Daddy. I'm afraid they'll ask for money. I can barely pay my bills. I don't have extra money for anyone."

"You're right. I'm sorry, Mara, I was wrong. But please don't go walking with Trent."

"I don't even like Trent, but I'll walk with whoever I want. I don't need my bossy sister telling me what to do. Get out of my apartment."

I walked back to the dorm with a heavy heart. I was used to being the protective older sister, but there was no way Mara would listen to me any more than Jake had listened to her. I couldn't blame them. We'd grown up in such a controlling environment that none of us wanted anyone to tell us what to do.

My New Year's resolution was to have more fun with my siblings, but that never happened. We each needed our own space to grow without interference from family. Thus, the year 1986 began without a word from either Jake or Mara.

A few months later, I saw Mara with a guy that I assumed was her boyfriend. We said hello like old friends, and there was no animosity between us. We were sisters, after all. We alone knew what we'd survived. But to keep up appearances with our friends, we never mentioned the past. I was relieved to see she wasn't with Trent. I still had no idea where Jake was or if he was even in town, and Mara didn't seem to know any more than I did.

In September, just before my twenty-third birthday, I decided to live in a house because I thought it was cheaper than living in a dorm. I was looking through the ads when a headline from the Walla Walla Union-Bulletin caught my eye. Over the weekend, Trent had gone to Debbie's house, taken out a gun, and shot her. Thoughtful, kind, Debbie—my first friend in College Place, was dead.

8 Girls Just Want To Have Fun

*The woman who walks alone
is likely to find herself
in places no one
has ever been before.
-Albert Einstein*

As I read about Debbie being murdered in her own home, a shock of electricity ran down my spine. Trent busted through her front door and shot her. Tears filled my eyes as I remembered how Debbie had calmed my fears about getting a social security number. She never made fun of me for thinking it was the mark of the beast, but gently led me on the path to normal.

It was hard for me to process that Debbie was gone. Daddy said girls who got hurt often asked for it, but I knew Debbie didn't ask for it. If Debbie had any fault, it was being too kind, but no woman should be condemned for dating an unsafe person. Mara could've ended up as Trent's target, but fortunately, she turned him down for that walk.

The college had given me permission to live outside the dorm, but when I read the news, a new fear consumed me. I began to see Momma's worst-case scenarios in every rental. How could I stay safe? One wrong choice, and my life might be over.

Thinking there is safety in numbers, I invited some friends to rent a large house with three bedrooms and two tiny apartments. It seemed perfect for six young women willing to share expenses.

The owner of the house was a bachelor in his mid-thirties named Sid. Sid seemed more interested in giving us personality tests than renting the house. I told him I just needed a place to live, but he wanted to know what kind of people were renting his house.

After I passed the personality test, Sid said he'd rent to the six of us if I'd be responsible for the bills. This meant I'd have to collect the rent from the other women and put the utilities in my name. I agreed to his conditions if he would allow us to put a fresh coat of paint on the walls.

I collected the first month's rent and signed the lease. Laurie and I shared the large bedroom. She was studying to be a grade schoolteacher. Candy and Jackie were pre-med majors who took the two smaller bedrooms. Lisa, a childhood friend, rented one downstairs apartment, and Rhonda rented the other. Rhonda, Lisa, and I were all in various stages of studying social work. The one thing we all had in common was our love for people and desire to serve others.

I organized the painting inside the main house while Rhonda led the others in clearing the brush from the yard and cleaning the basement. Someone found a used sofa and loveseat at a yard sale, so I sewed gray slipcovers to hide the ugly orange floral print. We put down new linoleum in the bathroom and bought blinds for the windows. I was the only one with a sewing machine, so I sewed valences to hang over the blinds, which added a cozy feeling to the drafty farmhouse.

I surveyed my handiwork with satisfaction. After bouncing all over College Place in various homes for three years, it was satisfying to see the house cleaned up and ready for us to move in. It awakened my desire to someday create a home with a man, but there was one man I had no interest in sharing a house with, and that was the landlord.

Sid did a walk-through and said the house looked great. Then he asked if I'd go to dinner with him. I told him I was busy getting everyone settled.

Move-in day was noisy as six young women got to know each other. A grocery store in Walla Walla sold cheap French bread, and someone picked up several loaves that first night. We minced garlic and toasted it in the oven, serving it with spaghetti and salad to celebrate our new place. Everybody loved the bread. Jackie suggested if any of us ever went by that store, they should buy several loaves and bring them home. It became a tradition. We often ripped the loaves apart and dipped the pieces in garlic butter. It was a holy communion between kindred spirits.

I didn't want to be paranoid, but the landlord kept showing up without warning even after we moved in. He said he needed to check the siding or a tree that could fall in a storm. It was nice that he was trying to keep the place safe, but he often overstayed and tried to engage us in conversation. Perhaps a houseful of girls was a temptation for an awkward bachelor, but none of us felt comfortable with him hanging around. I was getting vibes like I had with Debbie's murderer. The whole purpose of living in a crowd was to avoid stalkers.

My roommates occasionally shared their secrets. One was beaten in childhood, and another had been molested. Jackie was tired of being called racist names and slept with a golf club under her bed.

Even though I considered these women my friends, I never told any of them that I'd been beaten or that I missed out on a high school education. I'd spent so many years covering up for my parents that I almost forgot about my life in the woods. And even when I did remember, I pushed it to the back of my mind because I was still trying to fake it until I could make it.

It was Jackie's idea to call our new place "The White House." It soon had a reputation for being a fun place to hang out. The house was rarely quiet. We studied hard, but any given night could turn into a party. Our vices were card games, dancing to the radio, and eating ice cream straight from the container. The music was loud, but the house was somewhat isolated, so there was no one to complain about the noise.

One Saturday night, my roommates convinced me to attend the community college dance. I was nervous. This was another place where I'd been warned that angels would not protect me, but I wanted to be one of the girls. While I was dancing with my friends, I bumped into a guy with sunglasses wearing a Hawaiian shirt. I started to apologize, and when he took off his glasses, I screamed. It was Jake. My little brother was all grown up and out on the town with Carrie. We exchanged hugs and went on our way. Later, I was sorry I didn't get his phone number.

My heart grew heavy as we neared the holidays. Thanksgiving wasn't bad—it was only one weekend, and some of my roommates stayed in town to work—but I dreaded winter break because I didn't like to be alone.

Everyone had somewhere to go but me. Abby and my parents were still in Alaska. Mara had gone to Idaho with her boyfriend, and Jake and Carrie had completely disappeared. One of my roommates invited me to join her family, but I had to stay and work through the break.

Lisa came to tell me she had to move out. There was a dripping pipe downstairs, and she had to wear rubber boots and wade through the water to get to her apartment. Then her heater stopped working, and she had to sit on her bed swaddled in blankets to stay warm while she studied. I reported these issues to the landlord, but for all of his visits to fix it, the leak kept growing worse.

I was sad to see Lisa go. She was a kindred spirit. Her parents and mine had met in college, and we'd known each other since childhood. Like me, she'd moved a lot. I understood her need to find a safer place. Once she left, I'd be responsible for finding another roommate, and who would choose to live in such a dangerous situation? When another roommate came up short of her rent for that month, I discovered being responsible for collecting the rent wasn't working in my favor.

One of my social work classes required 30 hours of volunteer work by the end of the year, so I signed up to help with activities at a local care center.

I finished my last test of the quarter and trudged home with an armload of books. Candy and Jackie had left me a bag of oranges, a loaf of French bread, and a Christmas card. Their kindness touched me. I ripped off a piece of bread and stuffed it into my mouth while I walked around the empty house with a tight feeling in my chest. Everyone had somewhere to go but me. The loneliness was so overwhelming that I collapsed onto my bed sobbing.

When I woke up, It was pitch dark outside, and I'd left the blinds open. Hoping no one would see me walking through the house with the lights on, I moved as fast as I could from room to room, lowering the blinds.

A knock at the back door startled me. Trembling, I hesitated before going into the kitchen. I saw Sid waving at me through the glass. I had no choice but to find out what he wanted. Maybe he had finally fixed the leak.

"I was wondering if you'd like to go to dinner with me."

"I can't tonight. I have training in the morning."

As soon as he left, I ran around the house, locking the latches on all the windows along with bolting the doors—until I remembered that Sid was the landlord and had all the keys. Just in case, I went to Jackie's room, found her golf club, and put it beside my bed.

The White House was strangely quiet the next morning. The purpose of sharing this big house was so I'd never be alone, but here I was, spending the month of December alone with a landlord who seemed to be stalking me.

I'd often used the phrase "home" to mean wherever I was sleeping at the time, but whether it was a cabin, campground, or motel, none of those places were home. I realized I was homesick, but I'd never had a home. I wanted to throw myself down on the floor in protest and scream at God because life wasn't fair. But I had to set aside my self-pity because I'd signed up for that volunteer job. There was nothing to do but slip into a pink leopard-skin mini skirt, tie my hair in a lacy, black Madonna bow, and walk two miles to the care center.

9 Drive

*I am out with lanterns
looking for myself.*
-Emily Dickinson

Dolores, the activity director, was a motherly woman with a twinkle in her eye. While efficiently sorting the resident's mail into three stacks, she asked questions about my family and education. After we delivered the mail, she led me into the large activity room to call bingo while she continued her administrative tasks.

I'd never played bingo before, but a woman named Mabel was glad to teach me. As I spun the metal ball, calling out the letters and numbers, I glanced around the room. I figured these people covering their bingo squares were missing their loved ones as much as I was during the holidays.

While we played bingo, a young guy entered the room with a mop and pail and started cleaning the floor. I overheard him tell someone he was a senior at the Adventist Academy. As he moved closer to our side of the large room, he tossed his long blond hair out of his eyes and gave me a friendly smile.

He continued mopping, and I continued calling bingo. In the middle of the room, a large TV screen played the week's top songs on MTV. I was surprised these people weren't complaining about rock music. Some of them were hard of hearing, but most had no trouble hearing the bingo numbers. Perhaps they didn't share Daddy's conviction that syncopation came from the devil.

Dolores told me to let everyone choose a prize when the game ended. It was rewarding to watch people sort through the gadgets, notepads, and candy bars and leave with a smile.

While I collected the bingo cards, I heard Amy Grant's voice and stopped to watch the video. Lost in my thoughts, I turned to push the bingo cart and ran into the guy with the mop.

Embarrassed, I motioned toward the TV. "I shouldn't be listening to this on Sabbath."

He laughed. "I shouldn't either, but I don't care."

As I was leaving, I noticed someone had spilled their coffee on the floor.

I called out, "Hey boy, there's a mess over here."

"Name's Dylan. Like the singer."

"Mine's Cheri. So where are you from?"

He laughed. "Born right here in Walla Walla."

When I left the care center to walk home, the sun was setting. I passed a house with Christmas lights twinkling across the roofline and outlining every tree. Santa and his reindeer peered down at me from the roof, while a snowman and nativity scene filled the yard. I wondered what it would be like to live in such a house. I imagined the people inside were sitting around the table, laughing and telling stories until their stomachs and hearts were full.

I thought of that dance night at Mara's the year before. It had been such a rare moment of joy with my siblings, but my heart ached to realize we'd hardly seen each other since then.

College days were supposed to be one of the best times of my life, but I was tired of spending the holidays alone. I tried to remember good memories with my family, but I kept remembering how Daddy yelled at me for playing Christmas music.

The melancholy spirit that visited me every Christmas began to whisper in my ear that life was hopeless. That maybe there would never be any good holidays for me.

As the night closed in, I trudged down the railroad tracks, feeling sorry for myself.

I turned on the Walkman, and a song from the mix tape Lucas had given me came on. and I felt even worse. If a guy like Lucas hadn't found my polished appearance worth loving, why would anyone else value me? What was wrong with me? Why did everyone leave?

I turned up the music to drown the ache in my heart as a tear slid down my cheek. At any moment, a train might come racing down the track, but in my depression, I grew careless. I dared God to prove he cared for me. If I didn't hear the train, perhaps my life could slip away before I knew what hit me.

My breath caught when a car slowed down and pulled off onto the shoulder ahead of me. It was a weird-shaped, old-fashioned car. Maybe from the sixties. What kind of person drove such a car? An older man? What could he possibly want with me? Did he have a gun?

As the car rolled to a stop, Momma's worst-case scenarios kicked me into survival mode. Ripping my earphones from my head, I laced my keys through my fingers. I decided to keep walking. I wouldn't let him see how scared I was, and I wouldn't go down without a fight. My steps stumbled as I approached the car while I said a frantic prayer for help.

I saw the shadowy form of the driver reaching across to open the passenger door. He moved slowly, confidently, just as I suspected a murderer might do.

I was surprised to see the guy with the mop.

"Would you like a ride?"

"What? Oh, sure."

Relieved but still shaking, I got into the car and tried to act normal.

"Interesting car."

"Belongs to my grandparents. I'm house-sitting for them."

Despite the age difference, we had some things in common. His favorite classes were writing, drama, and psychology. He had a black cat and liked contemporary Christian music. I was surprised to hear his dad took him to an Amy Grant concert.

As he pulled up in front of the White House, my landlord walked by with his dog. Dylan seemed talkative, so I decided to keep the conversation going. Sid and his dog passed us again as he peered into the dark car. I hoped he thought I was on a date.

For the next two weeks, Dylan gave me a ride home whenever we worked the same shift. I was grateful since the December air was getting chilly. To my relief, Sid stopped hanging around.

On the last day I volunteered at the Care Center, Dylan gave me a final ride home. I wished him a good life, then ran inside to find the answering machine blinking next to the phone. Hoping it was my parents or one of my siblings, I eagerly punched the button.

"Hi Cheri, it's Dolores from the Care Center. I'm hiring an assistant—if you're interested, call me."

I glanced at the stack of bills next to the phone and knew what I needed to do.

When my roommates returned from the break, they were frustrated that Sid hadn't fixed the leak. Despite working many shifts at the cafeteria and volunteering hours, I didn't have enough money to pay the extra rent. As long as there was a leak, asking anyone else to rent that apartment was ridiculous. Without another roommate, we couldn't afford the rent.

It was a sad day when we all decided to move. I moved into an apartment with Jackie and Candy. The White House was fun while it lasted, but it was just a temporary sleeping space—like every other place I'd ever lived.

Dylan and I continued to be work friends, but we rarely spoke. He was busy with his friends and his senior year of high school while I juggled two jobs and several classes. Whenever he saw me walking, he gave me a ride, and whenever we ordered donuts, I saved him an apple fritter.

Sometime in early spring, I found him crying in the gazebo at work. When I asked what happened, he said an older employee had harassed him. I reported the man to the administrator, and the guy was immediately fired.

A few weeks later, I was walking back from the Friday evening church service when Dylan passed me with a car full of girls. He drove by slowly while I walked.

"Would you like to come over and hang out?"

I looked at the car full of girls and wondered why he was inviting me. But my feet ached from walking, and his grandparents' house was close to my apartment, so I slid into the front seat.

Dylan lit some candles, put on contemporary Christian music, and offered me a cup of tea. The other girls seemed at home while they sorted through the cupboards for snacks and began telling stories.

Dylan introduced me to musicians I'd never heard before. Rich Mullins and First Call were my favorites. The next day, he stopped by my apartment to give me a mix tape. It was the second time I'd been given such a gift, but this tape had no love songs—just various contemporary Christian artists.

That spring, Abby flew down from Alaska to join me. I was excited to share an apartment with her.

Each of my siblings left our parents more prepared than the last, but none of them followed me to Walla Walla College. Mara avoided my financial struggles by choosing to work full-time before going to school. Jake threw out the family's religion, vegetarian diet, and purity standards to set his own course from the start. And eighteen-year-old Abby arrived more savvy than I was at twenty with a GED, a social security number, and prior work experience. I was surprised that she was immediately hired at McDonald's.

It was early July, and I was lying on a blanket in the backyard, working on my tan, when Abby called from the back door.

"Some guy wants to know if you'd like to go to the carnival."

"What's he look like?"

"Tall blond. Seems polite."

"Oh, he's closer to your age. Why don't you go?"

A minute later, she came back and stood over me, speaking in a low, confidential tone. I squinted against the July sun, trying to make out her facial expression.

"I think you should go with him. He's not interested in me. He only has eyes for you."

I rolled my eyes, gathered my book, towel, and suntan lotion, and went to the front door. I wasn't interested in dating some guy who had just graduated from high school, but I wanted to be nice to the guy who'd given me so many rides and a great mix tape. I planned to let him down gently, but once I saw his earnest face, I decided it couldn't hurt to go. Besides, it wasn't a date—he was taking a carload of friends with him.

Dylan was driving his own car. It was a Dodge Aspen—an old police car with three paint colors and bondo, but the bones were good. It was sturdy and had more room than his grandparents' car, but it was hot and crowded with five other people. Fortunately, he had me riding up front, so I stuck my arm out the window to feel the breeze.

I'd never been to a carnival. It was on the list of places to avoid, but the idea of God's angels abandoning people when they needed protection wasn't making sense anymore. So, I jumped on the tilt-a-whirl, but as soon as the ride started, I panicked. What if this was how I died? I could hear Momma's sad voice saying, "She should never have gone down to the devil's playground."

My screams forced the attendant to stop the ride. Dylan and his friend Ben, who'd met us at the park, grabbed my arms and pulled me off the ride. I saw Ben mouthing the words, "How much fun is she?" But Dylan didn't join him in making fun of me.

While his friends enjoyed the hammer, Dylan took me on the kiddie rides. Then I sat on a bench while he joined his friends, hanging upside down and spinning until everyone was dizzy.

We went to Ben's house, where he made stir fry. The other girls fell asleep during the hour-long drive back to College Place while Dylan and I talked. He dropped them off one by one, leaving us alone at last. We continued our conversation in my driveway. The Milky Way shone brightly that night. We decided to stretch out on the seats—him in the front and me in the back with the doors open so we could hang our heads out for a better view.

"I love looking at the stars. My family used to camp in the desert when we lived in California." His voice sounded wistful.

"My great-grandfather discovered several comets." I decided not to tell him how much of my life I'd spent camping.

"Do you like having your sister as a roommate?"

"Yeah, we get along."

"I'm not that close to my family."

"Well, I could never live without my family." I failed to mention that I had no hometown, church family, or high school class. My family was everything to me.

We spoke about all kinds of things, many superficial, but somewhere in the conversation, in the dark—where he couldn't see my face, and I couldn't see him, I confessed a fear that was always on my mind.

"I feel like a fake."

In the silence, I held my breath, wondering if Dylan was shocked to find out I was a fake.

In a whisper, he answered.

"I feel like a hypocrite."

I didn't ask why he felt like a hypocrite because I didn't want to explain why I was a fake.

We stared at the stars in silence for a minute before I had an idea.

"Let's pray for God to lead our lives and help us be more authentic."

I shut the door and crawled over to the front seat, where we held hands like good Christian children and prayed a simple plea for God to guide our lives.

10 Sweet Child O'Mine

*A sister is like yourself
in a different movie,
a movie that stars you
in a different life.
-Deborah Tannen*

Abby was born when I was five. After she came along, I lost interest in all the other dolls. Momma said she was my real-life baby doll. By the time she came to Walla Walla, my baby sister had grown into a beautiful, witty, and kind-hearted young woman. She hated arguments and never found a stray puppy or kitten she wouldn't rescue.

I smiled when Abby told me about living alone with our parents. Her teen years in Alaska sounded a lot more fun than mine had been in Montana. Since we drove down the Alcan Highway, a lot had changed in the cabin. Momma took over my Avon territory, and Abby had moved back in with our parents and worked in fast food. The rest of us had flown the nest, and Daddy had given up most of his control, allowing hardworking Abby to keep her money.

With each of them working, there was enough money for necessities, and their lives settled down for a while. As Abby filled me in, I couldn't help but think my parents had started living like normal people.

"We usually had guests over after church and played table games on Saturday nights."

"That's the Momma I remember—before she got worn out from all the moving." I sighed.

Abby's stories gave me hope. If our parents were changing, perhaps things would be different for all of us in the future.

"Did you know Momma won a Mrs. Albee award for the highest sales in her Avon territory? You should've seen her putting on makeup and going out to eat with the other ladies."

My mouth dropped open in shock to hear that Momma went out to eat and wore makeup.

"What did Daddy say?"

"I'm not sure he noticed." Abby giggled.

It felt good to laugh with my sister, and for the first time since I'd moved to College Place, I felt at home. I thought about the constant moves in our childhood and realized the only home I'd truly known was the presence of my family. At the same time, while Abby was exploring her new life, I was getting tired of mine.

After four years of going to school part-time, I still lacked enough credits to graduate. I felt there was no way I could pass the required math and science classes. I still hadn't found a husband—not even a serious dating partner. I wasn't even sure what I wanted in a husband or career. I'd spent most of my energy trying to fit into a world where it seemed I'd never belong.

I envied the students who came to Walla Walla College with supportive parents, healthcare, and financial aid. They didn't have to work two jobs and go to school part-time to make ends meet. The most frustrating issue was that I couldn't keep up with the bills.

I was stunned when Dylan told me he was planning to go to community college because the tuition was much cheaper, and his money would stretch further. I felt tricked to realize I'd been paying extra to hang out with Adventists in a world that felt elite and beyond my reach. That summer, I decided to drop out of school to figure out who I was and what I wanted.

When Dolores took the day off, I had no idea it would change my life. She left a note for me to take the residents down to the activity room for a concert. The Reach Out Singers were a traveling choir that included people from all over the United States. Most had taken a year off from school or a job to sing about Jesus.

As I listened to the beautiful harmonies and watched the singers interact with the residents, I felt envious. I tried to imagine what it would be like to stop worrying about homework and bills and see the country by singing in a different town every night.

After the concert, a friendly woman came up to me with a smile.

"I noticed you were singing along with some of the songs. Have you thought of traveling?"

I shook my head. "Oh no, I could never afford it."

"You don't have to pay for it yourself. You can get sponsors. Why don't you just try out?"

If my boss had been standing there, I would never have auditioned, but she wasn't, and I was desperate for a way to improve my life. I could sing on key, but I wasn't a gifted singer. I sang a song for her, but I didn't expect much to come of it.

Three days later, I got a call from Jenny at The Reach Out Singers headquarters. She offered me an alto position and gave me a choice between several tours. One was a nine-month tour to Australia and New Zealand. My heart skipped. Perhaps this was an answer to the prayer I'd said in Dylan's car. I told her I'd pray about it.

I took a leap of faith when I left my family, but this leap could affect my faith in God. Up to this point, everybody I knew was an Adventist. Except for a few people at the care center, I'd never had a friend who wasn't connected to the Adventist church.

When I was a kid, Daddy had me memorize a quote from the Adventist prophet about Protestant Christians joining hands with Catholics at the end of the world. It warned against ecumenicism. Christians who did this would be lost. The Reach Out Singers included people from several different denominations. I wondered if joining them would cost me my salvation, but I didn't consult Daddy because I already knew what he'd say. There was a drummer in the band. If he didn't like the Heritage Singers, there was no way he'd approve of the Reach Out Singers. Besides, I wanted to explore other ways of thinking for myself.

Uniting with other Christians wasn't my only concern. I worried about what I'd eat. I'd been working at a vegetarian cafeteria, where most of my friends were vegetarian. I'd never tasted meat, fish, or eggs and didn't drink milk, coffee, or wine. Traveling around the country and across the world with people who ate meat and went to church on Sundays made me nervous. Despite my concerns, I was curious to see how other people lived.

Going on this tour might seem like running away from my problems, but it could also be a way to find myself. The more I thought about it, it seemed like an opportunity I couldn't turn down. I called the recruiter and chose Tour Z for Australia and New Zealand because kangaroos and koalas had always fascinated me. My soul was screaming to see the world. I was about to do something bigger than I'd ever done before, and I sensed this tour would change my life.

Abby had barely arrived. I'd hoped to offer her a safe place like Ruth and Earl had done for me, but I wasn't settled like them, and I didn't have the resources. It was stressful to tell Abby that I was leaving for nine months, but she seemed to take it well.

I returned from work a few days later to discover Abby had already moved out. She left a stack of dirty ice cream bowls in the sink and a pile of hulls where her parakeet's cage had been. My heart ached to realize she'd left no number or forwarding address.

Jake took off, Mara left, and now Abby had disappeared. Of course, she would probably say it was me who was leaving her, and that was true. She couldn't pay rent and come up with a new deposit at the same time. Our family never gave notice when we moved. Daddy taught us to disappear when we owed money. It was one thing to do this to strangers, but especially painful when it affected the way we treated each other. I understood that Abby hated any type of confrontation, so I didn't hold it against her.

The thought of my little sister wandering the streets of Walla Walla filled my mind with Momma's worst-case scenarios. Where had she gone? Was she sleeping at a state park? We'd grown up adjusting to many different living situations. I knew Abby was resourceful, but she was also naïve. I prayed she could stay safe.

While I was trying to figure out where Abby went, the phone rang.

It was my recruiter.

"Do you know a guy named Dylan?"

"Why?"

"He signed up for Tour Z. I figured since you live in the same town and are both Adventists, this must be more than a coincidence."

"What? I don't know what kind of joke he's playing, but I'm not going on any tour with him."

My trust in Dylan was based on his not having ulterior motives like some guys I had known. I appreciated the rides and the mixtape. I enjoyed our talks and didn't mind hanging out with him, but I shuddered when I remembered Debbie's murder and the pushy landlord. I wasn't dropping out of college and quitting my job to get stalked all the way to Australia.

I had no idea where Abby was, but I knew where Dylan was, so I put on my shoes, marched over to his place, and pounded on the door.

When Dylan opened, I didn't even bother to say hello.

"Look, I don't know what kind of game you're playing—but quit stalking me."

11 Livin' On a Prayer

Anything large enough
for a wish to light upon,
is large enough
to hang a prayer upon.
-George Macdonald

Dylan looked surprised to see me angry.

"I have no idea what you're talking about."

"You never told me you were following me on the tour to Australia."

"I didn't know you were going."

Then I remembered he wasn't working on the day of the concert.

"How did you even know about the singers?"

"I went to their concert at Village Hall."

"Oh, I see. So maybe it was a misunderstanding, but please stay away from me."

"That's going to be hard if we go on the same tour."

"I'm not switching tours; I specifically chose a country where I can understand the language."

"Me too, but I also wanted to go where no one knows me."

When I realized he was disappointed to know I was coming along, I felt sorry for yelling at him.

"Have you bought your airline ticket yet?"

I shook my head.

"I'll check the airlines and see if we can fly together."

"You'd do that? I'm terrified of flying."

"Maybe flying with someone you know will make it easier."

We agreed to meet the next week to discuss the trip.

A few days later, I came home from work to find a plate of homemade chocolate chip cookies on the counter with a Bible verse.

At first, I suspected Abby—no one else had the key. On closer inspection, there were eggs in the cookies, and none of Momma's daughters knew how to bake with eggs.

I called Dylan to confirm the time to meet. Before we hung up, I asked if he knew who might have made the cookies.

"It could be Kari; she likes to bake for people."

After we hung up, I opened the refrigerator and found fresh garden produce.

I called Dylan back.

"They also filled my fridge with food."

"That's cool." He sounded distracted and busy, so I said I'd see him on Thursday.

When I opened my nearly empty cupboards to find cans of soup and beans, I decided to look in the freezer and found my favorite vegetarian sandwich meat.

I called Dylan for the third time. "They even knew my favorite veggie meat."

"What is your favorite veggie meat?" He sounded curious.

"Baloney."

"You're lucky. I'm living off soda crackers, sweet relish, and fake chicken."

"Well, let me know if you get hungry because I've got plenty of food."

I asked around at work, and then among my friends at the college, but no one knew who my mysterious benefactor was. I finally gave up asking and accepted the gift. It gave me the feeling that God was leading.

I found Abby at McDonald's. She didn't seem to know anything about the food in my cupboards, and there wasn't much time to talk since she was at work. She'd found a cheap studio to rent. I thought she'd abandoned me by leaving me to pay double rent, but after we spoke, I realized she thought I was abandoning her by leaving town. Our situations were complicated, and we were at different places in our lives.

Since Dylan was coming over, I decided to cook. We needed to eat, and it might be the last time we had a homemade vegetarian meal for a while.

There were a few exceptions to the non-dairy rule in my family, and lasagna was one of them. I ran to the store and bought some mozzarella and a loaf of sourdough bread. A quick salad made from the produce in my fridge rounded out our delicious lasagna meal.

By the time Dylan arrived, the aroma of sautéed onions, roasted garlic, and chopped basil filled the room. I didn't worry about having garlic breath—this wasn't a date—it was just two friends comparing notes about a trip.

Dylan made an announcement.

"I got tickets leaving from Seattle the day before training camp starts."

"Then I guess we're going to Sioux Falls."

I went to my purse, took out most of the money I had, and gave it to him.

While we were eating, there was a knock on the back door. I turned to see my landlady pressing her nose against the glass. I knew she was looking for Abby's half of the rent. Not wanting Dylan to hear our conversation, I stepped outside.

"I got your note about paying the rest of the rent next Friday, but I'm concerned since you also gave your notice to move."

It was embarrassing to explain that I was going as a missionary when I couldn't even pay my rent on time.

"I'll be here for the rest of the month; my sister surprised me by moving out, and I'm short."

Her anxious eyes and wrinkled brow told me she wouldn't leave without a detailed explanation.

"Why can't your dad pay your sister's half?"

"He just can't."

"What kind of father doesn't help his daughters pay their bills?"

I realized she'd mistaken me for one of those girls whose father carried her boxes to the third floor of the dorm and took her out for dinner afterward. She didn't realize that Abby and I weren't those girls—we were on our own.

"I'm sorry. My father's low on funds because he's moving from Alaska to Seattle."

I spoke the truth, but my face burned with shame. Those words–moving, late rent, and leaving town–formed such a tight knot in my stomach that I began to feel nauseous. The landlady got back in her truck and slammed the door. I knew her anger was justified, but I had no money to pay her until the following week.

I went back inside to find Dylan's jaw twitching. He'd always appeared calm and almost carefree—I'd never seen this side of him. Concerned that he might have overheard our conversation and was thinking less of me, I decided to spill my guts.

"I don't know if I'm doing the right thing by going on this trip. My life's a total disaster, and I can't seem to graduate from college or connect with men. I don't know how to be authentic, and I'm so worried about what other people think that I screw everything up."

I paused to see if my confession had turned him off. His jaw continued to twitch. Had I said too much? Why did he seem so uncomfortable?

I held my breath. When he did speak, Dylan spoke fast, as if he wanted to say something before he changed his mind.

"I need to get my act together or move to San Francisco."

What was he talking about?

"Between the AIDS crisis and the fact that I could get rejected by everyone I've ever known, I think going on this tour might be the safest place for me."

He paused and stared at the carpet as if reading something on it.

"I know it's wrong, but the truth is that ever since I was three, I've dreamed of a man holding me."

A cold wave washed over me as if someone had thrown an ice pack against my shoulder. I felt scared. I'd never known anyone as kind as Dylan before, and I was terrified of him burning in the lake of fire—at least, that's what I'd been told would happen to people like him.

He was waiting for my response. Perhaps he was testing me to see if we could get along for the next nine months. I put on my most empathetic smile.

"God will help anyone who asks him. I'll pray for you."

The words were what every Christian fundamentalist girl was taught to say, but my heart felt hollow.

We prayed again. This is time for Abby to stay safe and for us to grow closer to God.

It felt good to pray and hand our problems over to God, but I found it hard to sleep with the fires of hell swirling in my head.

There was one word neither of us had used, and that was what some called people like Dylan. We'd been told it was such an abomination that neither of us dared to speak the word out loud. Daddy had never used any specific term, but he'd warned me that some people were different, and they would be lost because they went against God's natural order of things.

It was strange enough to be leaving the Adventist ghetto, but now I'd be hanging out with someone the church considered lost. I couldn't imagine Dylan lost. He seemed like one of the best Christians I'd ever met. Momma always said birds of a feather flock together. If I hung out with him, would I end up in the lake of fire, too?

Then I remembered how Momma didn't like me watching Mister Rogers' Neighborhood. She said he was odd. I was fascinated by his puppets and cheerful songs. I couldn't find anything wrong with Mister Rogers, but Momma said you can't always see it unless you pay close attention.

The more I thought about it, the more I realized how much Dylan and Mister Rogers had in common. They both liked to sing and play the piano, they both enjoyed performing drama, they both wore sweaters, and they both treated people with kindness.

I sat up straight in bed. "Oh, my word! I'm going on tour with Mister Rogers!"

12 That's What Friends Are For

*Walking with a friend
in the dark is better than
walking alone in the light.*
-Helen Keller

When we met at Sea-Tac airport, Dylan's family had come to see him off. His parents were friendly and hugged us as we said goodbye.

My hands were shaking as the plane lifted off, and I gasped when my stomach dropped. It felt like my entire life was passing before my eyes. I wondered if I was doing the right thing.

"What if the Sunday Christians don't like us?"

Dylan laughed, then grabbed my hand to hold it steady.

"I went to public high school for my junior year and joined a Christian club. People are basically the same no matter what church they go to. And Sunday Christians don't even think about all the stuff that Adventists are worried about."

"What if I can't find enough vegetarian food and I starve?"

"I'll help you."

"You're lucky to have the support of your family. I sent dozens of letters, but no one—not even my parents would support me because the Reach Out Singers isn't an Adventist organization."

He rolled his eyes. "Some people think they're the only ones going to heaven."

"My dad made me memorize that prophetic quote about Protestants holding hands across the gulf with Catholics at the end of the world. Do you think it's true?"

His eyes grew large. I could tell Dylan was beginning to wonder what kind of fanatic he was traveling with. I also got the feeling Daddy wouldn't approve of his parents. I slowly withdrew my hand from his, leaned back in my seat, and shut my eyes to pray.

I prayed the plane wouldn't crash, that I'd find enough to eat and that people would like me. Most of all, I prayed for God to forgive me if going on this tour was a mistake. Perhaps my decision to escape my problems had been in haste. Was Daddy right? Was I stepping on Satan's ground by singing syncopated music with Sunday Christians and a drummer? I especially begged God to protect me from holy rollers speaking in tongues and Catholics who wanted to persecute me.

When we arrived at the Reach Out Singers Training Camp in Sioux Falls, South Dakota, I discovered prejudice ran both ways. They'd never had any Adventists before. Our recruiter had to get special permission to invite us. The organization's founder allowed us, but he warned us not to proselytize. He said he wasn't sure if we'd fit in. I didn't blame him—I wasn't sure either.

Dylan and I met our teammates in a large room, where Jenny, the recruiter, introduced the Tour Z leaders, Glenn and Becky. Becky had a degree in piano performance and seemed a little uptight about Glenn. Every time he interrupted her, her face grew red, and she tossed her hands in exasperation. Glenn slumped in his chair as if he were lounging beside a pool. I questioned if they'd get along, but I kept my concerns to myself.

A tall blond girl named Lynn stood up and flashed us a friendly smile. As the only South Dakotan, she welcomed us to her state and sang a song in a clear, bell-like voice.

A guy in the row behind me whispered, "Wow! She's better than Sandi Patty."

He was right. Lynn's beautiful voice made me nervous about my limited talent, but she was so friendly and easygoing that I immediately liked her.

A chatty brunette named Sadie described how she'd once chased a thug on the streets of Chicago to get her purse back. I couldn't imagine living in a large city or hunting someone down to get my stuff back. Sadie seemed like a good person to have on my side in case any fights broke out.

Beth was a reserved Canadian. Her smoky alto voice perfectly complemented Lynn's soprano and Dylan's tenor. She also helped me find my way through our alto parts. Everyone laughed at her dry sense of humor.

Rob was a clown who played bass. He could do voice impressions, from Donald Duck to movie characters. If anyone had a bad day, Rob could make them laugh.

Steve was a football champ who came for one reason—to play the drums. When Jenny said he'd need to sit out the concert if the audience couldn't hear our voices over the drums, he scowled.

Tommy was an extrovert from Denmark who brought his European style and curiosity to the United States. I immediately connected with him because my grandfather was a Danish immigrant, and our family names were one letter off. We joked that we might be cousins.

The guys on Tour Z were nice-looking, but I'd been warned never to marry anyone unless they were an Adventist. Plus, I wasn't on tour to find a boyfriend—I was taking this trip to find out about myself. Studying the friendly faces around the circle, I decided I could handle living with them for nine months.

When the introductions were over, Jenny asked if someone could play the piano. Dylan raised his hand. I noticed he seemed confident—perhaps too confident. After all, we'd just heard that Becky was a piano performance major.

The first time through the song, Dylan missed some notes and hit a couple of sharps, and I felt nervous for him. As he stumbled through the next verse, I noticed a sly smile on Becky's lips. I was sure she could play the song better, but Dylan was my friend. I sat taller in my seat, preparing to defend him.

It turned out Dylan didn't need defending. By the third verse of the song, something changed. He'd filled out the chords and picked up the rhythm. By the fourth verse, the song sounded full and flowing, and people sang with enthusiasm. By then, Becky's smile had faded.

Later, when we were alone, I asked Dylan what happened.

"Were you just nervous?"

"It took a few tries to figure out the song because I play by ear."

When people discovered Dylan could play any tune by ear. They asked him to accompany them when they wanted to write a song or didn't have the music. When it came to improvising, Becky, with all of her training, could never compete with Dylan's raw talent. Some people called him a genius, but Dylan seemed unaffected by what people thought about his playing.

We spent the two weeks at training camp preparing for life on the road. There were voice lessons on breathing and harmonizing and classes to teach us the ropes of organizing, packing, and, most importantly, how to get along with each other. Jenny and a guy named Mike taught us the group rules. The first rule was a Bible verse.

"Let everyone be subject to the governing authorities, for there is no authority except that which God has established. God has established the authorities that exist" (Romans 13:1).

Jenny said this meant obeying Glenn and Becky. Obedience was necessary to keep order in the group because someone had to be in charge, and if we each did our own thing, it would lead to chaos.

The rules made sense, and no one seemed worried about obeying, so I signed the agreement.

The second rule was never to argue about doctrines. We had twelve people with eight denominations, and to avoid splitting the group, we were to focus on Jesus because he was the one thing we had in common. Not arguing over doctrines was a new thing for me. I had my proof texts, but it was a relief to set them aside.

It was vital for us not to be hypocrites. If we disagreed with a teammate, we were to resolve it before the concert. If we couldn't fix it, we would need to sit out the concert until our hearts were right. Jenny said people rarely sat out the concert, because differences could usually be resolved during the prayer hour before the concert.

There were lots of meetings at the training camp. During one session, I told Jenny I needed to use the restroom. She said to wait. Thirty minutes later, I was getting uncomfortable, but Jenny insisted I remain in the meeting. Finally, without permission, I dashed to the restroom and was back within three minutes.

After the meeting, Jenny approached me in front of the rest of Tour Z and slapped me in the face. Tears burned my eyes as I tried to understand what had just happened.

"I am sorry to punish you, but you disobeyed."

My face burned with shame while my teammates wondered what I'd done. I didn't defend myself because I'd been hit so many times while growing up that a part of me felt I deserved it. At the same time, neither of my parents had ever hit me in the face. My face was my identity, and I felt mortified for weeks whenever I thought about it.

There were several pianos at training camp, and Dylan usually played one of them. After he learned the concert songs, he moved on to arrangements for special music with different people. When no one required his help, he played whatever he wanted. My favorite was "Love Theme from St. Elmo's Fire." For the saxophone part, he played the highest keys on the piano, which sounded like chimes. As the notes rose, it created such a euphoria that I dropped whatever I was doing and sat mesmerized whenever I heard it.

Because I often listened while Dylan played the piano, one of our teammates started calling us Lucy and Schroeder from the Peanuts cartoon. Another guy called me "Snowpea." For the first time in my life, I began to feel like I belonged to a group. I was no longer an outsider—with my Tour Z teammates, I was an insider, and I had the nicknames to prove it.

After training camp, we hit the road in a 24-seat bus. We each had a section with two seats. I sat at the back, behind Dylan.

We started from Sioux Falls and drove slowly across the prairies and farmland of the Midwest. Some drives were only a couple of hours, while others took all day to reach the next concert venue. Most of our concerts were at a church, but sometimes, we sang in schools, nursing homes, and prisons.

Dylan liked maps, so he volunteered to be the navigator. Most of us were on tour to be tourists. We came to do concerts, but we also wanted to explore the highlights of each state as much as possible. Each day was an adventure with new territories to explore. Every time we drove over a state line, we cheered.

Road life was full of routines to protect our sanity and get us to the next destination on time. Our daily schedule included a quiet hour with God, worship with each other, hours riding the bus, exploring tourist attractions, setting up sound equipment, putting on a concert, and visiting with the host families who took us home. These were long and busy days.

Sadie liked to keep the group organized and on time, which led to some of the guys calling her bossy. I didn't think she was bossy at all—I thought she would make a great leader.

Glenn was a little older, and he wasn't as carefree as the rest of us. Perhaps it was too much pressure to oversee eleven other people. I found him hard to get along with because he didn't communicate well and never approved of the things I wanted to do.

Several of us wanted to stop by the Laura Ingalls Wilder Museum in Walnut Grove, Minnesota, but Glenn initially said no. This created a rebellion. Dylan, as the navigator and a peacemaker at heart, found a shortcut to take us past Walnut Grove. We had fun at the museum, and we were soon back on the bus with a grumpy leader. We usually had free time to get ready and stretch our legs when we arrived at the church before concerts. This time, Glenn singled me out to clean the inside of the bus. He specifically told me to do it by myself. I knew he was punishing me for getting Dylan to find a way to visit the museum.

Despite Glenn's passive-aggressive personality, we found ways to circumvent his control. One night, we stayed in a hotel and snuck out after he and Becky were asleep. We bought a few snacks and held a party in a car wash. It was the only place with enough light to see each other's faces. Getting to know each other gave us a sense of satisfaction and strengthened our bond.

We entertained ourselves with books and music during the long drives. I discovered no one cared if I rocked. Rob played his air guitar, Steve played imaginary drums, and Lynn sang along with her Walkman. Even Dylan played an imaginary keyboard with his fingers. No one was in sync with anyone else. Each person was in their private world, which made it easy for me to escape my body and rock away at the back of the bus.

Every potluck I'd attended before going on tour was strictly vegetarian. The sights and smells of meat were foreign to me. I ate lots of carrot sticks, white rolls, and potato chips. It wasn't a very healthy diet. Some of my tour mates worried that I wasn't getting good nutrition. Whenever Glenn allowed us to stop, Dylan bought me a vegetarian burrito at various fast-food chains.

One hour each morning was reserved for reading the Bible. Our leaders told us not to talk with each other during this quiet time. While my teammates cheerfully scattered across the church grounds or found a nearby park to read their Bibles, I felt trapped.

I'd memorized proof texts for Adventist doctrines, but I never read for the joy of knowing Jesus. The only Bible I'd ever read was the King James version, which I found hard to understand. I figured I must be doing it wrong, but I didn't mention this out of fear of looking like a worse Christian than everyone else.

We each had a part in each concert besides singing. Mine was to perform silly skits with Tommy to give the audience a break from the music.

When we introduced ourselves. I told people I was a former bag lady who'd been homeschooled without the books. The audience always laughed, but I wasn't joking. These statements hid the painful truth about my life—that I'd grown up without an education, and my family had often been homeless. I hadn't forgotten about my elephant memory and truth-telling ability, but I'd set them aside so I could fit in at college, and now it was getting harder to use them. I ached to be authentic, but I couldn't bring myself to share what I'd been through. I suspected others had secrets, too, but I didn't ask because I was too busy trying to hide my own.

Since his confession at my apartment, I carried Dylan's secret, too. Despite being the youngest member of Tour Z, Dylan became one of the main contributors to our concerts. He not only played the keyboard, but his tenor voice added harmonies unlike anyone else. The audience reported chills whenever Dylan arranged a hymn with his tenor, Lynn's soprano, and Beth's alto. It was like experiencing a taste of heaven.

Lynn organized our sleeping schedules with the host families. We stayed with all kinds of people. Most hosts took at least two team members to their homes. I enjoyed sharing a room with Lynn and Sadie where we could talk in private.

We met all kinds of pastors. As an empathic personality, I related to many of them as they cared for the people in their congregations. We met many self-sacrificing and charismatic leaders, but not one woman pastor. Daddy would say this was as it should be, but I couldn't shake the feeling that God called women, too. I, myself, had felt called, but I knew my parents would never accept me if I followed that call.

I was starting to realize other Christians were God's people, too, but there was one exception. I still viewed Catholics through the lens of the Dark Ages. Whenever we sang in a Catholic school or church, I felt anxious. While we sang, I thought of the Von Trapp Family in "The Sound of Music," planning to escape the Nazis by running out the back door. In my overactive imagination,

I imagined Tour Z running from priests who might torture or kill us.

One evening, it was my turn to give a short talk at a Catholic college. I don't recall what I spoke about, but I never asked for money. It was too embarrassing to admit that no one in the Adventist church would sponsor me.

It was already dusk as we coiled up the cords and carried our equipment outside. I was walking alone when a man began to follow me. I walked faster, and so did he. I looked for my friends, but they were inside, changing clothes, tearing down equipment, or leaving with their host families. I'd forgotten something on the bus, and now I was alone. Turning to face the man, I was shocked to see he was wearing a robe. I could barely make out the cross hanging from his neck in the dim light of the streetlamp. My breath caught as he held out his hand.

His voice was soft, and his words were cryptic.

"I see him in you."

"What?"

"Thank you for your talk. I see Jesus in you."

He pressed his hand closer.

"I'd like to sponsor you."

With a shaky hand, I reached out and took whatever he was offering.

When he turned to leave, I looked inside my hand and found three crisp one-hundred-dollar bills.

With my fear gone, I turned to shout, "Thank you," but he'd already disappeared.

I fell asleep that night, marveling how every Adventist I knew had refused to sponsor me because I was on an ecumenical mission. Their biggest fear was that I might unite with the Catholic church. Yet a priest who would never see me again provided for me with love. Surely, this was a sign that I belonged on this tour.

We celebrated Thanksgiving at Lynn's family farm. I'd been raised with Old Testament laws stating that people weren't supposed to touch a pig, let alone eat one. I'd even heard people at Walla Walla College arguing over whether playing with a football made of pigskin was okay. Despite this, I found myself fascinated with the pigs on their farm. The mama pigs seemed sweet, and the baby pigs were cute. I noticed it took very little to scare them. If I flapped my arms and ran toward them, hundreds of pigs ran to the other end of the field.

Lynn stared at me like I was crazy. She had no interest in chasing pigs, but I'd never had much power, and chasing pigs was a thrill.

One day, after the pigs ran squealing to the other side of the pasture, I noticed a shadow behind me. It was Lynn's dad. I waited, half expecting him to slap or yell at me for scaring his pigs, but he just stood beside me for a minute.

When he spoke, his voice was soft.

"I suppose it doesn't hurt to chase them a little, but it does send fear hormones coursing through their bodies."

Then he turned back to his tractor.

I thought about what a monster I must look like to those poor pigs. This was not the person I wanted to be. I didn't want to live my life making innocent creatures afraid of me.

I sat on a swing and stared at the farmhouse. Lynn had lived her entire life in that house. With six older siblings, a church family, and a high school class, she was guaranteed a place to belong. I wondered what that felt like. Her hard-working and loving parents lived a life of practical love for their neighbors. It seemed these Sunday-keeping, pig-eating Christians were as kind and close to Jesus as any people I'd met.

Going on Tour helped me realize that my attempts to be normal at Walla Walla College were motivated by my desire to be part of society. As a member of Tour Z, I felt like I belonged for the first time in my life.

A few days before we split up for Christmas break, Dylan and I stayed with the same host family. I woke up at four in the morning to get a glass of water and found Dylan sitting on the sofa. His hair was uncombed, and I'd never seen him look so disheveled. He looked tired like he'd been sitting up all night.

"Why are you up so early?"

He lowered his voice to a whisper.

"I can't sleep because Glenn keeps touching me."

13 All Out of Love

*If you think you are so enlightened,
spend a weekend with your family.*
-Ram Dass

For Christmas break, I stayed with Jake and Carrie, who lived near Portland, Oregon. It was my first time visiting my brother as an adult in his home. I was proud of him for getting his GED and driver's license. He and Carrie both had full-time jobs and were renting a small but cozy apartment.

They didn't have a guest room, but I didn't mind sleeping on the sofa. My thoughtful hosts provided vegetarian options for me even though they had started eating meat. Jake even found me a temporary job at a printing company. It was monotonous work, but I was grateful to earn money for my trip down under.

I wasn't sure what to think about Jake taking showers with his girlfriend and eating hamburgers, but I decided to treat them like I did my friends on tour. There was no universal law that people had to follow family rules once they grew up. Probably the hardest change for me to understand was that Jake had gone sour on religion. At the same time, it was his right to say how he felt. I couldn't blame him. I, too, had differences with the way we were raised.

I'd been working for two weeks, and it was almost Christmas when we sat down to a supper of vegetarian meatloaf, mashed potatoes, and green beans. Carrie was a good cook, and it was one of the most delicious meals I'd eaten since I'd been on tour.

When we were kids, Jake and I often shared our fears and insecurities. I'd always assumed the role of a wise older sister, but now I was the floundering one who had no clue how to spend my life once the tour ended. I shared how hard it had been to go to college without financial aid and a high school education.

Jake listened intently to my concerns and tried to encourage me.

"Did you know they have remedial classes for adults who never attended high school?"

This was news to me. If I'd told my advisor why I struggled, he might have offered this solution.

We were having a good conversation between siblings until Carrie said something that annoyed me.

"I think it's hard because you guys grew up in such a dysfunctional family."

"What? I wouldn't call our family dysfunctional." I looked to see if Jake agreed with her, but his eyes wouldn't meet mine.

"I'm not calling you dysfunctional. I mean your parents—you know, with all the moving and belting and no high school education."

Carrie didn't even know our parents.

"There were reasons for those things. It's not like our parents were jerks."

"I didn't say there were jerks—just dysfunctional."

I thought of Momma's rule about family togetherness. We were never to repeat family secrets to anyone outside the family. I glanced at Jake again, wondering what he'd been telling his girlfriend.

"I've taken social work classes and never called our family dysfunctional."

I noticed Jake glancing at Carrie like a secret passed between them. I was irritated to think my brother's allegiance had switched from our family to his girlfriend. Mara had warned me about this.

Carrie tried to correct the misunderstanding. "It's not your fault. I read that people who grow up in dysfunctional families can't always see it."

The room grew silent as I stared at a small ivy plant hanging from a macrame above Carrie's head.

"I won't sit here and let you bash my parents."

"I'm not bashing them. I'm just acknowledging what is."

Without thinking, I grabbed the macrame rope and dumped the plant, dirt, and all over Carrie's head.

She gasped as the dirt fell through her hair and onto her mashed potatoes.

I immediately regretted what I'd done and tried to apologize, but Jake wouldn't listen. He'd had enough.

"Get out! I won't allow you to be rude to my girlfriend in her own home."

The freezing wind hit me in the face just as the door slammed shut behind me. Standing on the porch in a stupor, I stared at the traffic until I realized I was freezing and needed a place to stay warm.

When the door reopened, I felt a rush of hope, but Jake was just tossing my coat out the door. With already frozen fingers, I fumbled to zip up my jacket, before walking to a pay phone where I called Abby. She and her boyfriend agreed to drive from Walla Walla to pick me up.

Daddy and Momma were living with Mara near Spokane, so I called them next. Daddy said he'd come get me in Walla Walla.

Jake allowed me to wait for Abby on the sofa while he and Carrie went to bed. It took Abby six hours to arrive, so I had a lot of time to think. I wasn't sure what compelled me to do such a crazy thing, but protecting my parents and keeping the family secrets left me feeling unhinged.

When Abby and her boyfriend arrived, they were in good spirits, considering it was the middle of the night. She told me how they'd met while she was working at McDonald's. My sister seemed to be in love, and I was happy for her.

When we stopped at a rest area and went inside, Abby informed me that she was using the rhythm method for birth control.

"Oh, Abby, I heard that doesn't work. Maybe you should get on the pill."

"Are you on the pill?"

"No. I've never had sex."

"Well, when you do have sex, let me know."

Silence filled the stalls between us. I couldn't believe my little sister was trumping my wisdom with her experience. As the oldest, I felt I should be telling her how birth control worked. My life was clearly not turning out the way I'd planned. It was time to face the reality that my siblings were well on their way to normal while I seemed to be falling further and further behind.

We arrived in Walla Walla as a rosy dawn filled the sky. I slept a few hours on the floor of Abby's studio apartment before Daddy drove me to Spokane. I was glad to see Daddy, but I didn't look forward to three hours of interrogation about life on tour.

"Hey, weren't you planning to stay at Jake's?"

"Yeah, but I want to see you guys too." I tried to sound casual like it was my plan all along.

"We're always glad to see you. Is everything ok?"

"Yeah, I just figured I'd see everyone on my break. It's easier now that you aren't in Alaska."

I answered his questions carefully without going into detail. I felt ashamed for dumping the plant over Carrie's head, plus I didn't want to hurt his feelings by telling him what she'd said about our family.

It seemed nobody in my family understood why I was on tour. Jake was no longer a believer and saw little reason for singing about Jesus. Abby was caught up in her new relationship. And Mara, who was in dental assisting school, had always craved stability. My life looked like a chaotic mess to them.

While my siblings showed little interest in my traveling adventures, Daddy seemed obsessed.

"How do you keep the Sabbath?"

"Saturdays are our day off."

This was true, but his idea of what was okay to do on Sabbath differed from mine.

"And what about drums? And the syncopated beat? Remember, the devil can write songs, too."

I tried not to roll my eyes.

"We've been over this before. I don't think Satan writes songs about Jesus just to get us hooked on a syncopated beat."

He sighed loudly and said nothing for several minutes to let me know he was annoyed by my point of view. Finally, I couldn't take his silence any longer.

"Daddy, why can't you just be proud of me? Right now, this tour is my one thing."

Daddy's face softened. "I am proud of you, honey, but remember, you're the firstborn. You need to set a good example for your siblings."

I cringed. He'd said that ever since I was a little girl, and it wasn't fair. My siblings were like wild horses freed from the barn. There wasn't much I could do to lead them back into Daddy's way of thinking at this point—even if I wanted to. I wished I could tell him that music was the least of our family's problems. I was the only one of his kids who hadn't tried sex or alcohol, but that would only leave the others open to scrutiny, so I changed the subject.

"Are you going to settle in Spokane?"

My parents and Mara lived in the country outside the city. He was excited about the prospect of making a living there. He was also into some multi-level marketing scheme where he peddled some vile-tasting health serum, and he thought I should try selling it, too. This gave him plenty to talk about on the rest of the drive.

I was glad to see Momma and Mara. We enjoyed a fun week of playing Scrabble and cooking our holiday favorites.

The week between Christmas and New Year's, Dylan left a message on the answering machine for me to call him. My parents didn't have long-distance on their phone, so I had to find a pay phone.

On the night of the call, a thick, icy fog blanketed the road.

Momma, imagining a worst-case scenario, questioned whether the call was necessary. I explained that Dylan had made my travel arrangements, and I counted on him to keep me informed.

"I can't imagine why he's calling, but what if my ticket has changed?"

It took Daddy twice as long as normal to drive the distance in the fog, but we finally made it to the phone booth. I jumped out of the warm car into the frigid air and pulled out a roll of quarters.

A man answered and put Dylan on the phone.

"Is everything okay?"

"Yeah, as much as it can be."

He lowered his voice. "I can't really talk right now. How are you?"

"I'm fine."

I wasn't sure if I was fine, but I couldn't talk either since I was within earshot of Daddy. Besides, even if I wasn't fine, what could Dylan do?

"I can't wait to get back on tour."

My heart leaped with understanding.

"Me too."

"I miss you."

"I miss you too."

I hung up, confident that despite the few words exchanged, we each understood what the other was feeling.

It was a relief to reverse my trip. Daddy drove me to Walla Walla. Then Abby and her boyfriend graciously returned me to Portland, where I boarded my flight back to Texas.

As the plane lifted off, I felt proud of myself for staying calm, but my heart was heavy. Thanks to one impulsive moment with a plant, my Christmas break had turned out nothing like I'd planned. My mind was full of questions. Would Jake and Carrie ever forgive me? Would my sisters and I learn to understand each other's choices? And would Daddy continue to think less of me for going on this ecumenical tour?

I looked forward to rejoining my tour family in Texas, where I could be myself. But I had a sinking feeling whenever I thought about Dylan. I wondered how he was going to deal with Glenn.

14 Can't Fight This Feeling

*We dance round
in a ring and suppose,
but the secret sits
in the middle and knows.*
–Robert Frost

Dylan had to report to Glenn every day because he was in charge of navigating road trips and organizing the concerts. I didn't know the details, but whatever happened in that bed had really upset Dylan. As his friend, I was determined to keep him safe, so I confided in Lynn. She adjusted the sleep schedule to ensure Dylan would never have to stay with Glenn again.

I also made it my business to be sure Dylan and Glenn were never alone. As a result, it seemed like Glenn singled me out for the most tedious tasks—especially when it would separate me from Dylan. Despite my extra duties, my plan to keep Dylan safe seemed to be working as we slowly continued our journey toward California.

Glenn was inconsistent. He appeared nice until he made some arbitrary rule to remind everyone that he was in charge. The fact that he and Becky barely got along gave us an excuse to either choose her authority over his or do whatever we wanted behind his back.

One Saturday, our teammates were shopping inside the mall while Dylan and I stayed on the bus. He was working on the concert schedule while I cleaned the floor.

"We have three concerts—two at a large Lutheran church, then an evening concert at a Pentecostal church. Do you want to do the same skit at each concert or mix it up?"

"Let me see what Tommy says. Did you notice Glenn asked me to clean the bus again?" I rolled my eyes and reached down to pick up some gum wrappers and a pop can off the floor.

Dylan picked up a candy bar wrapper and placed it in the trash bag I was holding. "He hasn't spoken to me for weeks except to correct the concert schedule."

"Do you think he wonders why you never stay with him?"

"I don't know, and I don't care."

Dylan and I had become allies to survive Glenn's abuse. While I was watching out for him, he took care of me. Dylan often asked Glenn to stop at places where we could get a vegetarian lunch for my sake.

One of my favorite people was Tommy. He never met a stranger without turning them into a friend. One day, someone's stereo was playing "Wake Me Up Before You Go-Go" by Wham, and I asked, "What is the jitterbug?"

Tommy jumped up, grabbed my hands, and pulled me to my feet.

"I'll show you!"

I wasn't very coordinated, but I loved how my full skirt billowed around me as we danced. Tommy patiently guided my moves, never mentioning my awkward feet—even when I stepped on his foot.

I'd never danced like that before, and I felt beautiful and free. At the song's end, Tommy smiled and hugged me. I liked Tommy because he was spontaneous and fun. He was also affectionate with everyone. Sometimes, when walking with one of the guys, he'd put his arm around them.

As I finished cleaning the bus, I looked up and saw Steve and Tommy walking out of the mall and holding hands. I thought about what happened between Glenn and Dylan. On the drive to the next church, Tommy and Steve fell asleep on the bus with their arms around each other. Acid rose in my throat. If men holding hands was acceptable, where would it end? And who would stand up against Glenn if he bothered Dylan again?

Other people's relationships were none of my business, but I couldn't stop thinking about what I perceived was a threat to all of us. I'd been taught that Satan was out to steal men's souls through "unnatural relationships." That teaching and the fear on Dylan's face that morning before Christmas break made me hyper-vigilant. Holding hands might seem innocent, but someone needed to stop the guys in our group from touching each other. I figured Tommy and Steve would be more careful if they realized we were dealing with a molester.

While we prepared for the concert with prayer and singing that night, Tommy held Steve's hand again. To be fair, we were all holding hands around the circle, but my fears were boiling over. Remembering how our recruiter told us to resolve stuff before the concert, I decided to confront Tommy. I figured if I did it in front of everyone else, it would stop this nonsense.

"Tommy, can you please stop holding hands? I'm tired of you acting like a faggot."

The group grew silent. No one had heard me use the word gay, let alone a slur. But I'd heard it somewhere, and that's what came out of my mouth.

I realized I'd made a mistake when I saw Tommy's face contort in pain.

"You don't know me, Cheri. You don't know my struggles and how hard I try to follow God."

My face burned with shame as he wiped the tears from his eyes.

I tried to apologize, and Tommy graciously said he'd forgive me, but a dark cloud hung over the group as we prepared to step out and sing. I had to stand next to Tommy, and we would perform a skit together. Something had changed between us, and I felt sick that it was my fault, but the show had to go on.

For the next few days, Tommy barely looked at me. I felt like he could see straight through me and see my petty, selfish heart. I ached to think how careless I'd been, but I couldn't erase my hateful words with more words, and any attempt to apologize again would only sound condescending.

Everybody loved Tommy, and no one liked that I'd made him cry. Glenn hid behind his own shame, and even Becky, who usually called people out for their rude behavior, said nothing. I never even considered how Dylan might feel. What if I'd spoken those insulting words to him?

If we could've been honest, we might've discussed how I'd insulted the hidden identities of half of the men in our group. I'd gone from trying to be normal at college to trying to look like a good Christian on tour. In the pecking order of traditional Christianity, gays were the least respected. The patriarchy had raised me to believe anything other than a man and a woman sharing affection was satanic. And I wasn't alone. We were on a traditional Christian tour, and most of Tour Z believed God himself would burn gays. Even the gays thought this. Most of them had come to serve God, hoping they might change.

Sadie was another person who had frustrations with Glenn. As the treasurer, she craved communication and order, but Glenn was so disorganized that he often sprang things on her at the last minute.

One morning, Glenn announced he'd be on the phone for an hour. He told Sadie to combine our meal stipends and go to the grocery store to buy bread, cheese, and luncheon meat for breakfast and lunch. We were used to spending our meal stipends however we liked, and no one wanted cold sandwiches for breakfast.

Sadie loved her morning coffee. "Why can't we just go across the street to McDonald's?"

"Just do as I said." Glenn went back into the church office, leaving us frustrated by his arbitrary command.

"Remember what the Bible says about submitting to the authorities," Steve spoke sarcastically.

"I'm not sure God put Glenn over us." I glanced at Dylan, waiting for him to agree, but he said nothing.

No one moved to get on the bus and drive to the store. After a moment of silence, Sadie jumped up.

"We have an hour. Who wants hot coffee? I've got the money."

Sadie swung her backpack over her shoulder and started to cross the street. We all followed except for Becky, who got on the bus by herself.

An hour later, Glenn called us into the church and directed us to sit in a circle on the floor.

"We aren't leaving until each of you says you respect me."

One by one, my teammates begrudgingly gave in and stated they respected him. Becky said it, too—even though I never saw Glenn accepting her authority as a co-leader. I didn't like the double standard that men—even if they were molesters—had authority over the rest of us, including our female leader.

Sadie and Dylan were the last to give in, but I knew they were lying. We sat in silence for half an hour while Glenn waited for me to say I respected him.

Glenn blew out through his lips. "We have a long drive, and the clock is ticking, so come on, Cheri, we need to get on the road, or we'll be late."

I glared back at him. "Well, I'm not going to say it because I know what you've done, and I don't respect you."

The red creeping up his neck told me he knew that I knew his secret.

Rolling eyes and exasperated looks between my teammates revealed that most had no idea what I was talking about. I said nothing more because I wanted to protect Dylan.

We continued to wait until Glenn had no choice but to leave, or we'd be late for our next concert.

"Okay, everyone, get on the bus. Cheri, you can sit out the concert."

When we arrived at the next church, no one spoke to me out of fear that Glenn might punish them, too.

I put on my concert uniform and tied my scarf in place. It was humiliating to dress like the others and sit out the concert. How would I explain this to my host family?

I went back and sat by myself in the darkened church sanctuary while my teammates practiced songs without me. Then, they all rushed off to put on their concert attire.

It hurt that everyone else claimed to respect Glenn when I knew they didn't. The rest of the team seemed ready to move on, and it seemed like everyone thought I was the problem. For the first time on tour, I felt alone.

I didn't want my mascara to run, but I was struggling to choke back the tears when Dylan entered the sanctuary and stepped up to the piano. I barely noticed the song he was playing at first, but my mood lifted when I realized it was "Love Theme from St. Elmo's Fire."

Our eyes met, and there was no need for words as his fingers spoke through the music. Having one heart that understood was enough for me to sit through that concert and keep my dignity.

After the concert, I was disappointed to find out I'd be rooming alone with my host family. After such an awful day, having a girlfriend to vent to would've been nice.

As I got into the car, my host dad glanced at me through the rearview mirror. "How are you?"

I tried to hold back my tears, but the whole story came blubbering out.

He drove slowly, while his wife turned to face me.

"We prayed for a singer who needed comfort tonight. We're professional counselors, and we have chocolate cake."

It was one of those moments in my life when I felt seen by God. Could God really be watching out for me? First, $300, and now chocolate cake?

We stayed up past midnight while I described tour life. I also told them about Glenn molesting Dylan.

The man pounded his fist onto the table. "I'll help you call Reach Out headquarters in the morning because having a leader molesting people is not okay."

My host mom slid another slice of cake in my direction. "It's okay to reject male authority figures who are abusive."

I marveled at her words long after I got in bed. No one had told me this before. Did this mean I could reject Daddy's authority, too? Then I felt a pang of guilt because I knew Momma would never approve of these counselors and their worldly ways of thinking.

True to his word, my host dad called headquarters and helped me explain everything—including what I knew about Glenn touching Dylan. I told them to ask Dylan because I knew he'd tell them in greater detail.

In the end, the man from headquarters said, "We need to keep Glenn because your team is about to go overseas, and it's too late to get another leader."

Irritated, I replied, "Honestly, I'm not sure what Glenn does as our leader. He doesn't plan the concert schedules. Dylan does that. He doesn't lead us in practice. Becky does that. He doesn't navigate the road trips. Dylan does that. He doesn't manage the money. Sadie does that. He doesn't set up and tear down equipment. Tommy and Rob do that. And he doesn't organize the housing. Lynn does that. I'm sure we can do fine without him."

The man on the other end of the phone spoke as though I was in a court of law. "Cheri, do you remember signing an agreement that you would submit to the authorities God places over you?"

I had to say yes. I realized arguing whether God had placed Glenn in authority over me meant nothing to the man at headquarters. My host counselors had done all they could, but I would be stuck with Glenn as my leader.

As we prepared to go overseas, we stayed near Loma Linda University, where my friend Lucas was in medical school. I hadn't spoken to him since he told me goodbye on the swing at Walla

Walla College. I called him to say hi, and we arranged to meet on my day off. He was still my favorite of all the guys I'd known at Walla Walla, and I looked forward to seeing him even though I knew we'd never be more than friends.

As we gathered to pray before the evening concert, Dylan slipped into the chair beside me and waved an envelope.

"My host dad gave me two tickets to Disneyland for tomorrow. I was wondering who might enjoy it the most, and since you've never been, I chose you."

Stunned, I wasn't sure what to say.

"Are you sure?" I thought about the tilt-a-whirl and also my plans with Lucas.

He laughed. "It's more than rides—you'll like it."

I wasn't sure if I should go with Dylan or keep my appointment with Lucas. I might never get the chance to go to Disneyland again, so I decided to cancel on Lucas.

Even though my first trip to a carnival was a disaster, I was able to redeem myself a little at Disneyland. Dylan started me slow on "It's a Small World" and the "Jungle Ride." Then we tried the Teacups. He held my hand on "Thunder Mountain Railroad" before we moved on to "The Matterhorn" and "Space Mountain."

When we took a lunch break, Dylan dipped his fries in ketchup while I dipped mine in a chocolate shake.

Dylan wrinkled his nose. "Don't you like ketchup?"

I shook my head. "I've never tasted ketchup."

"Who's never tasted ketchup?"

"People who grow up in families that think vinegar is bad for you."

"But don't you eat dill pickles?"

"Yeah, come to think of it, I do." I wondered why I'd never noticed the inconsistency of Momma's food rules before.

"I bet if you try it, you'll like it." He shoved the ketchup-laden side of his basket of fries toward me.

My brain split between what was forbidden and Dylan's generous, smiling face. Could he be trusted?

"Come on, try it!" Dylan dipped a fry into the red sauce and held it to my mouth. His blue eyes were so earnest as he anticipated my response that I couldn't say no.

I opened my mouth and tasted ketchup for the first time. As the tangy flavor exploded on my tongue, I decided it was the most delicious thing I'd ever experienced, and I quickly grabbed five ketchup packs and ripped them open, spreading them across my fries.

Dylan laughed. "A little fries with your ketchup?"

"I'm making up for lost time."

We took another spin on the teacups and rode the "Thunder Mountain Railroad" several more times.

At the end of the day, as we watched the Disney Parade, I was exhausted yet satisfied that I'd made the right choice. For the first time in my life, I felt like a carefree child.

Maybe it was the Magic Kingdom, but with his thoughtful and chivalrous ways, Dylan was starting to look a lot like Prince Charming. As I drifted off to sleep, I thought he'd make a great husband for somebody.

15 Down Under

Truth, like gold,
is to be obtained
not by its growth,
but by washing away
from it all that is not gold.
-Leo Tolstoy

Two things happened that changed my spiritual life before I went down under. The first was losing my Bible, and the second was a host dad's prayer.

As a child, my parents taught me to mark my Bible with proof texts for Adventist doctrines. I was proud of my well-marked Bible, but I liked holding it better than reading it.

I was superstitious that the plane wouldn't crash as long I held my Bible. I clung to it as if it were a talisman for protection. I felt a sense of doom when it went missing until Sadie came to my rescue.

Walking from her seat at the front of the bus, she sat beside me.

"My mom works at Moody Bible Book Store, and I can get a discount. What version of the Bible would you like?"

"I don't think my Bible is replaceable."

"Of course it is. You can always mark a new Bible. Let me know which version you'd like."

Up to that point in my life, I'd only read The King James. "I guess the KJV, what other versions are there?"

She laughed. "Do you think Jesus spoke in King James' language?"

She rattled off a list of translations and paraphrases, but I had no idea which one to choose. "I don't think my dad would approve of anything but the King James."

A mischievous smile crossed her face. "Then I'll get you a New King James."

A week later, when we arrived at a church, my new Bible was waiting. Sadie's face glowed as she presented her gift. I graciously accepted it, but I was nervous about reading a modern version. Would God still talk to me this way? Could this version deceive me? Would the proof texts I'd marked since childhood still hold up in this newer version?

Leafing through my new Bible, certain words immediately jumped off the page and caught my eye—modern words like you and yours instead of thee and thou. Unhindered by ancient terms, stories freed from the old King James language began to take on fresh meaning for me. Instead of marking a Bible to prove others wrong, I read to learn about Jesus for the first time.

The second thing that changed my life was a host dad's prayer over pizza at a restaurant in East LA. He prayed against the evil around us and for nothing in the food to make us sick. I liked how he prayed for specific things, but I was a little on edge when I heard him curse.

On the way home, he and his wife gave me a tour of their rough-looking neighborhood.

"We had another shooting across the street last week. A bullet came straight through the wall and killed my neighbor. Then, last night, someone stole my car right in front of the house."

I swallowed while I tried to breathe through my anxiety. "Can you pray with me before going to bed?"

This man prayed like he knew Jesus personally, but I barely slept. Throughout the night, I kept begging Jesus to protect me from any stray bullets that might come through the walls. If I could make it through a night in East LA, I might survive a flight to Australia.

The following day, I felt exhausted from lack of sleep, but I'd found a new way to pray.

I felt nervous boarding the Qantas plane. It was so huge, and I questioned its ability to carry enough fuel for a long flight. My brain spun between exotic images of sandy beaches and koala bears and Momma's worst-case scenarios of a plane spiraling into the ocean.

I hugged my new Bible and held onto Dylan's hand, which was my routine for every flight.

Glenn remained subdued since I'd called the home office, and Becky seemed to be taking more responsibilities. No one spoke about what happened, but Glenn left Dylan and me alone for the rest of the tour.

Our trip down under was a whirlwind of sightseeing and concerts. We flew over the Sydney Opera House, visited the Museum of Victoria, and grew enchanted with the Island State of Tasmania. We even held koalas and wombats at an animal preserve where we fed the kangaroos.

We walked on so many beaches that I made it a quest to find shells. Every shell I collected had its own story. One day, my host family's children were using large, beautiful shells to dig in their sandbox. I admired their "shovels," and they gave them to me. I hesitated to accept their gifts, but they reassured me they could find more.

One Tasmanian beach offered purple shells of every shape and size. A New Zealand host mom viewed me as a scavenger picking up discarded animal carcasses. She couldn't understand why I wanted to collect "deed feesh," as she called sand dollars.

Another time, I was afraid to step into the churning ocean when Dylan playfully grabbed my hand and pulled me into the surf. As we splashed in the knee-deep water, I felt something touch my foot and grabbed it with my toes. Lifting it out of the water, I discovered a beautiful coral-pink shell.

One of the most shocking moments occurred on a remote beach where Dylan and I noticed crunching with every step. We looked down to discover that we were standing on layers upon layers of sand dollars just beneath the surface of the sandy beach.

When Tommy found an abalone shell as large as a salad plate, the group stood around him admiring its silvery rainbow. Then Tommy held it out.

"Would you like it, Cheri?"

And that's how I knew Tommy had forgiven me for my careless and hateful words. He was my Danish brother, and I would always love him no matter what he did or who he was.

In Tasmania, Sadie and I discovered a hidden trail through the jungle. It was a wooden sidewalk barely visible from the picnic area. Once inside the jungle, we found exotic plants and singing birds we'd never seen or heard about. Remembering that Tommy loved unique experiences, we put a blindfold over his eyes and led him into the jungle. Once inside, we removed the cloth so he could see the beauty, then we covered his eyes and took him back outside. We took the blindfold off and asked him to find the trail's opening. Tommy was searching the edges of the jungle when one of our host dads ran up shouting.

"Stay out of the jungle. It's high snake season here in Tasmania. I just killed a deadly snake on my porch last night."

Horrified, we all shuddered and thanked God for his protection.

We visited the Glowworm Caves in New Zealand and took a rowboat down a river inside the caves. When the guide turned off the flashlights, we saw a million tiny worms suspended from the cave ceiling that resembled the Milky Way.

Rotorua, with its historic Maori buildings with geysers and mineral pools, reminded me of Yellowstone Park.

We discovered exotic flowers, unique birdsongs, and strange creatures everywhere we went in this enchanted world. Whether in the mountains, the bush, or the beaches, the landscapes were beautiful, and the people were so friendly that I felt tempted to look for an Aussie or New Zealand man and live there forever—except I'd miss my family.

The Reach Out Singers had a rule that nobody was to date on tour, but we had tour buddies, and Dylan was mine. I didn't think of us as a couple, but having a trusted friend to share these experiences was comforting.

Most of our group hiked to a waterfall in the hills above the beach at the resort town of Whangamata, while Dylan and I took the beach path carrying a picnic lunch. Walking barefoot through the sand, we came upon a private cove. There was no one on this beach but the two of us. We marveled at the beautiful waterfall pouring over the hill, making its way across the sand into the ocean. It was the perfect place to build a sand castle and eat lunch.

Dylan seemed a little wary of the cheese and beet sandwiches my host mom made for us, but once we removed the beets, he enjoyed them. We lay on the warm sand, listening to the sound of the surf with birds and waterfall sounds rounding out the symphony. It was a perfect temperature to doze. I'm not sure if it was the enchanted world around us or the culmination of all these exciting experiences, and I'm not sure who moved closer first, but we found ourselves kissing.

When we got up to meet our friends, we glanced nervously up and down the beach, hoping none of our tour mates had seen us.

My heart felt warm toward Dylan, but I was also confused. I wasn't looking for a relationship. I remembered what Lucas said about knowing ourselves first. Did Dylan and I even know each other enough to date, or were we just in love with New Zealand?

A few days later, we took a bus to a youth camp named Kiwi Ranch. It was Easter weekend, and families came from all over New Zealand to celebrate. The Reach Out Singers were providing music for the weekend. We discovered our hosts hadn't thought about how little a group of international travelers could carry with them. The locals brought bedding, sleeping bags, and pillows, but we came with only our suitcases. The camp provided one wool blanket for each of us with no pillows or cushions to sleep on the hard wooden bunks.

Fortunately, I'd just spent the night on a sheep ranch, where my host family had gifted me sheepskin. I planned to use it to lie on, with my jacket as a pillow. In the frigid temperatures, one wool blanket wasn't enough, so we all decided to sleep with our clothes on.

After the evening concert, Dylan asked if I wanted to go for a walk to look at the Southern Cross. I followed him up a trail lit with glowworms blinking in the bushes like fairy lights. We rounded a small peninsula and sat on a bench by the lake.

I zipped my jacket up to my throat. "It's chilly—you warm enough?"

Dylan pulled his hat down over his ears.

The Southern Cross was so bright it seemed I could touch it.

"Even the stars look different down here. Remember that night we prayed in your car? Look at where it's taken us."

Dylan smiled and nodded, but he seemed strangely quiet.

We took in the beauty of the lake, the glowworms, and the sky before Dylan broke the silence.

"Cheri, I don't want to hurt you, but I don't think I can spend my life with a woman. It's not you. I've had crushes on girls before, and if I was going to be with a woman, you're a wonderful person, but I'm attracted to guys, and I don't know how to change that."

I realized he was speaking from deep within his soul, and I respected him for it. His anguish was palpable. We believed, as our church had taught us, that if he chose to love a man, God would reject him forever. Tears blurred my eyes. Thinking of sweet, kind Dylan burning in the lake of fire was devastating. At that moment, I hated God.

Always chivalrous, Dylan walked me back to the girls' bunkhouse and bid me goodnight, while I tried to hide my grief. I wasn't sure if I was sad for him or me. It felt like I was losing my best friend for eternity and being rejected at the same time.

The sheepskin barely softened the hard bunk, and when I took my coat off to use it for a pillow, I couldn't stop shaking. Despite remaining fully dressed and covered with the wool blanket, I tried to sleep but was chilled from sitting in the cold. I wondered if I'd ever feel warm again or even survive the night. Perhaps I'd die from hypothermia, and my problems would all disappear.

We heard a knock at the door, and Becky called out, "Who is it?"

"Dylan. Can I come in for a minute?"

The other girls scrambled to make sure they were decently dressed while I lay flat on my stomach, hugging my sheepskin. I was too cold to get up, but I wondered what he wanted.

"Where's Cheri?"

Someone must have motioned to where I lay.

Footsteps came toward me, and then I heard Dylan's soft voice. "I found an extra blanket on my bunk and thought you could use it."

He gently laid it over me and slipped out the door. My feet and hands were still cold, but my heart felt warm.

Our time down under came to an end. I was relieved we'd survived so many flights, but we weren't safe until we landed on American soil. I was a little alarmed when the pilot said our flight home was taking a detour to Fiji. Fiji wasn't on our itinerary.

It was the middle of the night, and most of the passengers were sleeping, when I heard the pilot say that we were making an emergency landing. I glanced at my Bible in the seat pocket in front of me, but I didn't get a chance to grab it. I heard gasps and screams around me as the oxygen masks fell. Shutting my eyes, I waited for the crash, begging Jesus to hold me.

To my surprise, nothing happened. We sat on the tarmac for an hour while they did a maintenance check and then we took off again. Maybe I was getting used to flying, or perhaps facing my worst fear had cured my anxiety because I managed to land in LA without holding anyone's hand.

We got back on our bus and made our way back to South Dakota, where we had our final concert. It was an emotional occasion. We'd become family and made a lot of memories.

Going on tour taught me that other Christians know Jesus as much or more than I did. I stopped pretending to know everything about God. I discovered that God can reach us through any version of the Bible, and Jesus doesn't mind if we pray in everyday language. I also learned how to stand up against abuse and to let go of other people, even when it hurts.

As I looked at my teammates, from Glenn and Becky to Sadie, Steve, Beth, Lynn, Rob, Tommy, and Dylan, I tried to remember what my life had been like before I met them. We weren't strangers anymore. I understood their heartaches and quirks, and they knew some of mine. It was hard to say goodbye. We all cried as we sang our last song—which was "Friends" by Michael W. Smith. Only time would tell if we could remain friends forever.

16 Time After Time

*Insanity is doing the same thing
over and over again and
expecting different results.*
-Narcotics Anonymous

Before the end of the tour, a pastor called me to the church office to take a phone call. I nervously answered the phone to hear my sister's voice.

"It's Abby. I got the number from the Reach Out headquarters."

She paused. There was a long moment of silence. When I heard a sob, a chill raced down my spine as I wondered who died.

"What's going on?"

"I'm pregnant."

My heart sank. Abby was still a teenager and could barely afford a studio apartment. What would she do with a baby? Guilt washed over me. Perhaps she wouldn't be in this situation if I hadn't gone on tour, but it was too late for whatever might have been. I searched for a solution. Would she put it up for adoption? Could I take her child and raise it myself? Perhaps I should ask her.

"Do you want it?"

"Of course I want it. Don't be stupid. I just don't know how to tell Daddy. I wrote him a four-page letter, but I'm afraid he'll be upset with me."

Relief washed over me. "I'll talk to him if you'd like."

I called Daddy to discuss the fact that he was going to be a grandfather.

There was a long silence. When he finally spoke, I could tell he was crying, but his voice was filled with love.

"You tell Abby that we love her." He paused. "And we love her baby too."

I gave Daddy's message to a relieved Abby, who began surfing yard sales for baby clothes, while I boarded a Greyhound bus.

Dylan also took the bus home to Washington State. After two days of stopping at every town between Sioux Falls and Seattle, my parents met me at the bus depot while Dylan rode on to Sequim, where his family lived. I was so exhausted from lack of sleep that I could barely walk.

Going on tour was the most incredible experience of my life, but I hadn't considered the impact of dropping out of school, quitting my job, and running away from my bills. My problems were waiting for me, and now I was not only broke but homeless. My only option was to live with my parents, who were just a step away from being homeless themselves. In six months, they'd left Alaska, moved to Spokane, and then back to Seattle.

As I crammed my large suitcase into the back of their Toyota Corolla, Daddy explained they were living in a house Uncle Joe bought for one dollar.

"Your Uncle Joe's a wheeler-dealer. He can trade and swap anything with anyone."

I'd heard this my entire life. As the oldest son of a Danish immigrant, Uncle Joe believed anything was possible. My grandfather had many types of work, and his sons took after him. They were constantly moving and seeking new ways to make money.

When Uncle Joe heard of a house auctioned to make way for a shopping mall, he bid one dollar and won it. It needed to be moved by the time the contractor was ready to build the mall, but according to the newspaper, the mall contractors wouldn't start for at least two years. The lull in construction made it convenient for Uncle Joe and Daddy to use the garage as a shop and live in the house rent-free.

I noticed a boat outside the front door as we pulled up to the house.

"Why is there a boat on dry ground?"

Daddy laughed. "Your Uncle Joe traded a beater car for a beater boat. Neither work as they should, but Uncle Joe doesn't mind the leaky boat because he's using it as a bedroom."

"Goodness! He's got all kinds of surprises up his sleeve."

Uncle Joe stuck his head out of the boat as I exited the car and waved to me.

Inside the house, Daddy lowered his voice.

"Uncle Joe's sleeping in the boat so you can sleep on the hide-a-bed."

I nodded. I could see that the house came furnished with brown and green plaid furniture and orange floral drapes from 1965.

Daddy suddenly grabbed a newspaper and slapped a spider on the wall. "There are a few drawbacks, but it's a free place to live, and it's nothing we can't deal with."

Momma rolled her eyes. "Speak for yourself. I had to put masking tape on the bottom of the door to keep those varmints out of our room."

I was puzzled. "How does that work?"

Momma smiled. "They get stuck on the sticky side of the tape."

I took in the dingy room while Momma opened the hide-a-bed to put some thin but clean sheets on it. I cringed at a stain on the mattress. I could barely see it because the lamp was so dim. Perhaps the darkness was a mercy to spare me from all the frightening details of mismatched prints, mice droppings, and spiders on the wall.

"You'll want to wear shoes when you go to the bathroom at night because you never know when a rat might come up from the basement," Daddy spoke casually as if we'd always coexisted with rats.

Momma sighed. "Also, mushrooms are growing on the bathroom floor. I've tried to kill them, but they just keep coming back."

I shuddered as I lay down on the creaky hide-a-bed and tried to relax. I listened to my parents speaking in hushed voices while they brushed their teeth in the kitchen. When their footsteps faded down the hall, and I heard the bedroom door shut, I suddenly felt alone. I thought about my tour mates. We'd slept in many places, from kids' beds to wooden bunks and church floors, but nothing felt as creepy and strange as this house.

Even though I hadn't slept for two days, I couldn't sleep. Maybe it was the musty smell, the rats scurrying down the stairs, or the hide-a-bed support bar that kept jabbing me in my kidney. Since counting sheep didn't work, I began to count spiders. Every spot on the ceiling was suspect. With the faint light streaming through the window from a streetlamp, I tried to analyze each mark to see if it was moving.

A tear slid down my cheek. as I remembered that I'd left my parents once, and here I was, broke and living with them again. I ached for the comfort of my tour family. I already missed Dylan. I wondered how Sadie and Lynn were doing. A torrent of tears followed, leaving my pillow and ears wet in the already damp house. Finally, exhaustion overtook me, and I fell into a restless sleep.

The following day, I applied for work at a temp agency. My goal was to earn enough money to rent a place near Walla Walla College and get my old job back. Dolores had promised it would be waiting when I returned.

My first temp job was as a clown for a shoe store. It included walking along a busy highway in eight-five-degree heat, carrying balloons, and waving at traffic while wearing a striped suit and thick makeup on my face. Part of the job was blowing up balloons for kids in the store. It wasn't much fun. Some bratty kid demanded I remove my gloves to prove I was a real clown. When I refused, he started kicking me in the shins.

I returned to the temp agency and told them I hated the job, so they offered me a job as a secretary at South Seattle Auto Auction. Daddy and Uncle Joe were excited for me because they had bought and sold cars there for years. I had no enthusiasm because it wasn't my dream job. I answered the phone, and my lecherous boss kept asking me to wear miniskirts. I despised him and the job, but at least it was in an air-conditioned building.

Living with my parents after several years of college and traveling around the world felt almost as bad as living with them before college. Daddy drove me to and from work while Momma used her driver's license to cash my checks. I felt like kicking myself for closing my checking account before I traveled. What was I thinking?

When Daddy asked to borrow my hard-earned money, I began to feel hopeless. I wondered why I allowed myself to get into this situation again.

His arguments were persuasive.

"You don't have enough money to rent a place anyway. I can pay it back by the time you need it."

"How can I save money if I keep loaning it to you?"

"Tell you what, I'll fix up a car for you. Tell me what kind you want."

"Can you teach me to drive?"

I loaned him the money and paid for a Mustang at the auction. I felt like I'd made a good deal, but it set me back, and I still needed to earn more money to rent a place.

I kept begging my parents to teach me how to drive, and they kept making excuses. Daddy didn't have the time, and Momma thought learning in the big city was too dangerous. Plus, they didn't have car insurance, so we'd all get a ticket if I made a mistake.

I'd gotten to know my cousin Jessie while I was in college, and we had a special bond. She was fourteen that summer and looking for meaning in her life. Daddy agreed to let her come and stay for a few days. The only drawback was that she had to share the horrible hide-a-bed with me.

My cousin and I prayed every night that no spiders would bite us and no rats would touch our toes. Daddy's prayers were different. He saw Jessie's visit as an opportunity to make sure she followed God. He started reading long passages from the church prophet. Some of these passages were about the proper dress for young ladies, and others were about getting rid of every sin before Jesus came. He always prayed in the old King James English, addressing God with words like Thee, Thou, and Thine.

One morning, Jessie seemed upset. She was usually a very upbeat girl.

"What's wrong?"

"Your dad's always preaching at me and judging me for wearing shorts."

I didn't want to admit she was right. I tried to smooth things over by changing the subject, but as soon as Daddy called us for family worship, I sensed the tension between them. I also resented men who judged girls and women for what we wore. As he was about to pray, I saw an opportunity to turn the judgment on him.

"Daddy, Jesus didn't speak in King James' English. We don't have to say thee and thou. We can pray in regular, everyday language, and God will understand."

Daddy's lips formed a tight line as he shut the book. Then he got up and went to work in the garage. He never spoke another word about reading or praying for the rest of the summer. I was surprised that my words had such power as to shut him down. I didn't know what to think about his reaction.

Tour Z had been all about prayer, which only made me more homesick for my friends. One day, I was praying for guidance because I wasn't making any progress toward my goals. I was feeling depressed when Sadie called.

"Hey, girl! I never thought I'd say this, but I miss tour. And I miss you! I'm considering moving to Walla Walla to see what it's like to live in your half of the country."

My heart leaped to hear her voice.

"I'm planning to move back there myself as soon as I make enough money for a rental deposit."

"If you'd like to be roommates, I have enough savings for a deposit. You can pay me back when you get a job."

"I already have a job."

"Then let's do it."

I heard Sadie scream on the other end of the line. It was her happy scream, so I screamed too.

I went out to the garage to take a look at my Mustang. It lay in three pieces. The driver's door leaned against the wall, and the new hood, spray-painted with primer, lay on the floor. I looked at the broken windshield and wondered how long it would take for Daddy to put the car back together. I didn't want to wait that long. I needed to meet Sadie in Walla Walla as soon as she arrived. Dylan was heading back to Walla Walla. Maybe he could give me a ride.

17 Hard Habit to Break

*A good friend is
like a four-leaf clover,
hard to find and lucky to have.*
-Irish Proverb

Nine months of traveling together created a bond between Sadie, Dylan, and me that only a sibling could match. I connected with other friends, but Dylan and Sadie understood my daily struggles.

Sadie brought the mail in one day and tossed an envelope to me. It was a funny card from Dylan wishing me a great week.

Whenever she was suspicious about anything, Sadie raised one eyebrow.

"Do you get the feeling Dylan wants to be more than friends?"

"It's just a card. I wouldn't read much into it."

"Well, he's not sending cards to me."

She probably thought I was naive, but she didn't know what I knew. I'd managed to keep Dylan's secret throughout the tour. I let Sadie think whatever she wanted because it wasn't my story to tell.

To be honest, there were times when it did seem like Dylan was making a romantic gesture. He brought me a rose once, but I clarified that we were good friends. For one thing, there was the age difference. He was Abby's age, but as he quickly pointed out, Abby was mature enough to be a mother. I didn't think our relationship was going anywhere. I intended to keep my eyes open for a husband, but I had other things on my mind, like learning to drive and getting my Mustang from Daddy.

Momma never called anyone unless it was an emergency, so when I heard her voice, I immediately sat down.

"Abby felt dizzy and checked her blood pressure at the drugstore. It's dangerously high. Do you think you can check on her?"

Abby lived in Walla Walla, and I lived in College Place. Although we were several miles apart, I was willing to do anything for my very pregnant sister.

"Is she at her apartment?"

"She's walking home with groceries."

"I'll try to find her, but it would sure be easier if I had my car."

"You can't drive it without a driver's license."

"How can I do that without a car and no one to teach me?"

Momma sighed. "We're moving over there in a couple of weeks, and we'll figure it out. Meanwhile, I'm worried about Abby walking in the heat."

I hung up, trying to think of what I could do. It was mid-August, and the heat was suffocating. The thought of walking any distance outside overwhelmed me.

Every time I thought of Daddy driving my Mustang, I got angry. The car was in my name, and I had paid for the license and insurance, and I still had no access to it.

I tried to think of someone with a car who might give me a ride. Sadie didn't drive. She'd grown up riding the Chicago transit and now relied on a Walla Walla bus pass to get to work at Fabricland.

I couldn't think of anyone to call but Dylan. His roommate Jon answered.

"Dylan's not here, but I can give you a ride."

Jon took me into Walla Walla, where we searched up and down the streets for Abby. We eventually gave up and went to her apartment to leave a note.

That's when I saw my sister's heavy form, slowly carrying two bags of groceries up the steps into the old house where she rented a room. Tears blurred my vision as I realized how hard things were for her. I thanked Jon and jumped out to help my sister.

Abby's doctor had told her to go home and put her feet up to avoid a hospital stay. While Abby was resting, I looked around her apartment and decided to tidy it up. As I ran the dishes through the soapy water, I realized it was almost a year to the day when Abby had disappeared to start her own life. We had both changed quite a bit since then. She was becoming a mother and making me an aunt. My heart overflowed with affection for my sister and her unborn child.

One day, my friend Candy stopped by to ask me a favor.

"My boyfriend's best friend is depressed. His dog died, and he needs cheering. He hasn't dated anyone for months. Would you be willing to go on a date with him?"

"Oh, I don't know. I can't imagine going on a blind date."

"He's a fun guy, and it's just one night. What could go wrong?"

It might be all right if it was a double date.

"Are you guys going to be there?"

"No, we'll be out of town."

Despite my reservations, I agreed to meet the guy.

When my blind date pulled up to the curb in front of the house, I opened the door to find a nice-looking guy with blond hair and blue eyes getting out of a sports car. He approached the porch and threw a bouquet in my face. He spoke loud and fast as if he was on a TV commercial.

"I'm Lance. We're running late, so get in the car, and we'll talk later."

I handed the flowers to Sadie, who twitched her nose and raised her eyebrow. "Can't wait to hear all about it." She mouthed as I followed Lance to the car.

I hooked up my seat belt and asked, "Where are we going?"

"Demolition Derby."

"Oh wow, I've never been before."

"Never been to a demolition derby? Where have you been living? Under a rock?"

His loud laughter irritated me, but I was determined to be polite. But when he switched lanes to pass a car at breakneck speed, I couldn't resist making a joke.

"We're going to a demolition derby—not driving in one, right?"

He didn't laugh. Apparently, my joke wasn't funny.

"Do you know what a totaled car looks like?"

"Yeah, I've seen a few." I almost told him how my dad rebuilt totals for a living, but something in me said to wait.

At the fairgrounds, Lance stopped to buy popcorn and candy. He got a 32 oz orange soda to save money. He told me I could sip on it first, and then he'd finish it. It was a hot day, but I didn't plan to drink much. After seeing how far we had to climb in the bleachers, I didn't want to make too many trips to the restroom.

Once we sat down, Lance told me to start drinking the soda because he was getting thirsty. I'd been on a few dates before, but I'd never been forced to drink pop or even share one. Who did this guy think he was? The cup was so large I could barely wrap my hand around it. I took one sip to be friendly and told him he could have the rest. He seemed glad to take it back.

I tried to enjoy the show, but there was so much yelling that I grew annoyed. It was impossible to have a conversation, and I grit my teeth every time the cars crashed.

Lance tried to educate me by shouting above the crowd. "They fix them up just enough to drive them so they can crash the hell out of them. My hunting buddy is out there. The green beater with red stripes. I hope to join him next year if I can find a good total."

I smiled. It was a fake smile, but Lance didn't notice. I knew where to find totaled cars. Daddy could probably get a good deal for him. I almost said this, but when I glanced at Lance, my entire future swam before my eyes. How could I ever be with such a man? I despised sharing drinks with other people. I also couldn't see myself waiting around while he went hunting, and I was already hoping this would be my last demolition derby. It seemed like everything Lance liked involved destruction and death.

He took the lid off the soda, stuck his fingers inside, pulled out a piece of ice, and began crunching on it. Noticing my curious look, he chuckled. "I like to chew on ice, so bite me."

I was starting to feel like he had invited me along just to torment me. What had I done to deserve this rude date? Things were about to get worse. The giant cup was still full of orange soda. As Lance tried to put the lid back on, he fumbled with the straw and accidentally spilled it. I might have laughed, except most of the soda went down the back of the man sitting in front of us. As orange colored his white T-shirt, the man stood up slowly while I held my breath. I could only imagine how terrible the sticky soda felt on his back.

The man turned around to face Lance.

"What kind of ass are you? Come down here and let me punch your effen face."

I expected Lance to apologize. Instead, he responded by calling the man a punk. The two of them shouted insults at each other. I shrunk from embarrassment, but the crowd was so noisy no one else seemed to notice.

Thinking it was time to find the restrooms, I grabbed my purse and flew down the bleachers. I don't think Lance noticed me leaving.

I ran through a cement tunnel covered with colored gum and graffiti and stopped to catch my breath. Feeling nauseous in the heat, I stepped into the restroom to splash cold water on my face. I stared in the mirror, wondering how I could survive the evening.

I couldn't help but compare Lance to Dylan. Dylan—who drove an old police car with three paint colors on it. Dylan—who had too much class to spill pop down another person's back. Dylan—who never fought with anyone. Heck. Dylan would never be seen at a demolition derby in the first place. I looked for a pay phone, fumbled in my purse for a quarter, and punched in my emergency backup number. Dylan said he'd meet me out front.

18 A Groovy Kind of Love

One is loved because one is loved.
No reason is needed for loving.
        -Paulo Coelho

After spending my childhood scrambling to survive, I often struggled to share what I had with others. Sadie's generosity inspired me to give to others, and no one deserved it more than my sister.

I found a new admiration for my little sister. Abby was a dedicated mother. She searched yard sales to find baby clothes and accessories. She didn't have much money, but she made up for it with love for her unborn child. When I had the time, I tried to help her.

One day, I brought her a bag of yard sale clothes I'd found for a bargain to see if anything was worth keeping. Abby was folding a stack of onesies when she asked if I'd ever found out who baked me cookies and filled my cupboards with food before I left for tour.

"I'd almost forgotten about that. It seems a lifetime ago."

Abby laughed and patted her belly. "In reality, it's only been a year."

"I've always wondered who did it and how they got into my apartment."

"Didn't it seem obvious? I was the only person who had a key."

"Hey, you acted like you didn't know." I hit her with a burp rag.

She laughed. "I didn't want to ruin his fun."

"Who's fun?"

"Dylan's."

"Seriously? That guy is always full of surprises. I can't believe he's never told me."

A few days later, on my birthday, Sadie presented me with a beautiful silk fabric at breakfast.

"You always give such exquisite gifts." I ran my fingers over the delicate lavender and rose material. Then I stood up and gave her a warm hug. "I'll make a skirt."

"I knew it would be perfect for you."

"Can you believe we met just one year ago tomorrow?"

Sadie stirred her coffee and took a sip before staring dreamily out the window. "And to think I'd never even met a cow."

We laughed at her excitement to discover cows in a field on her way to work that first day. She'd called me to say, "I can't believe I have a job at a fabric store, and there are cows near our house!"

After living in rustic arrangements across five states, I took cows for granted. Sadie had lived in Chicago in one house for her entire childhood. Our friendship was filled with the contrast between a country mouse and a city mouse, but we always managed to have fun.

When Sadie pulled out some soft material for baby wraps, my heart warmed to realize her circle of love extended to Abby.

We enjoyed a peaceful dinner at home on my birthday, but I was sad because Dylan never called. I complained to Sadie.

"Even though we aren't dating, he's still good company, and I have more fun with him than I've had with any other guy."

"He cares about you enough to take you to the Michael Card concert tomorrow."

"I guess. It's a three-hour drive to Yakima and back both ways. Still, you'd think anyone worth spending six hours in the car with would be important enough to wish a happy birthday."

"Maybe he got busy at work."

"Maybe, but most friends find a way to wish each other a happy birthday."

Sadie cut another slice of chocolate cake and offered it to me.

It was hard to sleep that night. I couldn't get over the fact that Dylan sent me a casual card one week, yet he couldn't pick up the phone on my birthday.

When Dylan arrived to pick me up for the concert, he surprised me with a dozen pink roses and a card.

"Happy birthday!"

Sadie and I looked at each other and laughed.

"What's so funny?"

"My birthday was yesterday."

"Oh, I thought it was the first day of training camp."

"My birthday was the day we flew to training camp."

His face grew red.

Once we got in the car, Dylan apologized for the mix-up, but I was glad he remembered, even if it was on the wrong day.

Throughout the tour, one of our favorite hangouts was Pizza Hut. For old time's sake, he took me there for supper before the concert. While we waited for the pizza, Dylan went to the jukebox and put in a couple of quarters. The mellow voice of Phil Collins singing "A Groovy Kind of Love" filled the restaurant.

Back at our table, Dylan asked, "What do you think, Cheri? Don't you think we have a groovy kind of love?"

"I guess." I smiled, but to be honest, I didn't know the song, and I was caught off guard by his question. I wasn't even sure what the word groovy meant. I was so excited to see Michael Card that I could barely think about anything else.

The concert included a cellist, and my heart soared with the beauty of music and poetry. My favorite song was "Forgiving Eyes," about a woman caught in adultery. Since I'd read about her in the modern version of the Bible, I'd begun to look for grace everywhere.

On the way home, we talked about the concert and the George MacDonald novel I was reading. My heart was overflowing with joy for God and Dylan's friendship. It was a clear night, and the road had long stretches with no lights to obscure the stars. I marveled that the Milky Way—the same stars we'd prayed under that July night, seemed to be winking at us.

Two days later, Abby went into labor. Her boyfriend had promised to return from Mexico by the time the baby was due in October, but the baby had other plans.

Daddy and Momma drove from Seattle just in time for the birth. Dylan took me to the hospital, where we waited with the rest of the family until a nurse came out holding up a tiny red-faced baby. The minute I saw his little face, I fell in love. I promised him that I would always be on his side. This meant more than birthday presents and outings to the park. For me, this meant standing up against racism and never voting in a way that could harm him.

Relieved that Abby and the baby were healthy, I returned to work and registered for the school year. Dylan had convinced me to enroll at Walla Walla Community College. I no longer felt the need to spend three times as much to be surrounded by Adventists.

Dylan and I attended every contemporary Christian concert that came to town that year. We sometimes took Sadie and others with us. The three of us spent so much time together that it seemed like Tour Z had merged into real life.

Dylan's former high school classmate kept begging him to visit her in Seattle. I'd heard Brenda's desperate messages on his answering machine, and I wasn't impressed. Around the same time, we got a call from our Canadian tourmate Meg. She and her fiancé were visiting the West Coast and would love to see us if we could come to Vancouver.

Dylan planned a six-day trip to see Meg and invited Sadie and me. Sadie had to work, but I got the time off. A few days before we left, Dylan informed me that he'd be spending one night with Brenda when we got to Seattle. He wondered if I'd mind staying with my parents and Uncle Joe at the mushroom house for a couple of nights.

Of course, I minded. I hated that house and had no desire to stay there ever again.

"Is this what you mean by a groovy kind of love? Maybe I should just stay home."

"She's just an old friend, and it's only one day out of six. Ask Jon. He knows she's just a friend."

Jon was the one other person who knew about Dylan's secret. He'd also heard the answering machine messages. I found Jon walking on the Walla Walla College campus.

"I don't think Brenda's any threat to you—I've never seen anyone who seems like such a good match for Dylan as you. You guys were made for each other."

Jon encouraged me to go on the trip. At least I'd see Meg and have some fun.

We had a great time in Canada, but by the time we crossed the border, I was less optimistic. The thought of Dylan spending the night with Brenda began to bother me.

"I can't believe you're sending me back to that mushroom house."

I didn't mention it, but I was embarrassed to tell my parents that Dylan was spending the night with another girl.

Dylan dropped me off, and I did my best to enjoy catching up with Momma and Daddy. As I walked past the green Mustang in the driveway, I thought it would be nice to jump in it and drive back to Walla Walla, leaving Dylan with that girl.

"When can I get my car?"

"As soon as you get your driver's license." Daddy smiled like we were playing a game.

"How can I do that without a car?"

"We're planning to move to Walla Walla next month. It will be easier to learn in a smaller town."

I'd heard it before, but I hoped this time, their new grandson would inspire them to move to Walla Walla.

The following day, I was in no hurry to shower with the mushrooms. Dylan was planning to spend the day with Brenda, so I lazed around.

I was finishing breakfast when Momma said, "Oh, look, Dylan's here!"

Tossing my dishes in the sink, I ran to the bathroom. "Tell him I'm in the shower."

I jumped over those ugly mushrooms and took the fastest shower of my life. When I came out, Dylan sat on a chair, talking with Momma like old friends. I was glad to see they were getting along. I gathered my stuff, hugged Momma, and followed Dylan out the door.

The rain was coming down in buckets by the time we got in the car, but I didn't mind. Dylan turned the heater on and hit defrost. While we waited for the fog to clear from the windows, he turned to me.

"I decided I'd rather spend the day with you."

I smiled and listened.

"People are starting to call you my girlfriend. How do you feel about that?"

"I don't know. How do you feel?"

"I think it's fine if you don't mind."

"Well, I don't mind—if you don't mind."

We smiled at each other. Then I noticed the raindrops flooding the windshield and asked, "Look at this crazy rain. What are we going to do?"

"When it's raining in Seattle, starting with a mocha is always appropriate."

I couldn't think of anything I'd love to do more—as long as I was with Dylan.

"Would you also like to get lunch at Pike Place, then take the ferry to Sequim and see where I used to live?"

"Sure. I used to live there too."

He laughed. "You used to live everywhere."

Despite the rain, or perhaps because of the rain, we had a magical day exploring the shops at Pike Place Market before taking the ferry to Sequim. His parents were out of town, so we had the house to ourselves. The next morning, Dylan took me on a tour of several places he'd lived and the high school. It also brought back memories from when I was ten years old.

"Your family moves almost as often as mine does."

He nodded, but unlike me, he didn't make any excuses for his family moving.

"I didn't want to switch schools at first, but attending public high school was a good experience."

"Well, at least you got to high school. I was homeschooled without the books."

He turned to me. "What does that even mean?"

I shrugged my shoulders. "No textbooks."

Dylan shook his head. "That's crazy."

For the first time, I was dating someone I felt I could be myself with. At the same time, Momma had cautioned me to never tell the family secrets. She said there was no point in dredging up the past. I knew from experience that Jake had told Carrie too much, and now she thought we had a dysfunctional family. I decided not to say too much to Dylan about my childhood because I wanted him to like my parents. Perhaps if I kept quiet, they would get along.

Once we established that we were dating, life became a rhythm of joyful experiences throughout the following year. Dylan planned to be a humanities teacher and took me places I'd never been. He invited me to my first symphony and presentation of "Handel's Messiah." Every weekend, we attended art galleries, plays, and concerts. If we took any trips, he asked me to read his literature assignments while he drove. I loved the stories, plays, and music that we shared.

These shared experiences opened new ideas to me—a world my parents had always scorned because they thought secular plays, music, and literature—including Shakespeare, were dangerous and lacking in Christian values. The more I learned, the more I saw flaws in their thinking.

I wasn't worried about Dylan's attraction to men because the Bible forbade same-gender relationships. At least, that's what we'd been taught. I never heard him call himself gay. He mentioned having "same-sex attractions," but since it was a sin, there wasn't much point in discussing it. We shared a passion for so many things that sexuality was just one piece of the relationship puzzle.

Throughout that year, we had a lot of fun. For Christmas, Dylan had a special present for me on the tree. I could barely view it through the opalescent wrapping, but I knew it was a watch. My parents and grandparents never had engagement rings or wedding bands because traditional Adventists never wore jewelry. Dylan followed the Adventist tradition of giving me an expensive watch resembling a sparkly bracelet. We didn't question the traditions. We just followed them because we wanted to be good Christians.

When Dylan asked me to marry him, I didn't hesitate because we had so much in common. He was my best friend, and he was also everything Daddy wasn't. He held down a job and was planning a career. He never tried to control me or told me what to do. He never raised a hand to me, even when we disagreed. Even though I was a woman, I knew he considered me one hundred percent his equal.

We were secretly engaged for most of a year before we told anyone. During this time, my parents, along with Jake and Carrie, had moved back to Walla Walla. Everyone in the family lived nearby except for Mara. It seemed this new baby—the first of his generation—had brought our family closer together.

Jake and Carrie moved in two houses down from where I lived with Sadie. It was awkward, but Carrie and I eventually overcame the plant incident and became friends. We often went to each other's house to play cards.

That summer, while we were camping in the Wallowa Mountains, Dylan and I planned our wedding. We decided to announce it on my birthday—a year after the Michael Card concert and two years after we flew to training camp.

Dylan wanted to throw me a birthday party and surprise our families with the announcement. His plan made me nervous because my family didn't do birthday parties. I couldn't remember ever having one. I felt more comfortable throwing parties than accepting one, but Dylan was so excited that I didn't have the heart to refuse him. We invited my family to Dylan's parents' house for the party. Everyone except Mara, who still lived in Spokane, was there.

Our landlady had a backyard full of roses and often brought us flowers and vegetables from her garden. She also baked wedding cakes for students. Everybody called her Grandma G. When we told her we were planning to announce our engagement on my birthday, she offered to make me a birthday cake.

Now, Grandma G did a sneaky thing with that cake. She probably just forgot to tell us, and I'm sure she meant well, but our announcement didn't go as planned.

When we uncovered the cake, instead of announcing "Happy Birthday," the beautiful cake decorated in our wedding colors of peach and lavender flowers announced our wedding date.

"Dylan and Cheri, June 24, 1990."

Everyone saw it at once. There were lots of cheers, but there was also an angry gasp as Dylan's grandmother jumped to her feet and stumbled across the room.

With spit foaming on her lips, she shook her fist in my face and hissed, "If he doesn't graduate from college, I will kill you."

19 Everybody Wants to Rule the World

*All happy families are alike,
but every unhappy family
is unhappy in its own way.*
-Leo Tolstoy

Our engagement seemed to disrupt Dylan's entire family. His siblings complained they never saw him anymore, his father tried to talk me out of marrying him, and his mother and grandmother told people they were going to wear black to our wedding.

I told my boss how his grandmother had threatened to kill me.

"It's the worst thing that's ever happened." I shuddered.

Dolores' smile reflected wisdom as she shook her head. "You're young. Much worse things are going to happen throughout your life. Hard things, weird things, and things you will have zero control over. This is just a small thing, so keep it in perspective."

Dylan grew up watching his parents argue over his grandmother's demands. His coping mechanism was to avoid confrontation.

For Christmas, the "Grandmonster," as I christened her, gave Dylan a red shirt and red jeans, and she demanded that he wear them to the family New Year's party. Dylan didn't argue with her, but he returned the clothes for cash the next day. I thought it seemed rude, but he said it wasn't as rude as telling people what to wear.

His father's request bothered me the most. Once, when I was speaking at a church, he told me he was proud of me. Now that I was marrying his son, he wanted me to disappear.

I was delivering the mail at work when Dylan's father approached me in the hall of the care center.

"Are you sure you want to marry my son?"

"Of course." I grinned. I thought he was joking until I realized he wasn't smiling back.

"Have you considered the advice of your elders?"

"I'm not sure who you're talking about."

"Do your parents think this is a good idea?"

"It's my decision, not theirs."

"Some people are concerned that your family doesn't have high morals."

I was caught off guard by this remark.

"What are you trying to say?"

"Some people in our family are concerned about your siblings' lifestyles."

I imagined he might be against our marriage because I was a little older than Dylan, but when I realized he was referring to Jake and Abby, I saw red.

"Are you judging me because my brother is living with his girlfriend? Or because my sister's an unwed mother? You don't know anything about us or what we've been through. My family has a lot more love than yours."

He looked down at the floor and sighed.

"What would it take for you to break up with my son?"

"The only person who could convince me to do that is Dylan. Do you want to call him?"

"No, I'd rather you don't even tell him that we spoke."

Disgusted, I waved him off.

"I need to get back to work."

Meanwhile, my parents moved to Walla Walla. Daddy was driving my Mustang around town. He had several cars he was working on in various stages of repair, and I couldn't understand why he couldn't drive one of those. Whenever I asked for my car, he said I couldn't drive it without a license. If I asked either of my parents to teach me how to drive, they were too busy.

One day, Dylan and I saw the Mustang in a grocery store parking lot, so he parked next to it. As I got out of his car, I looked inside the Mustang. I was so close that I could almost smell the interior, but I didn't have a key.

"I wonder if I'll ever get to drive it."

"Didn't your dad say he'd teach you?"

"Yeah, but I think he's busy."

I always tried to sound positive about my family, but it hurt that Daddy wouldn't help me learn to drive. I didn't say it out loud, but my mind went back to all the times Daddy promised to buy me textbooks for homeschooling, but he never did.

"Did he teach Mara or Jake?"

"Come to think of it, no."

Dylan laughed. "Come on, I'll show you how to drive."

That afternoon, I learned to parallel park in Dylan's recycled police car.

"I'll find it ironic and laugh in the officer's face if I make a mistake and get pulled over in your police car."

"You won't make a mistake, and you won't get pulled over."

He was right. Thanks to my patient teacher, I was soon parallel parking like a professional.

It was a big day when I passed my driver's test. Dylan rode shotgun while I drove his car to my parents' place.

I found Daddy on the ground with his head under a car.

"I need the keys to the Mustang."

I flashed my driver's license at him.

Nothing was said between us as the keys exchanged hands, but we both knew this was about more than a car. I was switching my trust from one man to another. I'd finally found someone who wouldn't say I was too much—a man who recognized my intelligence and treated me equally.

We celebrated by going to Pizza Hut, where we made a list of expenses for the wedding. I was an activity assistant, and Dylan was a waiter. We had no one to help us, and we refused to go into debt, so we were on a tight budget.

"I can sew my dress. Momma will sew Lynn's dress, and Mara can make hers. I'd love to have Abby in the wedding too, but I think she'll probably have her hands full with the new baby."

Dylan nodded. "If we have only two attendants, it will save on the cost of the tuxes."

I had an idea. "What if we get married in a country church like the ones on tour?"

We drove around the valley and eventually settled on a tiny country church with a bell tower. We both loved the idea of ringing the bell at the start of the wedding.

Satisfied that we could create the wedding we wanted—even on our tight budget—we ordered the supplies.

We had to sign up for pre-marital counseling because the state of Washington required six sessions to get married. We chose our favorite pastor at the Walla Walla College Church. As a prerequisite, we filled out the Prepare/Enrich Assessment tool and went to meet him.

The college church had over two thousand members. Even though he was our favorite preacher, he didn't know us personally. We spent five minutes in his office, where he told us that he didn't recommend we get married because I was an extrovert and Dylan was an introvert.

"It'll never last," he said.

I'd taken enough relationship classes to know he was wrong. As I left his office, it was hard to hold back the tears. Why was everyone against our marriage? It felt like even God was against us. And what motive did this pastor have to treat us so rudely? Later, we found out he was an old friend of Dylan's dad.

The church receptionist was a friend of mine, and I confided in her as we left the office.

Lowering her voice, she suggested we try a different pastor. She sorted through her file and gave me a number. I went home and made an appointment.

The new counselor thought we seemed compatible.

Dylan's mom wanted us to join her in a counseling session, but. I felt uneasy about it, and Dylan had no desire to go to counseling with his mom.

Our counselor suggested we follow Dylan's gut instinct.

"You guys are just starting out, and you don't need to drag his parents' baggage into your marriage."

We talked about all the opposition to our wedding. He explained how a controller can manipulate an entire family. He said the secret to dealing with someone like the Grandmonster was to ignore her.

"Dylan seems to know how to rise above his family's fighting. Cheri, can you take your cues from your future husband and follow him?"

I wasn't sure, but I agreed to try.

A few days later, Dylan's mom called.

"Is Dylan there?"

"He's at work."

"I need to ask you something. Have you guys had sex yet?"

Shocked by her audacity, I told her she should ask Dylan, and she immediately hung up.

Not long after our engagement, Sadie moved back to Chicago. She missed her family. I'd been blessed to have her as a roommate, but now I missed our conversations. I was looking for someone to talk to about all the family drama, so I decided to visit Momma.

"Are you sure you have enough time to drive all the way over here on your lunch break?" Daddy glanced nervously at the clock.

"Yeah, why?"

"Nothing, we're just not used to you having a car and popping in on us."

Were they mad at me for taking the Mustang?

The phone rang, and Daddy answered it. When he hung up, he shouted to Momma from the other room.

"Jake's car broke down, and he needs help. Can you record "The Young and the Restless?"

I turned to Momma. "So, you guys are watching soap operas now?"

Momma looked sheepish. "We were hoping you'd leave so we could watch our show."

I couldn't believe it. Soap operas had always been taboo while I was growing up. It bothered me that Daddy was worried about me reading Christian novels by George MacDonald while he was watching soap operas. I was beginning to wonder if I knew my parents at all.

At our next counseling session, we discussed how to handle family conflicts.

"If your parents want the privilege of having you in their lives, they need to treat you like they do their friends."

He suggested we confront our parents and tell them they were hurting us.

I know the counselor meant well, but my parents had never shown much concern for my feelings. Whether I was asking to go to high school or to learn to drive, they brushed aside my concerns. and said I was overreacting. My feelings just weren't on their priority list.

The thought of confronting his parents gave Dylan a migraine. He'd grown up with adults fighting, and he despised conflict. The counselor encouraged him to take his time, and only do it when he felt ready.

A few nights later, Dylan was at work, and I had gone to sleep when the phone rang at eleven-thirty. We had no caller ID back then, so I got out of bed to answer it.

"Did I interrupt you having sex?"

When I recognized the voice of the Grandmonster, I hung up.

Our nine-month engagement flew by. A few weeks before we married, the college church held its quarterly communion. Adventists practice the ordinance of humility, following Jesus's example by washing each other's feet. At the time, if you wanted to wash your spouse's feet at church, you had to be married.

Since we planned to be married within the month and hoped to enter marriage with hearts of service toward each other, I bought grape juice and crackers. This way, we could wash each other's feet at my house by following the service from home while listening to the college radio station.

We'd already washed each other's feet during the second service when there was a loud pounding on the door. It was Dylan's dad.

"Can I come in? I need help."

Dylan reluctantly opened the door to let him in.

"We just went to the first service and had communion when I got mad. I'm sick of dog hair in the car. I shouldn't have yelled, but your mother got upset and walked to Grandma's. Now I'm stuck with two cars in the church parking lot. Dylan, can you drive one of them home?"

Dylan hesitated. "Dad, we're in the middle of something."

His father glanced around the room. When his eyes fell on the grape juice and crackers, he raised his voice even louder.

"This is wrong. You should only do this at church with the elders present."

Feeling shamed, we put on our shoes and followed him to the car. Dylan and his dad drove the family cars while I followed in the Mustang so I could give Dylan a ride back to my place. Later, I wondered how his mom got home. Did we add to her stress by moving her car?

I was pulling lasagna out of the oven the next evening when Dylan made an announcement.

"I'm ready to confront my parents."

Setting the oven to warm, I followed him out the door and got in the car.

Dylan nervously asked his parents to stop what they were doing and listen.

"If you want me in your life, you'll need to stop talking about us because we deserve respect. That means no more gossip or putting down our relationship."

I was surprised they listened. After that, they seemed to treat us with respect. I was proud of Dylan for standing up to his parents. I wished I could do the same, but I knew mine would never understand.

It felt like half of the people coming to our wedding had been against us getting married at some point. Dylan was my best friend, and I was happy to be his wife, but I'd also be glad when this wedding and all the hullabaloo that came with it was over.

Our wedding rehearsal went smoothly until the Grandmonster showed up and kissed Dylan on the lips.

When I saw Dylan wince with disgust, I felt angry.

"Why don't you tell her to stop?"

He shrugged his shoulders. "You know what our counselor said about ignoring people like her. Besides, my parents have been fighting with her for years, and it's much easier to ignore her."

"Well, I can't ignore her. If you want to marry me, you'd better make sure that never happens again."

I didn't say this for my sake—but for his.

20 Glory of Love

*Few delights can equal
the presence of one
whom we trust utterly.
-George MacDonald*

On our wedding day, I woke to the sound of a robin singing. One glance out the window revealed a pink dawn in a cloudless sky. The weatherman had forecast a hot day, so I lingered in the cool sheets as long as possible, contemplating the progress we'd made to arrive at this day.

My parents were supportive of our marriage. Momma thought Dylan was friendly and fun to play Scrabble with, and she especially enjoyed his talent on the piano.

The only advice Daddy gave me about finding a husband was to find a sincere man. He believed anyone could be worthy if they were honest and willing to change their mind. If Daddy had any concerns when I confided that Dylan was attracted to men, he said nothing. He never treated Dylan any differently than the rest of the family. Besides, what better proof of sincerity than a man trying to obey the Bible and marry a woman in the hope of becoming straight?

Our wedding week stretched my parents beyond their comfort zone. Momma was nervous about looking old in the photos, so I suggested we color her hair. I wasn't sure if it helped since she'd never colored it and considered her own mother vain for doing so. My parents, who never ate at restaurants, came out to dinner with the wedding party, but they were annoyed by the silly songs we sang.

It was a relief that our parents had mellowed some, and we'd enjoyed a friendly dinner with both families the day before.

Dylan's great-grandmother supplied the reception hall at the recreation center where she lived. She was friendlier than the Grandmonster. An efficient woman in her eighties, she made sure we had everything we needed before we turned the decorating over to my coworkers from the care center.

Grandma G made our wedding cake for the cost of the ingredients. We chose a carrot cake with cream cheese icing. She offered to decorate it with peach lace and lavender pansies. I couldn't wait to see it. She'd also offered free roses from her garden. Dylan volunteered to get up early and cut peach, lavender, and white roses before taking them to our friend Susie, who was arranging them for free.

The small Adventist church we attended gave us a night in a jacuzzi suite at a local hotel. Since we planned to drive to the Oregon

Coast for our honeymoon, we decided to stay in the suite after the wedding.

I decided to add my first-born nephew to the wedding party. I'd sewn him a pair of gray trousers and a lavender bow tie to wear with suspenders. I knew he'd look adorable carrying a lavender balloon next to the other children.

As I checked each item off the list, I marveled that we'd managed to pull this wedding together despite our tight budget. Everything was in place. What could possibly go wrong?

When I remembered Grandpa and Grandma were driving over from Oregon City, I got up to write a card thanking them for coming. I set it next to the bouquet of roses and the basket of snacks I planned to slip into their hotel room.

The wedding wasn't until six o'clock in the evening, but I had things to do, so I tiptoed past Sadie and Lynn, sleeping on the living room floor, to get to the kitchen.

As I put a bagel into the toaster, I heard a tap on the window and turned around to see Dylan. He was pouring water into a five-gallon bucket for the roses. He gave me an excited smile, and I blew a kiss before he left for Grandma G's to get the roses.

Sadie stumbled into the kitchen to make coffee and wagged her finger at me with a grin.

"Hasn't anyone told you that seeing the groom before the wedding is bad luck?"

I laughed. "I don't believe in bad luck."

After a happy sigh, I asked her, "Did you ever think I'd marry Dylan?"

Sadie rolled her eyes. "I think everyone on tour saw that coming."

Sipping a mug of coffee, Sadie took in my homemade wedding dress, then offered to iron it as soon as we got to the church.

Lynn got up and tried on the peach satin dress Momma had sewn for her. I was glad to see the fit was perfect. The presence of these two wonderful friends was an extra gift. Our families knew and loved Sadie, and we felt honored that Lynn would grace our wedding with her beautiful singing.

When we arrived at the church, we discovered the air conditioner had broken on the hottest day of the year. A maintenance man ran around frantically trying to fix it, but he kept shaking his head.

The heat opened the roses as our guests filled the tiny church. Dylan's best friend Jon and his brother stood patiently beside the groom. Mara and Lynn looked beautiful in their peach dresses. Daddy joined me at the back of the church with Sadie. Her job was to pull on the thick rope and ring the bell six times to signal the start of the wedding.

After Sadie's first pull, she flew up and nearly disappeared into the belfry. I tried to stifle my laughter while Daddy grabbed her feet and pulled her back to the floor. Together, they rang the bell five more times. Daddy had to hold her feet and pull her back down each time. After the sixth ring, Daddy had to wait for me to get my giggles under control before we could walk down the aisle.

When he held his arm out to me, Daddy's eyes filled with tears and whispered, "I always wished I could have given you more."

"It's okay, Daddy. I love you."

He patted my arm. "I love you, too."

Daddy's words filled me with joy, but I saw a different love in Dylan's eyes as he watched me walk down the aisle. As I looked into those eyes, I felt no fear. I knew I was marrying an honest man with a kind heart, and I felt safe. The napkins I'd chosen for the reception reflected my heart: "This day, I marry my friend, the one I laugh with, dream with, live for, love." We'd made a pact to build a home and shelter each other through the storms of life.

Despite the sweltering heat, the wedding was beautiful. Lynn sang the "Wedding Song" and "When I Think of Home" by Bryan Duncan. I chose that song because I'd never had a building to call home, but wherever Dylan was felt like home.

We wrote our own vows, and I didn't promise to obey Dylan any more than he promised to obey me. We pledged to serve each other in love with the freedom to grow.

When we left the church, we drove the Mustang to the reception, with our guests honking behind us.

Our families and friends mingled for several hours, and everyone was getting along when the pastor asked if we were ready to sign the marriage license. Dylan searched through a stack of bulletins but couldn't find it.

Jon and another friend offered to drive back and search at the church. While they were gone, I broke a wisdom tooth on a walnut nutshell in the carrot cake. It didn't hurt, but I was scared it might start.

Jon returned without the marriage license. I asked the pastor what would happen if we couldn't find it.

"The date of your marriage will be whatever day we sign it. Right now, you've got an hour before midnight."

I panicked. I wanted the correct date on that piece of paper. Dylan raced back to the church to search for himself. Meanwhile, the pastor went home. He said if we found the document to knock on his door.

Dylan's mother showed her support by decorating the Mustang. She'd sprayed "Just Married" in white letters on the back window and tied tin cans to the bumper to make a lot of noise. She was blowing up condoms like balloons when Dylan interrupted her to take the car.

Mara's husband went along to help Dylan search, while Daddy and Momma took me to wait in the pastor's driveway. I found myself sitting in the back seat with Mara, which made me groan.

Momma turned to look at me. "Are you okay? Is it your tooth?"

"No, my tooth doesn't even hurt, but I've spent my entire childhood sitting in the back seat with Mara, and this is not how I pictured my wedding night."

We all laughed. It felt good to be laughing with Mara and my parents on my wedding night. For the first time in a long time, I felt their love.

A few minutes before midnight, Dylan came rattling into the pastor's driveway with the Mustang, dragging all the tin cans behind him. The church organist had tucked our marriage license inside some sheet music. Fortunately, Dylan thought to look inside the bench.

The pastor's wife opened the door in her nightgown and graciously let us into her home. Along with our witnesses, we signed the license just minutes before midnight.

Most of our guests were home in bed. Grandpa and Grandma had long been asleep in their room. Mara and her husband left with my parents while Lynn and Sadie went to our house.

Finally, alone at last, Dylan and I headed for the jacuzzi suite. We passed the grocery store and hoped it would stay open just a little longer so we could buy some sparkling cider.

When we entered the store, it was midnight. Dylan was still in his tux while I held the train of my wedding dress as we rushed through the automatic doors.

Despite the late hour, quite a few people were in the store. Everybody loves a bride and groom. Strangers started calling out, "Congratulations!" as we ran through the aisles.

The beverage aisle was crowded. As Dylan reached for a bottle of cider, it slipped through his hand and flew through the air, but he caught it with his other hand just before it hit the floor.

Others witnessed the near mishap, while a woman further down the aisle shouted, "Lucky in love!"

Other people applauded. Dylan made a quick bow as we headed for the checkout, while I said to myself, "Lucky for sure!"

21 Papa Don't Preach

*A lot of parents will do
anything for their kids
except let them be themselves.*
-Banksy

Our honeymoon on the Oregon Coast was everything I'd dreamed it would be. To save money, we stayed in a hotel for one week and spent another week camping. The camping week was our favorite. There was something about sleeping in a forest next to the ocean. It was romantic to make love with the surf roaring in the background. In the mornings, we fried potatoes and covered our pancakes with fresh local strawberries, remembering to share a few tidbits with the jays.

We enjoyed the restaurants and shops in Old Town Newport. We also drove down to the Sea Lion Caves, went on a whale tour to view humongous gray whales, and spent an afternoon at the aquarium.

In the evenings, we roasted vegetarian hot dogs and marshmallows over the campfire before taking long walks on the beach at sunset, talking and dreaming about our future. Then we returned to camp, where we fell asleep in each other's arms, listening to the ocean's lullaby.

Newport also had impressive fireworks for the Fourth of July. We set our lawn chairs on a dock and met interesting people. As I snuggled under a warm blanket and watched the sky light up with Dylan's arm around me, he shared his thoughts.

"After taking those aptitude tests at the career center, I'm thinking about changing my major."

I sucked in a deep breath of the salty air and held it. "What would you do instead?"

"Maybe become a physical therapist."

"But I thought you wanted to be a teacher?"

"It's a sort of teaching, but on a one-to-one basis instead of one-to-many. I'm not sure I'd like standing in front of class every day."

"Where would you go to school?"

He sighed. "I probably have the best shot of getting accepted into an Adventist school. Maybe Andrews University in Michigan. But how would moving affect you?"

My heart seemed suspended between my husband and my family.

I tried to keep my voice from wavering. "I don't think I can live that far away from my family."

He reached for my hand. "We still have months to decide. Let's think about it."

We watched the climax of the fireworks before walking back to the car in silence. We were deep in our thoughts because we wanted the other to be happy.

The week after we returned from our honeymoon, I got promoted to Activity Director. Proud of myself and thrilled to be a full-time employee with healthcare benefits, I stopped by to tell Momma.

Instead of sharing my joy, her face looked pinched. "Are you sure this is what you want?"

Bracing for one of her worst-case scenarios, I smiled through my teeth.

"It's a fun job, and I enjoy helping people."

"Oh, I could never work in such a germy place." Momma shuddered.

"I always wash my hands."

"Being around the sick and dying makes me depressed."

"I don't see them as sick and dying. Besides, it's a good job until I return to school."

"Oh, I thought you'd be a stay-at-home wife."

"Someone has to pay the rent while Dylan's studying full time."

"As soon as I got married, I quit school and never looked back. Mrs. White says a woman's most important job is being a wife and mother."

Momma often pulled out quotes from the prophet and founder of the Adventist church to make a point whenever we disagreed.

Feeling defensive, I raised my voice. "Look, I came to share my good news, but it seems all you can do is criticize me."

Daddy had been working on a car outside. At the sound of our voices, he rushed through the back door.

"Cheri, can you tone it down a bit? Our neighbor has a microphone called the "Whisper 2000," which amplifies sounds and allows her to hear everything you're saying."

I rolled my eyes. "Are you serious?"

My parents exchanged looks as if I were a disobedient child. Grabbing my purse, I stood up to leave. "I'll go find someone who cares about my news."

Daddy closed the kitchen window. "I'm not kidding. The landlord has the neighbor spying on us."

I got in the car and slammed the door extra hard. In my parents' eyes, the only respectable status for a woman was as a wife and mother. As a single woman, they'd never listened to me, but now that I was married, I'd hoped they'd respect me.

I turned the key in the ignition and started to pull out of the driveway when I noticed their backyard covered with black and white garbage bags. Their dog was chained to a tree, but he'd ripped open some of the bags.

I cringed. There were things I hadn't told Dylan to save my parents' dignity—and mine. I was afraid if he saw that yard, he'd mistake us for hillbillies. Why couldn't Daddy stick to a job and pay for garbage service like normal people?

Looking at the mess, I realized we could not have a nice dinner at their place. I thought of our tiny kitchen table, which could only fit four people. If I were going to host a family dinner, I'd need to get a longer table.

The following day, I used my lunch break to drive to an antique store across town. I found a maple dining set for eight. It had a few scratches, but with a little TLC, it would be perfect. Then I saw the price tag: three hundred sixty dollars. That was more than a month's rent. How could we afford it?

Back at work, my eyes fell on the glass case where Dolores sold crafts. I decided to sew some crafts to raise money for the table.

Jake and Carrie moved two doors down from us on the same side of the street. She'd forgiven me for the plant incident, and when an activity assistant job opened, she applied for it. Most of the candidates seemed either clueless or careless. Even though Carrie was pregnant, she was the best person for the job, so I hired her. I never regretted it. She turned out to be a compassionate and responsible worker. It wasn't long before we got to know each other and talked like old friends.

One lunch break, I told her about my dream of having family celebrations around a table.

"Sounds fun, but I wonder if your parents will show up. Jake says they're kind of weird about holidays."

"I don't think they're weird. When I was younger, we had Christmas. Then Daddy decided Christmas trees were pagan, but Momma says he was mostly depressed because he didn't have money for gifts. Now that we've grown and have jobs, that shouldn't be a problem."

"I hope not. Now that Jake and I are going to have a baby, I want my kids to have Christmas."

She paused. It was almost like she was afraid to ask me something.

"Do you think your dad might have bipolar disorder? I have a sister who takes medication for that."

"If he does, he'd never take meds because my parents think Jesus and natural remedies are enough."

"It seems like they ignore their options. Jake and I believe in science."

I didn't want to get into another argument defending my parents with my pregnant sister-in-law, so I let Carrie think whatever she wanted.

My crafts were selling as fast as I could make them, and the dollar jar kept growing. Every week, I drove across town to check on the dining set to see if it was still there. When I'd raised half the money, I sighed with relief to see the antique dealer place a sign on the table with the words, "sale pending."

That year, we celebrated Christmas Eve with my family and Christmas morning with Dylan's family. We gathered at my parents' house and enjoyed doting on Abby's babies. Dylan's mom surprised me with her creativity in decorating presents, and I discovered we had more in common than I thought.

I couldn't wait to have people over to our place, but I knew there was one person I'd never invite. The Grandmonster seemed to have gotten the memo that Dylan didn't enjoy her kisses, but she had no end of petty remarks and childish scowls for me. I could tell we would never be friends.

Early in the new year, when the dining set was paid off, Dylan helped me carry it into the house. I eagerly pulled out the box with our wedding dishes. My heart leaped to see my Pfaltzgraff, with its grapevine pattern in lilac, rose, and sage green. I pulled a plate out of the box and ran my finger over the surface before setting it on the table. I cherished it as others did their expensive china.

Dylan came through the door with the last chair and a stack of mail in his hand. His face was red with excitement.

"I got accepted into the PT program at Andrews University."

He grabbed me in a warm embrace while I hugged him back.

"Congratulations!"

Then reality sunk in. "I finally have a good job with most of my family living in one town. How can I move to Michigan?"

Dylan was sympathetic to my feelings and reassured me that we didn't have to decide yet. We could put it off for another year, and he would explore other options.

Dylan often worked late at the restaurant while I had to get up early for my job. One evening, he was working, and I had already gone to sleep when the phone rang. It was almost midnight, and I expected him home any minute, but just in case his car broke down, I answered. No one spoke, but I heard creepy, heavy breathing before the caller hung up.

A chill ran across my shoulders. Thinking of Debbie and her untimely death, I jumped up and locked all the doors and windows before I called Dylan. He was still at work. He couldn't imagine us having a stalker, but he promised to look around the neighborhood when he came home. When he came through the door, he saw nothing. The streets were empty and quiet as usual.

We had no caller ID back then, so we decided If he wanted to call me in the future, he'd let the phone ring twice and hang up, and then he'd call right back so I'd know it was him.

A few days later, when I heard Abby was in town, I rushed to my parents' house with some baby clothes I'd found on sale. When Abby came into the room, I didn't recognize her. It looked like her body, but her face was red and purple, and her eyes were nearly swollen shut. The only time I'd seen a person look like that was from an allergic reaction to a bee sting.

"What happened?"

"We got into an argument, and he grabbed my hair and slammed my face onto the floor."

I felt sick to my stomach and filled with rage. Any man who did this to my precious sister didn't deserve her.

"You can't go back, Abby."

"I don't have a choice. Where would I go? Besides, he's my kids' dad."

"We'll find you a place. He could've killed you."

She shook her head. "You don't understand."

Since she wouldn't leave him for herself, I tried to make her leave him for the kids. "What if he hurts the boys?"

"He's never touched them, and he would never have done this if I hadn't gotten upset over some idiotic woman."

"Was this an isolated incident, or has he hit you before?"

Abby remained silent. I could tell she wasn't ready to tell us everything.

I glanced at our parents. Momma was ripping her fingernails apart. Daddy looked angry, but his red face gave me a chill. Why did I feel so uneasy? Then I realized the Persuader was always lurking. Even though Daddy didn't dare to touch us with the belt, it still hung on an invisible hook in the room. I wanted to blame it for Abby's pain, but I knew those marks were from her boyfriend. Perhaps if there'd never been a Persuader, Abby would recognize that no man—not her boyfriend or her father—had a right to hit her.

Nauseous and overcome with emotions that I couldn't process, I grabbed the kids' clothes and fled. It wasn't my finest moment. The babies needed those clothes, but I felt it was the only leverage I had to persuade Abby to leave their father and stay safe. Of course, it didn't work.

I couldn't sleep for weeks. Dylan was my world, but my sister's face continued to haunt me. I'd left her once when I went on tour—how could I move to Michigan and leave her behind again?

I looked forward to Abby's birthday, but it was a quiet evening. I'd invited the entire family, Mara couldn't make it due to winter weather, Jake had to work, and Abby's boyfriend was spending time in jail because she finally reported him. It was the first gathering around the new dining table, and I'd hoped for a better turnout. Instead, it was just Abby, my parents, Dylan, and me.

Daddy looked through our bookcases, while I set the food on the table. I was careful not to play my music while my parents were visiting, but I'd forgotten one of the rules from my childhood was to read only true stories.

"Who is George MacDonald? You have quite a few books written by him."

"He was a minister in Scotland in the nineteenth century." I set a basket of rolls on the table.

"They look like novels." His face tightened with concern.

Novels were considered sensational and untrue. I glanced around the room. Our bookshelves were full of Dylan's literature books, which included a giant volume of Shakespeare. My parents criticized people who attended such plays. And now, I was one of them.

I set the salad on the table. "Daddy, they're religious stories about redemption and God's love."

"Do they teach about getting rid of known sin?"

"They teach about God's unconditional love."

His eyes narrowed. "How unconditional?"

I was afraid he was going to give a lecture and ruin the meal.

"Daddy, I didn't invite you over for a debate. It's Abby's birthday.

"So, they aren't true stories?" Momma looked at Daddy's furrowed brow and shook her head.

"No." I wanted to share that I was finding new ways to see God's love through those books, but I knew they wouldn't understand.

Hoping to change the subject as we sat down to eat, I asked, "Daddy, would you say a blessing over Abby and the food?"

Daddy's eyes dropped to the table and refused to meet mine. He spoke in a low voice. "I'd rather not."

Confused, I searched Momma's face. She, too, wouldn't look at me. I'd been taught it was proper for the head of the family to pray, but Dylan barely knew my sister. I cleared my throat and decided to take up the mantle Daddy had tossed aside.

I thought of my host dad in East LA, and I prayed in a Pentecostal style, hoping to bless my sister's socks off. Desperate times call for extreme measures, and I wasn't taking any chances after what happened to Abby's face. I prayed for her health, her relationship, and her children. I got so carried away that I almost forgot to pray for the food.

When I finally said, "Amen," I opened my eyes to see anxiety on Momma's face, and I realized my new way of praying was probably scaring her.

After dinner, Momma helped me clean the kitchen while Daddy went to get a map out of the car.

I spoke softly. "What's wrong with Daddy? Why wouldn't he pray the blessing?"

"Oh, Cheri, you have no idea how much you hurt his feelings when you told him how to pray."

My mouth dropped open. "I remember saying we don't need to say thee and thou when we pray, but I can't believe he's been holding a grudge for two years."

"Well maybe some things are just better left unsaid."

"Are you asking me to apologize? Daddy never apologizes to me."

She sighed. "It seems like you've changed a lot. And spouting off all your new ideas isn't helping."

So, my parents thought I was being a know-it-all.

"Momma, I love reading modern versions of the Bible. And those novels are about God as a loving father. I feel like I've been in the dark about God, and now I can see more clearly in the light. I just want to share that with the rest of the family."

Her eyes grew large. "I hope you're careful. Remember that Satan himself comes as an angel of light."

After Abby and my parents went home, I turned to Dylan. "Why are my parents so critical of me? I've tried to be a good Christian my entire life, yet in their eyes, I'm never good enough."

Dylan shrugged his shoulders. "I don't think they are critical as much as they're scared of new ideas."

Jake's birthday was a month after Abby's. Despite my disappointment over her birthday, I wanted to try again for him. I was making a list of people to call when Jake called me. The minute I heard his voice, I knew something was wrong.

"Dad and Mom moved without taking their garbage, so their landlord dumped it all over my lawn. He even ripped the bags open."

A knot formed in my stomach. "They moved again? I thought Daddy said they were settling down."

"If this is the result of them living near us, who cares where they move?"

I understood his frustration.

He continued his rant. "It's not enough that I have to struggle to go to college with no high school education and put up with all their religious rules. They judge me for doing what's best for my family, but this garbage on my lawn is just one more way I'm stuck dealing with all the crap Dad leaves behind. I'm done pretending that we're a family."

It felt like Jake had punched me in the gut, but I couldn't blame him. My dream of bringing the family together was fading. Everything he complained about was true, but I couldn't believe he might disown the family. Then, a new thought struck fear into my heart. What if Dylan saw that mess? What would he think about my family?

"Jake, if I were you, I'd take it to the dump as soon as possible."

"How am I supposed to haul all this shit with a Honda Civic?"

"Do you know of anyone with a truck?"

"I'll look for someone, but it's embarrassing."

"Tell me about it."

"Jake, try not to let this make you bitter. We all need to forgive and forget."

"You can do whatever you want, sister, but I'm done."

When Jake hung up, I realized it was hopeless to plan a party for him since he was angry with Daddy. Perhaps Mara was smarter than the rest of us for keeping her distance.

My biggest dream had been to gather my family around the table to eat, laugh, and love, like those cute signs at the antique store. It was a nice idea, but it wasn't going to happen in this family.

As we got ready for bed one night, the phone rang. Since Dylan was home, I answered. Once again, it was the heavy breathing. This time, I decided to call the bluff of whoever it was. I shouted, "I know who you are, and you're pitiful."

"What's wrong? Did I interrupt while you were having sex?"

Surprised to hear the Grandmonster's voice, I slammed the receiver down. When I told Dylan who it was. He shook his head. "At least it wasn't a psycho that we don't know."

I felt like I was suffocating whenever I spent time with my parents. Momma expected me to be just like her, and Daddy thought my soul was in danger if I didn't believe like him. It felt like they wanted to crush me back into the box I'd been raised in, but it was impossible because I'd already seen the light. I finally told Dylan I was ready to live in Michigan. Maybe a new place would allow us to grow without all the family stress.

I made a haystack dinner to celebrate our new adventure. As I set the table with the grapevine dishes, I felt a pang of sadness for all the gatherings that never happened. I lit some candles, and Dylan opened a bottle of root beer.

Lifting his tumbler to mine, he smiled. "To Michigan, where we can escape our crazy families and start a new life!"

22 Nothing's Gonna Stop Us Now

*Life is what happens
to you while you're busy
making other plans
-John Lennon*

There were three things we felt we couldn't live without—Dylan's Baldwin Spinet piano, my maple dining set, and our hand-me-down queen-sized bed. With something to sleep on, music to lift our spirits, and a table to entertain others, we planned to enjoy life no matter where we lived. But first, we had to haul our belongings two thousand miles and find a place.

We reserved a fifteen-foot moving truck and were given a larger one for the same price. Since we were towing our car, it would be harder to find a parking space, but the larger truck was also a gift.

By laying our mattress flat in the back, we could sleep in it and save money.

We stayed with Mara and her husband in Spokane. Mara was the last physical connection to my family, and I felt sad as I hugged my first friend in this life goodbye—even if it was only for a while. The next three years looming over us felt like an eternity.

Dylan was eager to hit the road, but we didn't get far. When we stopped at Walmart to get some flashlight batteries, we locked the keys inside the cab. Pacing around the truck in circles, we tried to be patient while we waited for the locksmith. He arrived within minutes and quickly retrieved the key.

Back on the road, we played music and passed the time while I read to Dylan as he drove. That evening, we took showers at a truck stop before snuggling into bed at the back of the truck. I prayed no one would notice the door propped open with Dylan's shoe while I set a can of mace and a crowbar above our heads. Dylan's eyes grew large when I announced my intentions to attack any intruders, but fortunately, we had a peaceful night.

The next evening, we stopped in eastern Montana to grab a pizza. It felt good to get out of the truck and stretch our legs. As we finished our supper, the radio station announced that a big storm was heading our way. We looked out the window to see dark clouds filling the sky. Rushing to pay, we figured we'd try to outrun the storm until we discovered the keys locked inside the truck again.

"We can't keep doing this," I yelled above a loud crack of thunder.

"You try driving this thing and see if you can do better."

The restaurant manager was turning out the lights and locking the door when she noticed us arguing.

"Are you guys, okay?"

She unlocked the door and gave Dylan the number of the only locksmith in town.

When Dylan got off the phone, he rolled his eyes.

"He has to round up his cattle first."

The manager jumped in her jeep and drove off just as a bolt of lightning struck the field across the road, and huge drops of water began to pelt us. Waiting on a locksmith was one thing, but standing in a thunderstorm without shelter was beyond my comfort zone.

"Maybe we should leave a window open next time we get out of the truck."

Dylan pulled his sweatshirt over his head like a hoodie.

"Relax, the locksmith will be here soon."

"Soon? It can't be soon enough. Soon has come and gone. We need to find shelter."

The restaurant sat by itself on the outskirts of town. My eyes searched the landscape.

"There's not even a tree."

"Trees get hit by lightning. Here, crawl under the truck."

Dylan slid under the truck and motioned for me to follow.

The truck was high enough off the ground to sit under, but the parking lot was filling with water. The locksmith arrived just as the water began to seep under the truck.

With the heater on high, blowing our wet hair, we drove through the storm. Tornadoes were rare where we came from, so we never thought of that possibility. The country station faded out as we drove on through the night. Left with no radio, we began to sing every song we could think of while the thunder crashed, and lightning danced around us.

By early in the morning, the storm had passed, and we pulled into a rest area. We soon fell into a cozy sleep, dreaming about our new home.

The rest of the trip was uneventful until we reached Chicago. Cars swiftly darted in and out of the lanes around us making it awkward to tow our car behind the long truck. Dylan found it challenging to switch lanes, but we were a good team. I called out the route from the atlas while Dylan negotiated the traffic. Once we got through the city, we exhaled with relief.

We arrived in Berrien Springs at dusk, parked at the Apple Valley Market, and once again snuggled into our cozy bed at the back of the truck.

The next day, Dylan unhooked the car, and we began to explore our new community from the Andrews University campus to the surrounding vicinity. Hundreds of international students gave Andrews the feel of a big city, but the farms and orchards in the countryside around the school made us feel right at home.

We spent several days looking for an apartment to rent. It was harder than we imagined. We were getting nervous because it was almost time to return the truck, and we had no idea where we would sleep. An Adventist woman invited us to her church prayer meeting. It was 30 miles north of the school, but we couldn't afford to be picky.

At the meeting, we met an elderly couple who were shocked to learn we were sleeping in the back of the truck. They invited us to stay in their guest room. The next day, they had us unload our belongings into their garage so we could return the truck on time. We ended up staying with them for a few weeks.

One day, the pastor stopped by to tell us about a cute, tiny house we could afford to rent. It was thirty minutes from campus, which seemed farther than we wanted, but the pastor reassured us it was a good deal. Our hosts loaned us their pickup to move our stuff. Eager to have our own space, we moved in without paying much attention to the house or its location.

Dylan hauled our washer and dryer down to the basement via a narrow stairway. I shuddered at the spiders and mice droppings and wondered how to keep the clothes clean, climbing past the mildewed walls.

The only bedroom was on the third floor, and we couldn't get the queen bed base up the stairs, so we had to sleep on the floor. The piano barely fit on the main level, and we could feel the entire house shake whenever we walked across the floor. I was worried that the piano had overtaxed the weight limit. As for my dining set, there was simply no room to set it up.

The house sat about forty feet from the railroad tracks. This fact went unnoticed when we paid the deposit, but it became apparent the first time the train blew its whistle and startled us out of bed.

We soon discovered the train came through all hours of the day and night.

The stench of mildew was so pungent it made my nose burn. We bought some paint that was supposed to seal over the mildew. We had a week before Dylan's first term started, and the tensions were mounting because we had to pay rent, and I still hadn't found a job.

Despite the drive to school, the tight spaces, the mildew, and the train, we were determined to make that house a home. The pastor said it was a good deal, and we had no reason to doubt him.

I brought up a concern while we were rolling paint over the walls.

"My mom forwarded our mail, and there was a notice for a bounced check."

"Did the rent go through?"

"Yes, this check was for the grocery store, but what happened?"

"I'll be getting my financial aid check, and we will set it straight."

"I don't think you understand how much this upsets me. My parents always bounced checks, and I do everything I can to make sure that we don't."

"It's okay, Cheri, we'll cover it."

"But how did it happen? Did you take out money and not tell me?"

"I didn't say anything because I didn't want you to stress out."

"Remember Billy Joel's song "Honesty? I can't handle you lying to me."

"I think you have unrealistic expectations."

He sounded annoyed, but he wasn't as irritated as I was.

"Unrealistic expectations? How could you marry me and not tell me that you are a liar?"

"I'm not a liar. I'm just saying that you're the most scary, honest person I've ever met."

"Then you are the sneakiest liar I've ever met."

"I'm done here." Dylan rolled his eyes, grabbed the keys from the kitchen counter, and jumped into the car.

I ran out the door behind him, feeling desperate. "First, you lied, then refused to admit it, and now you're running away? How dare you call me scary, honest."

He drove off anyway. Tears streamed down my face as I wondered how the one person I trusted the most, could say such things and drive away. I felt he must not love me after all.

When I heard the train whistle, I considered throwing myself in front of it, but that would have been too final. Seeing the hammer on the back porch, I removed my engagement watch and pounded its face.

Dylan drove back into the driveway just in time to see me crush the symbol of his love.

His eyes were cold as he got out of the car. "So that's how you treat the gifts I give you?"

"Which is more important, trust or a watch?"

"Love is more important."

"What do liars know about love?"

Startled by footsteps in the gravel behind me, I turned to see the pastor walking up to the porch carrying two brown bags of groceries. How long had he been there? I was embarrassed to think he heard us shouting at each other.

A voice in my mind said, "The pastor must think you're a terrible Christian."

"We thought you kids could use some groceries." He paused to look at Dylan, standing with his hands on his hips. Then he turned toward me, looking at the broken watch in one hand before staring at the hammer in the other.

I set the objects on the railing and reached out with my shaking hands to take the groceries.

"My wife works at the University cafeteria and says to stop by the office if you want a job."

I remembered he'd written a book about prayer, so I decided to swallow my pride and ask him to pray with us.

His smile faded at my request, then he began to walk backward toward his car.

"I think such matters are better handled in private. See you in church."

After the pastor left, Dylan's eyes met mine. This time, he looked empathetic as he took the groceries and carried them inside.

"I'm sorry, Dylan."

"I'm sorry, too."

"If you just tell me what happened, I'll never bring it up again."

"I wish I could. I have no idea what happened. I didn't lie about anything."

Tears filled my eyes as I realized I'd destroyed my engagement watch over nothing.

Dylan looked like he was going to cry, too.

"Why do you always have to imagine the worst?"

"I don't know."

I'd always taken pride in being honest, but I couldn't answer his question because I couldn't understand myself.

So far, things seemed much worse in Michigan, and I was beginning to wish we'd never moved. We were about to celebrate our first wedding anniversary, and we'd had two fights within a week. It was devastating to realize my watch hadn't survived the first year, and I had no one to blame but myself.

I'd always felt shame when Daddy couldn't pay his bills. Now, I felt even more shame for bouncing a check and accusing Dylan of lying. I wished I hadn't destroyed my watch, and I especially wished I hadn't asked the pastor for prayer.

I didn't know what to do with so much pain, so I turned to food for comfort. I fried up veggie burgers and threw some fries in the oven. Dylan put a movie in the VCR, and we sat down to forget about our stressful move.

I'd barely tasted my burger when the train whistle drowned out the movie and shook the entire house while we hung onto our plates.

When the train finally passed, and we could hear each other speak again, I set my plate down.

"I don't think there are enough prayers in the world to help our nerves as long as that train keeps roaring past us several times a day."

Dylan dug into his cold fries.

"Driving 23 miles back and forth every day is expensive."

I groaned. "We should've known better than to take the advice of a pastor who won't even pray with us."

"We might have to make the best of it for at least the summer."

I had no intention of staying in that stinky, shaky house. I was determined to find a better place to live, but we'd fought enough for one day, so I kept my thoughts to myself.

We turned the movie back on and escaped our chaotic life with heaping bowls of mocha almond fudge.

The following day, Dylan had an early appointment at Andrews University while I stayed behind. The freshly painted walls still reeked of mildew, and the Michigan humidity made everything feel sticky. My heart still felt heavy from the events the day before, so I went outside to get some fresh air.

The early morning sun painted the fields a golden pink, but the land was flat as far as I could see. A dairy farm down the road explained why it was so hard to find fresh air depending on which direction the wind was blowing.

We hadn't been gone for a month, but I already missed Washington. I was homesick for my family, Grandma G, her cozy rental, and the dry climate of Walla Walla. Most of all, I missed myself—the person who had proudly worn her engagement watch, performed the duties of a professional activity director, and had a place for everything in her well-organized home.

I didn't like the woman I was becoming. She was anxious and insecure, and I hated to admit it, but I'd acted more like Daddy than I'd ever dreamed possible.

Everything about the move and this house seemed like a mistake. I'd broken Momma's rule of keeping family secrets by telling the pastor we'd been fighting. What was wrong with me?

I thought about the pastor and his book on prayer. Had I been wrong to ask him to pray for us? It still hurt to remember that Daddy had refused to pray a blessing over Abby's birthday dinner because of me. It was hard not to take these prayer refusals personally. All my life, men—Daddy, church elders, and pastors—had prayed whenever a crisis occurred. My parents taught me that leading worship was the husband's role. It bothered me that Dylan wouldn't take on the patriarchal role in our marriage. How could we be blessed if we didn't follow God's rules for marriage? Feeling lost and alone, I decided to pray for myself.

I apologized to God for starting with my needs, but it was my needs that drove me to him. I prayed for a job, a better place to live, and faith to trust my husband. I poured out my heart, begging Jesus to fix everything.

I got up to examine my beautiful engagement watch, but it was broken beyond repair, so I tossed it into the garbage can. Trying not to cry, I turned to go inside. That's when I noticed the oak next to the house was full of goldfinches. I'd never seen so many in one place, and their singing was so vibrant that it flooded me with a surge of hope.

Dylan returned an hour later with a smile.

"I found a place across from the University. The good news is it's cheap, but the bad news is that it's a basement apartment. What do you think?"

"I don't know. My nose is still burning from mildew in this house. I can't imagine living in a basement could be better. Plus, it's probably full of spiders." I shuddered.

"Who says there has to be mildew and spiders?"

"A lady at church warned me that Michigan basements are damp and non-habitable."

"Let's just check it out. It's cheap, and it could save us money on gas."

I jumped into the car, and he drove us back to Berrien Springs.

The main house was a large colonial-style home with two floors above the basement. The entry to the apartment was off to the side and looked like it led to a hole in the ground. I hesitated at the top of the narrow steps, but once inside, it reminded me of a dollhouse.

The kitchen and living room were one room. I was relieved to see it had windows, even if they were up next to the ceiling. It felt less dark when we opened the blinds and let in the natural light.

"It smells like something died in here. Do these windows open?"

Dylan cracked a window and examined the screen. "No holes."

"It doesn't matter. The spiders are already inside."

I pointed to the ceiling, which looked like a prop for a Halloween party. I turned my attention to the appliances. A tiny stove with a doll-sized oven sat beside an ancient refrigerator with only two feet of counter space.

"How can we even cook in such a small space?"

"We'll use the table."

I glanced around the room.

"If we open up the table, there won't be room for anything else."

"I think the fridge is working."

Dylan opened the door, took a whiff, and shut it quickly.

"But I'm sure you'll want to bleach it out."

I felt heartsick. Was this how God answered my prayers? I wished we'd never left Walla Walla.

Dylan stepped into the bedroom.

"The bed will fit if we put it against the wall on one side."

I entered the bathroom and discovered a full bath with a shower, tub, and sink. The counter and mirror ran the length of the wall.

I'd grown up in places without running water, so the thought of a hot bath on a cold winter night inspired me to consider living in such a tight space.

Dylan stuck his head inside the bathroom.

"This counter is long enough to cook on."

"Stop it!"

I swatted him back out the door so I could reassess the main room.

"It's bigger than the cabin I grew up in. At least there's electricity and hot water." I was beginning to see the potential.

"The owner says we can paint the walls and do anything we want to make it livable."

Dylan tugged at a piece of ancient wallpaper dangling from the wall.

"Why doesn't he fix it up? He could get more rent from it."

"They just want to cover property taxes."

I thought of the long Michigan winter and how it might be nice to escape by watching movies.

"Where would we fit a sofa and TV in this tiny room?"

"Maybe if we put the TV in the closet and open it when we want to watch it."

Dylan opened the closet door, and I gasped as a four-inch daddy-longlegs stepped out and slowly crossed the ceiling above our heads.

"There's a carpet store on the highway that sells remnants. It wouldn't cost much to get a cheap carpet to fit this space."

Dylan stepped off the length of the living area like I'd seen Daddy do. "I'd get a ten by sixteen piece of linoleum for the kitchen side."

"Can you even get your piano down here?"

"I think we can roll it on a couple of boards, over the stairway, and straight through the front door."

I felt edgy as we signed the lease. As soon as we were beyond earshot of our new landlord, I turned to Dylan, "I didn't think it was possible to downgrade our housing to a spider-infested hole in the ground. We'd better save on gas."

An advantage to renting such a small space was that it took only a remnant of wallpaper and one gallon of paint to cover all three rooms. I was excited to discover we could buy the plushest carpet with the thickest pad for under a hundred bucks.

The first thing we did was prep the walls and ceiling for painting by washing them with bleach. I'd heard enough about Michigan basements to make sure we had no way for mildew to grow.

When Dylan pulled out the stove, he found an electrocuted mouse hanging from his teeth, which were still clenched around the wire. Removing that mouse immediately improved the air quality.

Dylan removed the baseboards and took them outside to paint while I filled the space between the foundation and walls with spackling paste to discourage spiders from entering the premises.

Working to create a comfortable space had drawn us closer to each other. We were a team—we'd always been a team—and this move at the end of our first year of marriage only strengthened us. We soon forgot the house by the railroad tracks and any angry words that passed between us.

When the paint was dry, Dylan stretched across the sand-colored carpet across the floor and pounded the last nail into the trim. Then he lay down on the floor.

"Come, feel how thick this is. We could sleep on it."

I knelt to experience the luxury for myself. Looking around at our remodeled space, I smiled with satisfaction. We had a clean and cozy home.

I got a job at the cafeteria managing the student cashiers. My boss told me it was my job to hire, fire, train, and maintain twelve students who came from all over the world. I found the work challenging at first, but my coworkers were fascinating people who taught me many things about different cultures.

We settled into the rhythm of university life. I went to work, and Dylan studied hard. On the weekends, we had other couples over for dinner and played table games.

Before Christmas, Dylan brought me a box of Christmas cards.

I smiled at the scene of a chipmunk couple making their home in the ground, complete with a table, bed, and tiny Christmas tree.

"It's just like our little apartment in the ground."

I looked around our cozy home. Whenever there was a tornado warning, I felt safe because we were in the basement. It seemed God had answered my prayer. We had a comfortable, safe, and affordable place to live near campus. I had a pleasant job, and we were even beginning to make some friends.

23 That's What Love Is For

*One heart is not connected to
another through harmony alone.
They are, instead, linked deeply
through their wounds.*
-Haruki Murakami

Dylan kept his promise that we could visit my family every summer. We didn't spend the entire summer in Walla Walla because the Physical Therapy Program only took a month off. We had just enough time to drive the 2000 miles to Walla Walla, visit family for two weeks, then drive back to Andrews.

Each trip was a struggle with our student budget and aging car. We saved expenses by setting up our tent in free forest service campgrounds and eating simple foods. We enjoyed the adventure of the open road and took different routes each way to hit as many tourist stops as possible. It was fun to discover new pockets of the American landscape.

One year, we arrived in Walla Walla with car trouble. What a relief to have Daddy repair it. Two weeks later, we wondered if we'd have enough gas money to get back to school. To be safe, we decided to ask our fathers for a small loan.

When Dylan finally got up the nerve to ask his dad for money, his father stared at us like we were beggars off the street.

He handed Dylan a twenty-dollar bill and said, "You guys will feel better about yourselves if you never have to ask anyone for help."

Dylan wasn't bothered by his father's comment, but my face burned with shame as we got into the car.

"We asked to borrow money, not steal it."

"Don't worry about it, Babe. We aren't planning on borrowing money from him in the future."

I hesitated to ask Daddy because he was always short and didn't have a regular paycheck, but he immediately reached into his wallet and gave me two twenty-dollar bills. I saw it was most of what he had and worried I was taking Momma's grocery money.

"Wait. What if you and Momma need this?"

"We'll be okay. I can always borrow from Uncle Joe. Just stay safe."

Tears filled Daddy's eyes and mine, too, as I hugged him goodbye.

The long drive gave me lots of time to think. Perhaps I was too quick to judge both of our fathers. Dylan's dad was right. I never wanted to beg anyone for money again. And I felt ashamed to think I'd moved away, thinking Daddy didn't care about me because of our differences.

Back in Michigan, Dylan and I fell into the rhythm of school and work again, but we felt like tourists. On weekends, we made short trips to visit Michigan's Upper Peninsula, Amish country in Indiana, and Chicago zoos and museums.

My staff position at the cafeteria allowed me to take time off when Dylan had breaks, so we took advantage of those to drive further and explore the eastern states. Campgrounds were cheap, and we had to eat anyway. Gas was our main expense as long as we could pitch a tent and cook meals on our camp stove.

We played a game to see how far we could travel on a budget. During one break, we learned about history in Colonial Williamsburg and Washington, DC, and explored the Great Smoky Mountains the following year.

During the last spring break of Dylan's education, we decided to drive to Disney World. Florida was our ultimate destination because it was the farthest from our home state of Washington.

We survived camping in the snow in Tennessee and were thrilled to pitch our tent on the warm sand of South Carolina. After exploring the gardens in Savannah, we cheered as we crossed the Florida state line.

We planned to stay at a Florida State Park while we explored Disney World. The Everglades, complete with Spanish moss and alligators, allowed us to experience Florida's natural side along with Disney World.

We arrived at the campground at dusk. New places always make me nervous in the dark. Dylan walked to the pay station while I ran my flashlight over the sign to read the campground rules. He returned with a ticket and set it on the car dash.

"Okay, let's get the tent up."

"Wait. Did you read this sign?"

He stepped closer. "What's it say?"

"It's a warning about alligators, rattlesnakes, scorpions, and fire ants."

"Fire ants? I've never heard of those."

"Me neither, but if they're listed in that company, they can't be good."

"I'm tired. Let's get to bed and worry about fire ants in the morning."

"Since we're pitching our tent in the dark, how will we know if any of these creepy things are in our campsite?"

Dylan sighed.

While we analyzed the situation, two men stepped out of the bushes. From the reflective patch on their shirts, I figured they must be park rangers. They paused under a light next to the bathrooms.

"Hey, Jim, you've got a tick on your arm."

I watched with alarm as they took off their shirts and checked each other's backs. When they noticed we were watching, one laughed.

"Beware, it's tick season!"

His co-worker shook out his shirt and put it back on.

"Are you guys here to watch the launch?"

Dylan glanced at me while I shrugged my shoulders.

"What launch?"

"The space shuttle's going up at dawn. Lots of people are staying here to see it. We can tell you the best places to view it."

"Oh, I didn't realize we were that close."

My mind flashed back to the Challenger accident.

"Being this close is only a concern if it blows up." The ranger chuckled.

"So, what are fire ants?"

Dylan nudged me to be quiet, but I had to know.

"Only the most hellish thing I've ever experienced."

The rangers didn't laugh or make jokes about fire ants. That's how I knew we were in grave danger.

After a short lecture, I decided Florida was a creepy state. I was terrified to use the restroom. Dylan stood outside the restroom door while I did my business, and then I ran back to the car, shaking myself to make sure no ticks were hanging from my clothing.

Dylan bravely set up the tent by himself. He convinced me to run to the tent and zip the door behind me. I lay on my foam pad inside the tent but stayed awake for a while. I begged God to protect us from alligators, rattlesnakes, scorpions, ticks, fire ants, and the Space Shuttle Discovery.

The shuttle went up without incident while we were sleeping. We enjoyed our first day at Epcot Center, and I enjoyed the rides on the second day. Now that we'd survived two nights in the park without incident, we congratulated ourselves on how smart we were to camp and save our money for Disney World.

We were in The Haunted Mansion when it quit in the middle of the ride. A ticket agent stepped out of the shadows and told us to get off because a tornado was heading for Disney World. Soon, we were being pushed and shoved by hundreds of people trying to get on the monorail. I wasn't used to tornadoes, and riding up in the air didn't seem safe. Panic rose in my throat, but I kept moving with the crowd.

It was a relief to get off the monorail and stand under a large metal roof as the rain began to fall. After a loud crack of thunder, lightning began flashing from one end of the parking lot to the other. Next came hail the size of grapefruit. There was nothing anyone could do but huddle under the metal roof, listening to the sound of hail smashing the windows and roofs of our cars.

The storm passed as quickly as it came. We walked through the melting ice, past car after car, with windshields and back windows punched out by the hail. We were relieved to discover our windshield was barely cracked.

Glad to be spared, we headed to the campsite, where our tent had collapsed, and our sleeping bags were floating in several inches of water. I was resigned to sleeping in the car when Dylan called his mom.

My mother-in-law graciously paid for a hotel room, and we were able to take warm showers and sleep in a comfortable bed that night. Since we foolishly had no savings or backup plan, we were grateful for her generosity.

By the time we returned to Andrews, our windshield crack had taken off in several directions and now resembled a giant spider web.

While we stared at the windshield, Dylan gave me advice.

"The next time you pray about rattlesnakes, scorpions, alligators, fire ants, ticks, and the Space Shuttle, please add tornados, floods, and hail to the list."

We were always grateful for our basement apartment whenever we returned from these trips. I couldn't wait to grab a roll of quarters and stand at the pay phone to tell Momma about our adventures. Sometimes, my legs ached from standing on the concrete, but it was worth it. I enjoyed talking with her, and we always had a good visit. Sometimes, Daddy even said hi, but Momma took the time to listen.

Dylan said putting two thousand miles between us and our families was one of the best things we'd ever done. I agreed. I enjoyed the freedom without Daddy looking over my shoulder. He couldn't hear the songs I played, see the books I read, or know when I went to the movies.

In our last year at Andrews, our little Ford Escort was still purring along despite all it had been through. It might have made it one more trip west if it weren't for the accident.

Dylan was driving home from class when a boy chased a ball across the road. There was no time to stop, but Dylan was able to swerve away from the child and hit a parked car. Our car was totaled since it was old and wasn't worth much. We could walk to campus and carry groceries home but couldn't take our laundry to the laundromat.

I walked to a pay phone–this time to call Daddy. I knew he was too far away to fix the car, but I wanted his advice.

"Don't bother to fix that one. Let me see what I can find."

"How can you help me from so far away?"

"Don't worry. We'll figure something out. Here, talk to Momma. She's anxious to hear from you.

I hung up, comforted to know my parents cared about me. When I called back a few days later, Daddy was working on a black Ford Tempo, which he offered to sell at his cost. He'd even drive it to Michigan if we paid his airfare back home.

Grateful for his help, we bought him an airline ticket.

When Daddy arrived, I was glad for the car, but I longed to share my life with him and show him where I worked. He didn't want to go on campus. I was sad that he wasn't like other people's dads. He only ate things he was used to, so he wasn't interested in food from the cafeteria. He didn't dress fashionably. His clothes were a simple T-shirt and jeans. His hands were stained black from working on cars, but despite everything, I loved him, and I didn't care what anyone thought.

I realized fathers with regular jobs might not be able to take time to fix a car and spend three days driving across the country to deliver it. Some might think what he did was crazy, but I saw that no matter how much he disagreed with me, Daddy wanted me to have a safe car. And I felt his love because of it.

For most of my life, Daddy seemed larger than everything else in my world. It was more than the fact that he was six feet and two inches. From my earliest memories, when he first swung me around and tossed me in the air, I loved him. Even though he belted me, he also shared whatever he had with me, whether it was cookies, peaches, or water on a road trip. He had stories to entertain me whenever I was sick or scared.

I'd always imagined Daddy as big and strong. I thought nobody could overpower him. But watching him board the plane, he seemed small and vulnerable. He'd often told me how he had an inferiority complex, but I never saw it until that day.

I hugged him goodbye and watched him stand in line with passengers dressed in business suits, flashy Hawaiian shirts, and designer sweaters. Out of all the passengers, one man stood out–and that was my Daddy holding his gym bag, dressed in old jeans and a plain white T-shirt.

When it came to making a home, Dylan and I managed to make do with what we had. I decided to do the same when it came to having a dad. Daddy wasn't like other dads, but he was mine. Nobody else's dad would rebuild a car and drive it two thousand miles, sleeping at rest stops for three days to deliver it. Daddy was doing the best with what he had, and I loved him for it.

24 Stay For Awhile

A half-truth is a whole lie.
-Yiddish Proverb

Moving west was easier than moving to Michigan. For starters, we were going home. This time we were wiser and decided to skip the rental truck and sell our used furniture. It was hardest to sell Dylan's piano and my dining set, but they didn't justify renting a truck. We kept three boxes of books and shipped them to Grandma's house. By the time we stuffed the car with bedding, pans, and clothing, we couldn't see out the back window.

Among the keepers were the grapevine dishes from our wedding and four pewter candlesticks I'd collected from staff Christmas bonuses. These treasures could be placed on any table. After spending the holidays apart for three years, I hoped we could gather my family together to eat, laugh, and love, like those cute country signs.

With his education behind us, Dylan found a job with a sign-on bonus that would enable us to buy new furniture for the first time in our marriage. Sunnyside, Washington, was in the middle of the state. Neither of us could remember being there before, but it was near Yakima and nearly equal driving distance between my parents in Portland, Jake, and Abby in Walla Walla, and Mara in Spokane.

We were excited to be back in Washington state with evergreens, mountains, and family, but finding a house to rent proved harder than we'd planned. The first drive through town gave me an ominous feeling. It could have been all the feedlots that made the town stink. Or perhaps it was poverty. Every day, we drove past what locals called "the shanty town," where migrant workers built tiny shelters with wooden pallets and plywood. Some even used sticks and cardboard. It reminded me of the slums we saw in El Paso, Texas, when we were on Tour, and I was filled with overwhelming empathy and grief every time we passed that part of town.

Dylan's job didn't start right away, so we spent two weeks in a hotel searching for a house to rent. We hoped to find one by the time he started work, but there was a housing shortage. Even when an ad looked promising, it was snapped up before we could call.

Three weeks later, we were running out of money from spending it all on the hotel and still didn't have a place to rent. Driving by the shanty town was starting to feel scary because we were only a few dollars away from being homeless ourselves.

We were finally able to walk through a cute little house the evening before Dylan started work. The landlord required the first and last month's rent, and we had only enough for one month. Fortunately, he accepted our story about the job and said we could move in with one month's rent and pay the other when Dylan got paid.

We'd already paid for one more night at the hotel when the landlord left us with the keys. We sat in the driveway trying to decide what to do since we had twenty dollars left to buy groceries and gas for the next three weeks.

"It's a nice little house." My eyes wandered down the road in the direction of the shanty town while I tried to block out all the worst-case scenarios. "Things could be worse. At least you have a job, and we have a house."

Dylan turned the key in the ignition with a sigh.

"Not much gas in the tank, and twenty dollars won't be enough to get me to work and back for three weeks."

"Could your dad loan us some money? We could pay him back in three weeks."

"I doubt it."

When I remembered what his dad said about not asking for help, I didn't blame Dylan for not wanting to ask him.

"Well, my parents are camping in a tent on my Grandparents' land. I could never ask them."

"I hate the idea of begging for money, but we might have to go to the Adventist church and ask for help."

We sat in silence for a minute. Off in the distance, I heard a whippoorwill.

"Let's head back to the hotel. We'd better enjoy the bed because we're gonna be sleeping on the floor for several weeks."

Dylan turned the key in the ignition.

"Wait, I feel sick at the thought of introducing ourselves to church people and asking for money—can we just pray about it?"

"Go ahead." He turned the car off.

A childhood of poverty taught me that God doesn't always answer prayers the way we'd like him to. One book warned that we shouldn't treat God like a catering service, but Jesus did tell us to ask. I believed prayer could somehow unlock possibilities that might never happen without prayer.

After saying amen, I was overcome with a craving for grape juice.

"I sure wish I had a glass of grape juice right now."

"In three weeks, you can have all the grape juice you want!"

"Dylan, what if God can't hear our prayers because we haven't been good enough Christians?"

"What do you mean?"

"We haven't returned tithe for three years. We went to the theater to see Schindler's List on Sabbath. What if our sins are keeping God from hearing our prayers?"

"That's not why we don't have money. We just needed to plan better."

"After you pray, can we buy a can of frozen grape juice? If we're going to ask the church for help, spending a dollar and thirty-five cents on a can of frozen juice won't make much difference."

It was getting dark, but I thought I could see him roll his eyes.

While Dylan prayed, I could barely hear what he was saying because I was obsessed with my craving for grape juice.

After Dylan said amen, he turned to me.

"If you buy grape juice, you should get a cheaper brand than Welch's."

"It has to be Welch's—that's the only kind my mom ever buys."

"Okay, let's go to the store. You check the Welch's, and I'll check the other brands."

The sign in the window said they were closing at nine. We had only fifteen minutes to spare, so we raced to the frozen juice aisle. The Welch's juices were separate from the generic brands.

Dylan ran to the far end of the aisle, while my eyes scanned a row of purple cans. There it was—but what was on top of the cans?

I squinted as I reached down to pick it up. Two green bills rolled tightly as if they'd been wound around a finger. I unrolled them slowly. One, zero, zero. It wasn't just a single dollar bill, but two one-hundred-dollar bills. Holding my breath, I slipped them into my pocket.

Dylan met me in the middle of the aisle with a generic white can of grape juice, while I triumphantly held up the Welch's.

My heart was beating so hard I could almost hear it as I whispered. "Just buy this with the twenty. I found two hundred dollars."

His eyes grew large in astonishment as he set the generic can back in its place and followed me to the checkout aisle.

I told the girl we'd found some money and gave her our new address. "If anyone lost some money and can identify the amount, we'll return it."

As a former head cashier, I knew better than to tell how much money, because the amount was the way to identify it.

Back at the hotel, I filled our pitcher with water and stirred the grape juice. I took a long sip, smacked my lips, and savored its sweetness while I reflected on what had just happened.

I'd been raised to believe the only way to get a good answer to prayer was to be a perfect Christian. This meant having no known sins, but my list of sins was long. I'd once stolen some money, I hadn't returned tithe, and I'd gone to the movies on Sabbath, yet God still answered my prayer. It felt exhilarating to think God loved me despite not being a "good Christian." For the first time in my life, I felt God saw me because he'd answered my prayer in what I could only view as a miracle.

A month later, Dylan cashed his sign-on bonus, and we went to the local furniture store. We'd never bought anything new bigger than a TV. The prospect of buying furniture was exciting, but it also came with the responsibility of finding quality items that would last.

The first thing we found was a teal-green sofa. It was velvety soft and had a recliner on each end, which we both immediately tried out. Stretched like royalty, we reclined until we couldn't see each other. Staring at my elevated feet, I laughed.

"I can't see you, or anything but my feet, but it's like heaven after sitting on that hide-a-bed with its sharp springs poking my butt for three years.

A young man peered down into my face.

"Can I help you?"

Embarrassed, I sat up and looked around for Dylan, who'd already wandered off to the bed section.

I smiled. "I think we'll take this, but we're also shopping for a bed."

The guy took the ticket from the arm of the sofa and followed me across the aisle, where Dylan was bouncing up and down on a king-sized bed.

"What do you think about this one? Not too soft and not too hard."

I stretched out in it. "Anything will be better than the GrandMonster's old cast-off. You know I despised that bed."

We tried several beds until we found the sweet spot on a bed, we both liked."

The salesman rang up our prizes. "Will this be cash or charge?"

Dylan proudly opened his wallet and answered by placing four thousand dollars on the counter.

In just a month, we'd gone from praying for gas money to buying furniture. For the first time in my life, I was going to sleep on a brand-new mattress and sit on a sofa that no one else had owned. We were finally going to live like normal people, and I couldn't wait to tell Momma.

"Finally, after all these years of putting Dylan through school, it was worth it," I chirped.

"I'm glad for you, honey."

Momma sounded genuinely happy for me.

"Can you guys come for Thanksgiving?"

"I'll check with Daddy and let you know."

The next day, I called each of my siblings and invited them for the holiday dinner. Thanksgiving was still a couple of months away, but I wanted to make sure they didn't make other plans.

When I called Abby, her voice sounded a little tense. After a few questions, I got her to tell me what was happening.

"Daddy's upset because you bought a new sofa when you owe Grandma money."

"What? I don't owe Grandma money! Daddy borrowed that money in my name. I thought he was going to pay her back."

We hung up, and I called Momma. "Why is Daddy talking about me to other people? If he had a problem with me buying a new sofa, then why doesn't he talk to me?"

Momma sounded surprised. "I have no idea what you're talking about."

Thinking Abby must be confused, I changed the subject. We spoke about the weather and my new neighborhood before hanging up. I wasn't off the phone for more than ten minutes when Abby called back.

"Hey, Momma just called and asked if I'd told you what Daddy said, and I said no."

"Why?"

"Because I don't want to get in the middle of this."

"So, you and Momma both know what Daddy said, and you both know that I know, but none of us can talk about it? That's ridiculous!"

"I'm sorry. Just leave me out of it."

That night, sinking into our cozy new bed, I found it hard not to think about my family.

"I guess my dad thinks we should spend our money the way he would."

"Well, if your dad doesn't like the way we spend our money, he can get a regular job and buy his own sofa."

"I feel frustrated that Momma and Abby think they have to lie so we can all tiptoe around Daddy while he gets away with criticizing me."

"It's probably just a misunderstanding. Can you just forget about them for tonight? I have to get up early for work in the morning."

I doubted it was a misunderstanding, but I rarely spoke about my childhood because I didn't want Dylan to disrespect Daddy.

I drifted off to sleep and woke up with nightmares about arguing with my parents.

After selling everything in Michigan, I had to do a lot of shopping to prepare our new home for guests. I found a cheap lamp, bookcase, end table, and a TV at Walmart.

A local store had a simple dining table. I set the chairs around it with a pang of regret. I missed the old maple table I'd once worked so hard to get, but as soon as I pulled out our wedding dishes and the pewter candlesticks, my spirits soared. I traced my finger over the grapevine pattern. Those grapes had taken on more meaning than ever after I found the two hundred dollars in the grape juice aisle.

I spent a weekend in Spokane shopping with Mara. It was fun to see her place and get to know her husband. We were in a store sorting through housewares and kitchen appliances when I saw a white industrial-strength Kitchen-Aid mixer. Every time I saw one at the cafeteria, I'd dreamed of having my own. I lifted the bowl out of its cradle and imagined mixing cookies, whipping cream, and kneading bread with such a powerful machine.

I wanted it more than anything else in my cart, but I hesitated when I saw the price tag. Several hundred dollars for a mixer seemed extravagant. It cost more than half the price of our new sofa.

Mara came back to find out what was taking me so long to get in line.

"Are you getting that? It'd be great for baking."

"I feel guilty spending the money."

"Oh, come on, you know you want it. And you can finally afford it. It's a good investment. You'll make bread with it for years."

"I don't want Daddy to think I'm a spendthrift. He was already talking about me behind my back for buying a sofa."

"Don't be so sensitive."

I was irritated by her remark. Daddy often accused me of being too sensitive.

"Why do you say that?"

Mara shrugged her shoulders.

"When I left home, I didn't speak to them for months, but you wrote home every week telling them your business."

"Do you think I share too much?"

"Maybe. Perhaps it bothers Daddy that you have what he's never been able to provide."

Grief flooded my heart as I realized how insensitive I'd been to talk about my brand-new sofa while my parents were living in a tent.

"What can we do, Mara? We can't stop buying the things we need."

"Once, when I got a different car, Daddy said I looked like a rich person, but I'm not rich, and it was a used car. I decided not to let his words bother me. We can't spend the rest of our lives justifying everything we buy. At some point, we have to live our lives."

I went home with the mixer and a renewed awareness of Mara's wisdom. I also saw the need to say less about whatever I bought in the future. All I wanted was for our home to be comfortable for our guests, but after selling everything in Michigan, it would be impossible to hide the fact that nearly everything in the house was new.

I hoped Thanksgiving would be perfect. I wanted my family to enjoy a delicious dinner and have a good visit. It depressed me to think the very item I bought so my parents could sit comfortably in my home would offend them because it was new.

A few weeks later, the smell of sautéed mushrooms and onions filled the house as I spooned them over the gluten steaks before slathering them with sour cream.

Dylan paused from connecting the video player to the new TV. "It sure smells good in here."

"Momma made this dish for every holiday since I can remember."

"I thought you guys were vegan?"

"We were most of the time, but not on holidays."

Dylan slipped a Veggie Tales DVD into the VCR and placed it on pause. This was to ensure our nephews had entertainment while the grownups talked.

Once the large casserole dish was filled, I wiped the edges with a paper towel, just as Momma had always done.

"It's quite heavy, Dylan, can you put this in the oven?"

He jumped up and set it beside the yams, which were already bubbling in margarine and brown sugar.

Together, we moved a long plastic table to meet the end of the dining table and covered both with a white tablecloth.

I lovingly lay down the grapevine plates on top of the rose placemats and silently said a little prayer of thanksgiving. They looked great with the pewter candlesticks.

Dylan set a goblet by each plate and carefully began pouring the grape juice, while I set a handmade place card in front of each plate with a name for everyone—well, nearly everyone. Jake had called the day before to let me know he couldn't make it. I was disappointed but excited for whoever was willing to show up.

I'd spent the day before prepping and baking for what felt like the most important meal of my married life. I'd started by baking. First, I made homemade dinner rolls, then apple and pumpkin pies.

I'd also made vegetarian stuffing for Dylan. Momma had never made stuffing, but I hoped each person would find something they enjoyed at our table.

By the time the casserole and yams were baked to golden perfection, the mashed potatoes had been creamed, and the table was filled with a veggie platter, cranberry sauce, and a sour cream fruit salad called ambrosia.

I looked over the table with satisfaction just as I heard a car door slam shut. These were our family favorites. In a lifetime of scrambling to find enough food, Momma had always managed to make a feast for Thanksgiving, and I felt proud to have followed in her footsteps.

Mara and her husband, Kip, arrived first, followed by Abby and her two boys. Daddy and Momma were notorious for being late, but I kept the food warm for over an hour. Just as we were about to eat without them, they arrived.

As we sat down around the table, Daddy seemed to be in a good mood. Abby's boys were skeptical of most of the food, but I pointed them to carrot sticks and mashed potatoes, reassuring them they didn't have to eat anything they didn't like. My parents raised their eyebrows as I spoke. Their house rule was that kids had to taste everything at least once, but I was a doting aunt, and I had no intentions of falling out of favor with a five-year-old.

Everybody was talking at once and making jokes until Daddy passed me the cranberry sauce and said, "I wish Jake were here."

"I hoped he would join us, but he said they want to start their own family traditions." I tried to hide my concern that my sisters might do that in the future.

Mara passed the basket of dinner rolls to Daddy. "Well, if you ask me, I think it's the fact that he eats turkey now."

"Lots of people eat turkey for Thanksgiving. I'm sure he knows Mom and Dad wouldn't enjoy watching him eat a bird." Abby fed one of her kids a taste from her plate.

For Momma's sake, I tried to make light of eating turkey.

"I tasted turkey on tour, and I think it's an acquired taste."

As soon as I said it, I realized Momma was concerned that I had eaten turkey.

Daddy cleared his throat. "I'm not as worried about what Jake eats as I'm concerned that he's rejected God."

"At least he's being honest, people can't pretend to believe in God if they don't." I felt someone should stand up for Jake since he wasn't there to defend himself.

"Maybe that's why he gets depressed." Momma sighed and set her fork down.

Mara and I exchanged glances. We'd recently been talking about the ways our parents' choices had affected our lives. We didn't blame Jake. We got depressed, too.

"It's not something to take lightly, Jake ended up in the psych ward because he was depressed. Who wants pie?"

Momma handed me her plate. "I just wish Jake would focus on the positive instead of the negative. Jesus is coming soon, and he seems to be stuck in the past."

Daddy shook his head. "I know we made mistakes, but it seems if we want to be ready for Jesus, we need to learn to forgive and forget." He looked at me for some reason, and I froze. Did he think I hadn't forgiven him?

I bit my lip and imagined myself trying to pull the bandage off of a very painful wound.

"I think we can forgive, at least I do, but until Jesus does come, we have to live with the results of our choices every day."

I'd never spoken so boldly and began cutting up slices of pumpkin pie as fast as I could, hoping everyone would stay for dessert.

Daddy seemed to take my remark in stride, but Momma raised her voice.

"Cheri, you guys have no idea of the kind of pressure Daddy was under when you were kids. We tried over and over to find ways to get you an education."

"But you never bought one book."

I knew I was pushing the limits, but it had to be said. Jake wasn't the only one who was struggling.

Daddy opened his mouth like he was going to say something, then abruptly got up from the table and put his plate in the sink.

"I'm going to look at the Tempo. Did you guys say it was making a noise?"

I could tell Daddy was finished with this conversation, and by the look on Momma's face, I knew she was upset. I felt a sinking feeling in the pit of my stomach as I put cream on the pie and passed plates around the table.

I wished Daddy would apologize to all of us, especially Jake. Maybe then we could all forgive and forget, but as long as the past couldn't be acknowledged, it festered like a fevered wound.

After we finished the pie, Abby got up and searched for the kids' coats.

"I need to get the boys home."

Mara and Kip were already taking dishes off the table. I quickly made some plates up with the leftovers to send home with everyone. Dylan was the only one who had tried the stuffing.

When I hugged Momma goodbye, she spoke into my ear softly, "I just wish everyone could get along."

The beautiful meal I'd planned hadn't ended the way I'd hoped. After everyone left, I was so emotionally torn by the conversation that I decided to write a book. I didn't know what kind of book or if it would ever be published, but I needed to sort out my feelings. Maybe if I saw the words on paper things would begin to make sense.

A few days later, I bought a word processor and became obsessed with writing down my memories. Some days, it felt good, and other times, it required indulgent amounts of chocolate cake to process my feelings. Despite all my writing, I never once read it to Dylan.

These were my private thoughts, and I wasn't ready to share them with anyone.

We lived in Sunnyside for six months, but no one in my family visited us again. I told myself that if I'd only kept my mouth shut, things might have been different.

One night, after Dylan went to sleep, I couldn't sleep, so I got up to write in the living room. I'd been typing for an hour when I heard a sound at the door. I looked across the room to see the doorknob moving from the outside. Then, a credit card moved in and out, searching to disengage the lock. Terrified, I slammed a book down on the table to let the intruder know that someone was awake inside. Then I ran to the bedroom to wake Dylan and called the police.

They never found the intruder, but my peace was shattered.

"Probably a homeless person looking for shelter."

Dylan was trying to reassure me, but his remark only depressed me.

"You mean like my parents?"

"No. I mean, there are a lot of homeless people around here. Where is your can of mace?"

"I can't carry mace around the house all day."

"Well, it might be wise to keep it nearby."

"The only reason we moved here was to be closer to my family. The new sofa, table, and bed mean nothing if we can't even share life with them."

"What do you want me to do?"

"Remember how you wanted to be a traveling therapist? Do you still wanna do that? We could travel, see new places, and pay our school loans."

And that's how we put our stuff into a storage unit and found ourselves on the road again.

25 I Just Called to Say I Love You

*The hardest thing to learn
in life is which bridge to cross
and which bridge to burn.
-David Russell*

When Dylan locked the padlock on the storage unit, a wave of relief washed over me. It was almost like I'd stowed my parents' expectations inside that locker with my journal and the grapevine dishes. Of course, it was only a fleeting victory because once we hit the road, I had hours upon miles to think about Thanksgiving dinner and wonder what I could have done differently to help my family members get along.

If there was one thing that Dylan and I did well together, it was traveling. We'd bonded on the road while crossing the country with Tour Z, and we were still tourists at heart. Packing light and sleeping in strange places came naturally to us. Dylan's family had moved a few times in childhood, while mine had moved constantly. As I stared ahead at the open highway, I realized my life had been a lonely, wandering road until I met Dylan. Being with him had turned my life into an adventure.

Dylan chose a job in Connecticut so we could enjoy summer on the Atlantic Coast and experience the fall colors. Connecticut was as far east as we could get from Washington State, but half the fun was getting there.

We had two weeks to get to the temporary location. Dylan marked the atlas with a yellow highlighter so I could follow the route. Our itinerary had no set reservations, so we had the freedom to drive as long as we wanted. The disadvantage was that we never knew for sure where we'd sleep each night.

The travel agency provided a travel budget, but we planned to save money by camping as much as possible. We told ourselves as long as we could pitch a tent, we could sleep anywhere. I liked camping because motels and hotels left me with anxious feelings. If we stayed in an older motel, it reminded me of feeling trapped living in a motel as a teenager. If we stayed in a fancy hotel, I would feel guilty for staying in such a nice place.

No matter where we went, Momma was always on my mind. I wished we could take her with us and share the interesting sights along the road. Determined to stay in touch, I kept a roll of quarters in the car. I often asked Dylan to stop whenever I saw a phone booth.

As soon as the car rolled to a stop, I'd jump out, punch in a few quarters, and dial Grandma's number. When Grandma answered, we'd chat while Grandpa went down to where my parents were camping to get Momma. When Momma took the phone from Grandma, I'd say, "I just called to say I love you!"

After I gave Momma a report on our latest adventure, I'd tell her goodbye, hang up the phone, and we'd be on our way. Dylan had no interest in calling his family, but he never complained when I called mine.

We pulled into a state park in North Dakota when the sunset was filling the sky with bright fuchsia and orange. We rushed to set up our tent under what looked like the only tree in the campground before it was too dark to see.

With camp set up, we paused to take in the beauty around us. A full moon was rising, and in the fading sunset, we watched a flock of pelicans flying over the river below us. It was a tranquil scene and we marveled at the contrast between this wild and natural place and Sunnyside with its noxious air from the feedlots. As we snuggled into our sleeping bags, we told each other we'd made the right decision.

Three hours later, I woke up to something tickling my nose. Opening my eyes in the dark, I discovered something seemed to be floating over my face. Reaching for my flashlight, I gasped to discover the tent had blown down over us, and a strong wind was blowing it across us. Panicked, I nudged Dylan.

"Hey, wake up! The tent's blown down over us."

Annoyed to be awakened, Dylan turned away from me. "I don't care. I just wanna sleep."

"But what if it blows away?"

"As long as we're in it, it won't blow away."

Wondering if it was the right thing to do, but feeling tired myself, I turned over and went back to sleep.

An hour later, I woke to the sound of thunder and poked Dylan this time.

"Can you hear the thunder? We're under the only tree around. Don't you think we should go to the car?"

Frustrated to be awakened again, Dylan groaned.

"If we both get out of the tent, it'll blow away. We're in the middle of nowhere, and this is the only tent we have."

A flash of lightning lit up the tent, setting my hair on edge. When a second flash coordinated with the thunder, I panicked and scrambled, sliding across the plastic floor, groping for my shoes and jacket.

"Dylan, did you hear how close that was?"

"Oh, come on, I just want sleep."

"I'm going to the car. Where are the keys?"

"In my shoe."

I found his shoes, grabbed the keys, and spun around, trying to find the door. Throwing the tent off of my shoulders, I crawled onto the grass, only to be blinded by another flash of lightning. I stood up and froze in place, hovering between the tent and the car.

"Dylan, I think you should get up. What if lightning strikes the tree?"

A muffled voice answered from inside the tent.

"Tell your mother and her worst-case scenarios to let me sleep. Besides, someone needs to hold down the tent."

When the next flash of lightning lit the campsite, I could make out Dylan's form on one side of the flattened tent, so I picked up the picnic table and threw it on the opposite side."

"What in the world? Are you trying to kill me?"

He continued yelling from inside the tent, while I walked to the car.

I sat alone for over an hour, hoping that Dylan would come to his senses and join me, but apparently, he was able to sleep through the storm.

Then came the rain. It was raining so hard that I could barely make out a form crawling out from under the tent. Dylan might have been swimming to the car because, by the time he joined me, he was dripping wet.

I turned the engine and then the heat to warm him up, but Dylan turned it off.

"We need to be careful, I'm not sure how far we'll have to drive to find gas."

We shivered and listened to the rain pounding on the roof while we stared at our once cozy tent, which was now sitting in a puddle with a picnic table on top of it.

As soon as dawn broke, we went to the restrooms and warmed up with hot showers. Then we went back, gathered our sleeping bags, and threw the wet tent in the back of the car.

As we drove out of the campground in the early light, we discovered hundreds of bluish salamanders lying on the white gravel road. A couple of pickup trucks had driven out ahead of us and had run over them, leaving the road red, white, and blue.

Dylan squinted at the road. "That's the worst patriotic display I've ever seen."

Tired, yet relieved to be warm, we laughed until we cried.

That night, we arrived in the beautiful state of Minnesota, where we set up camp and made supper next to a beautiful lake. We went to bed early because we were tired from our lack of sleep. We'd only been in bed for an hour when we sustained multiple bites from mosquitos. We double-checked the zipper on the door and wondered why we had an entire cloud of them inside the tent with us. Upon closer inspection, Dylan discovered I'd ripped a hole in the tent when I threw the picnic table on top of it. We got up and drove into the nearest town, where we found a cozy log motel and booked a room.

Wide awake and unable to sleep, we decided to go to the little theater and watch, "A Walk in the Clouds." It was a sweet movie. Later, while sipping hot chocolate in our room, I was grateful for such a fun day despite all the stress from that storm.

As I snuggled into a soft bed and listened to Dylan's gentle snoring, I marveled that he had never blamed me for the ripped tent. Not one put-down or angry word. I thought about all the stressful moving in my childhood, with Daddy yelling and swinging the belt. The fear of not knowing where I would sleep used to tie my stomach in knots. But despite sleeping in a different town every night, I felt a sense of peace lying next to my best friend.

The next morning, we went back to the campsite and collected our bedding. Dylan wadded up the empty tent and tossed it into a dumpster.

"I'm done with tent camping. We deserve sleep."

We traveled on through quaint towns in Northern Wisconsin and the Upper Peninsula of Michigan. Since we no longer had a tent, we had to find lodging, but I was starting to feel safe no matter where we stayed.

At Sault Ste. Marie, we crossed the International Bridge, entered Canada, and continued our journey through Ontario.

In Ottawa, we spent a day exploring Parliament Hill's Victorian architecture and visited with the "Cat Man of Ottawa," who fed all the homeless cats around the nation's capital.

We enjoyed viewing art in the Canadian National Gallery, and inside the museum, we found a delightful cafeteria-style restaurant serving delicious foods from all over the world.

We spent a day exploring the beauty of Quebec and managed to shop and eat out even though I'd forgotten most of the traveler's French I'd learned in college. It was such a beautiful city that we wished we had more time to enjoy it. From there, we headed south into the States.

As we drove through a small town in Vermont, I was excited to see a phone booth. I hadn't called Momma while we were in Canada.

"Can we stop? I want to tell Momma about the Cat Man of Ottawa."

Like an invisible umbilical cord, those pay phones were my lifeline to Momma.

Moving into the furnished condo provided for us was quick and easy. We tucked our few belongings away and bought an extra frying pan, but we weren't under any illusions that this place was home—we were tourists on a mission to see as much as we could.

We spent a few weekends at the beach overlooking Long Island Sound and checked out the seaport town of Mystic. On other weekends, we drove north to explore Massachusetts and Plymouth Rock. We visited the Norman Rockwell Museum and Walden Woods. We also explored Vermont and upstate New York. It felt like one long vacation, but Dylan worked five days a week while I did the shopping, cooking, and laundry.

As summer faded, the Autumn colors brought more wonder to the New England landscape. For my birthday, we decided to take a long weekend to the Maritimes. As a fan of L.M. Montgomery, I looked forward to seeing where she lived and wrote on Prince Edward Island.

Before we took off for the trip, I called to discover that Momma was in the hospital. Daddy told me she had to take an ambulance, and they were giving her some tests. Filled with concern, I gave him our hotel itinerary with phone numbers.

As we drove through Massachusetts, New Hampshire, and Maine, we took delight in every quaint town, stone fence, and rustic farmhouse. The landscapes were dotted with sheep, red barns, and private boarding schools, along with the ever-changing backdrop of green pastures and winding rivers, all sprinkled with the glory of autumn. Our excitement and joy only increased as we crossed into Canada to explore the Maritime Provinces. The rocky coastlines reminded me of the San Juan Islands in Washington State—only larger.

We explored the Bay of Fundy, New Brunswick, and Nova Scotia. Each day was packed with beauty and adventure, but the most anticipated part of our trip—visiting Green Gables on Prince Edward Island—was scheduled for my birthday.

I woke up so excited that I could barely swallow my bagel. I showered early and got dressed. We were ready to take the first ferry to Prince Edward Island when the phone rang in our hotel room. I was glad to hear Momma's voice, thinking she was just calling to wish me a happy birthday, but all of my plans came to a screeching halt when I heard the word "cancer." I no longer cared about our trip—I was filled with remorse for being thirty-five hundred miles away from her.

Later that day, my hair blew across my face as I stood on the ferry, looking back at Prince Edward Island. The cool air felt good against my tear-streaked face. I took a deep breath of the salty air and marveled as the ferry came so close to the red and white lighthouse that I could almost touch it.

My birthday had been full of delights that only a fan of Anne could appreciate. I'd visited the red sandstone cliffs of Cavendish, toured Green Gables, and discovered lighthouses on every corner. I also enjoyed lots of ice cream, thanks to multiple dairies on the island. Best of all, I carried several new Avonlea books in my bag.

Dylan had offered to buy anything I wanted from the gift shops and restaurants. He did his best to give me a wonderful day, but the one thing I wanted he couldn't provide, and that was reassurance that Momma would be okay.

While I'd spent most of the day crying and asking God why, Dylan had remained calm and patient.

"Why'd we have to move so far away? What if she dies and I never see her again?"

"We'll get an airline ticket, and you can visit her."

"Where would I stay? I can't handle sleeping on my grandparents' floor, and my parents live in a camp trailer."

This last sentence brought a new flood of tears.

"Plus, I'm not sure I can handle my parents without you."

When I left my journal inside the storage unit, I figured I could stash my feelings with it, but now that Momma had cancer, everything changed. All the fear and disappointment that I'd ever experienced rose up like a bad genie trying to escape a bottle, and I wasn't sure what to do with it.

26 I Want to Know What Love Is

*Family is supposed to be
our safe haven. Very often,
it's the place where we
find the deepest heartache.
-Iyanla Vanzant*

Since I was a child, I'd felt responsible for taking care of Momma. She was kind-hearted and gentle, but she had anxiety when it came to answering the phone or talking to strangers. As her firstborn, I did my best to take care of things for her. It was hard to be so far away while she was in surgery and not be able to do anything. Prayer was one way I could feel close to her.

When we returned from our trip, I bought paint and canvas. Since Momma loved blue, I started with an indigo sky and added a cabin with a small stream. I painted and repeated the twenty-third Psalm the entire time she was in surgery. I wasn't ready to let Momma go. I begged God to extend her life. My wrist grew sore, but I kept painting and praying, hoping she would live long enough for me to give her the painting.

Daddy called to tell me how Momma was doing.

"She's awake, and Mara's here."

"I'm glad Mara can be there." I wondered where Mara was sleeping, but I didn't ask.

"Are you okay?"

"Yeah," his voice cracked, and I could tell he'd been crying. "I'm not sure how to make her comfortable once she leaves the hospital. The bunk in the trailer is too hard."

I knew recovering from surgery would be challenging, but it would be even worse without a comfortable bed.

"What if we got a recliner for her to sleep on?"

"I don't have the money for one. Plus, where would I put it?"

"I'll send you some money. Can you remove the trailer's table?"

"I guess, but I'll need to measure to make sure a recliner can fit through the door."

The next morning, I went to FedEx and sent a money order to Daddy. He didn't have a bank account, so this was the only way he could get it. I sent enough for the recliner along with extra for groceries and supplies. I knew Daddy couldn't work much while caring for Momma, and I wanted to lighten his load.

The weeks flew by. While we enjoyed exploring New England, Momma slowly recovered from the surgery. Every time Dylan got paid, I continued to send money. The good news was that the doctor thought he had removed all the cancer. The bad news was that we were giving Daddy the money we'd planned to put on our school loans. Dylan had been generous and understanding, but I wasn't sure how to wean Daddy off our income after nearly three months of us taking care of them.

As autumn turned toward winter, the Connecticut weather changed—reminding us it was time to go south. Dylan chose a traveling job in Louisiana and reserved a hotel room in Gatlinburg, Tennessee, for the week before Thanksgiving.

Our stay in the Smoky Mountains was beautiful and otherworldly. We explored the park and Cades Cove until it snowed. We watched the snow falling from large windows while we enjoyed the intoxicating scent of cedar logs on the fire and soaked in a hot tub.

After several days of relaxing, we drove south and enjoyed a sparse, but joyful Thanksgiving in Mississippi. We made our Thanksgiving dinner in the hotel room with the microwave. Our meal consisted of instant mashed potatoes, a can of creamed corn, and a can of fake chicken. We marveled at how satisfying it was to enjoy our own company after all the hard work and disappointment of the last Thanksgiving.

By the time we got to Louisiana, I'd devised a plan to help Daddy regain his independence. He'd been working on a car to sell when Momma got sick, but now he hadn't worked for months. I called him to ask if he still planned to sell it.

"I'd like to, but I don't have the money to buy parts yet."

"What does it need?"

"Well, it needs a fender, a hood, and a new windshield."

"How much will that cost?"

Daddy estimated the amounts, while I wrote them down.

"I can't place an ad in the paper until I pay the past due bill."

"How much do you owe?"

"About two hundred and thirty dollars."

I sucked in my breath and added that amount to the list—along with paint and a couple hundred more dollars for groceries.

When we finished, I added the numbers and realized it would take most of our December budget. I reasoned if Dylan and I could survive on rice and beans for the month, it would be worth it to help Daddy get back on his feet.

I told Daddy I'd get back to him after I spoke with Dylan. Ever generous and thoughtful of others, Dylan went along with my plan. We agreed to skip Christmas gifts that year, and I drove to FedEx to send the money.

The next day, I was making a salad when the phone rang. I pushed the button on the speakerphone while I continued to chop carrots.

When I heard Abby's voice, I took a deep breath.

"Is Momma okay?"

"Yeah, I just wanted to ask you something."

She paused as if she was afraid to say what was on her mind.

"Did you just send Daddy money?"

"Yeah, why?"

"Did you know they moved in with us?"

"No."

The thought of my parents living with Abby and her family in a two-bedroom apartment sounded like a disaster, but winter was coming, and I was relieved they'd have a roof over their heads.

Abby continued.

"I just wondered because they seem to be on a shopping spree. They just bought a bunch of household things."

I didn't need the details. I could tell Daddy wasn't using the money to fix the car. After we hung up, I was confused and upset. It felt like he'd tricked me into giving him our money, but I wasn't sure how to confront him.

I decided to call while Dylan was home in case we argued, and I needed backup.

"How's it going, Daddy?"

"Well…" He laughed nervously. "Why do you ask?"

Not wanting to involve Abby in our dispute, I acted like I was just checking to make sure he had received the money and was buying the parts we'd discussed.

"I've decided not to finish the car right now. I'm waiting until January."

"But you've always said that January is the worst time to sell a car."

"Well, I've changed my mind."

"Daddy, I don't think you understand. I gave you every extra dollar we had. We were sacrificing to help you get on your feet. That means we don't have money for Christmas or an emergency fund. We barely have enough money for food and gas until the next paycheck."

"Calm down, you're overreacting. I'll pay you back."

"I'm not overreacting. I remember how you borrowed money when I was a kid. Now, I know how your bill collectors felt."

I spoke fast and without thinking, and I began to regret it as soon as I heard Daddy clearing his throat.

"Is your husband around?"

"Yeah, he's here."

"I'd like to speak to him."

"Just a minute."

I motioned for Dylan to step closer to the speakerphone.

For some reason, I expected Daddy to apologize for taking Dylan's hard-earned money, but he caught me off guard.

"Dylan, how long have you guys been married? Five years?"

"Yeah."

"Her mother and I—and the rest of the family, have wanted to talk with you for some time. It's hard because you two are always together, and we can't get you alone. We think you have a right to know that your wife has a mental illness. You can't trust a word she says because she makes up stories—all kinds of stories, but mostly about her childhood."

My heart stopped beating while my father's voice faded into a dark tunnel. My hands grew damp, and I felt tiny and far away. I tried to catch my breath, but I could barely make out Dylan's face. while Daddy continued.

"Now, she'll ask what we're talking about, so we need to think of something."

Dylan's face came back into focus. He was staring at me—possibly in shock, but I couldn't tell what he was thinking, so I stared back, hoping he didn't believe the lies.

It felt like we were in a hostage standoff.

Daddy continued.

"I know. Let's say we were discussing the ball game."

Regaining my equilibrium, I tightened my jaw and clenched my fist as I spoke loudly into the speaker.

"You don't have to do that, Daddy. You're on the speakerphone."

I heard a click as he hung up.

It felt like a bomb went off in my head, and I screamed.

Daddy's betrayal destroyed everything I'd believed about him, me, and God. My Daddy, the one who carried me on his shoulders and taught me about love, had tried to destroy my relationship with my husband. That's not what fathers are supposed to do. I always thought Daddy had my back, but now I knew the truth—he would betray me—his firstborn daughter, to cover up his own sins.

My body held so much tension that I had to move, or I would implode. I was afraid I might cut myself or jump off the balcony, so I decided to run. I had no idea where I was going, but I stumbled out the door and ran. Dylan followed with my coat. Once he caught up, he walked beside me while I sobbed until I was cold and hoarse. The sky grew dark, but the physical darkness was no match for the blight inflicted on my soul. The only thing that kept me alive was Dylan's steady arm across my shoulders while he gently led me back inside and made me a warm cup of tea.

27 It's All Coming Back to Me Now

Unless we remember,
we cannot understand.
-E.M. Forster

Three days went by without a sound from my family. I suspected neither Momma nor Abby knew what Daddy had done. And since they lived in such tight quarters, it would be hard to talk to either of them privately. I'd watched Momma defend Daddy throughout my childhood, so there wasn't much point in discussing it with her.

During those three days, I walked around our apartment complex crying while Dylan went to work. On the third day, I finally took a shower, made breakfast, and sat down to read the newspaper. I hoped it would distract from the hollow ache in my chest.

I was two thousand miles away from family and had no friends in Louisiana. The South was like a foreign country compared to my native Washington State. The landscape was full of moss-covered oaks and swampy bayous with an occasional raccoon or alligator. The people spoke in strange accents. The towns maintained drive-up daiquiri stands like Seattle had coffee houses. Even the laws were questionable. When Dylan got a speeding ticket, his coworkers suggested he give the judge his favorite liquor. If Dylan believed Daddy's lies or had been an abusive husband, I could've been in a vulnerable situation.

I was walking outside again when the rain came. Buckets of water pouring from the sky forced me to go back inside. By the time Dylan got home, the temperature was falling, and we started to wish we'd brought winter clothes. The temp agency had promised we'd be living below the frost line, but this was a freak storm.

The next morning, we woke to a silver thaw. The rain had saturated everything, and the temperature froze it. When we stepped onto the balcony, we looked up to see the icicles hanging over our heads like daggers hanging from the roof. Pink camellias on the bushes outside our apartment shone gloriously in the morning sun despite being encased in ice. The grass had turned into a fuzzy frost carpet, and everything from cars to tree branches wore shiny, sparkling coats of ice. The frozen road resembled a shiny river, and since no one dared to drive on it, the neighbor kids had turned it into an ice rink.

Shivering, I turned back inside, grateful for our warm apartment. Dylan called work to discover his co-workers were staying home, too.

We decided to make a holiday out of Dylan's day off. We put on coffee and cooked a delicious brunch. After we ate, we played cards with Mariah Carey's Christmas album in the background. Everything felt cozy, and I could almost feel my heart starting to mend when the power went out.

Dylan put batteries into the boom box and turned on the radio so we could catch the weather report. The reporter announced that the ice storm was breaking records throughout southern Louisiana. The news anchor warned everyone to stay home because the roads were dangerous.

We thought the power would return in a few hours, so we turned the radio off to conserve batteries and continued our game.

"You know how my dad said I make up stuff? Well, he's just saying that to cover his butt."

Dylan set down a run of cards. "I figured."

"I try not to think about my childhood. It makes me feel guilty because I don't want to hurt my parents."

"What happened?"

"My dad used to beat me with the belt."

"Oh, I hate that. My mom went crazy once and belted all of us, but she eventually came to her senses and apologized."

"It was more than once, and Daddy has never apologized."

I tossed a card on the discard pile.

"And when we were on Tour, you remember how I used to say I was a bag lady? That was my way of saying my family was homeless. I left home, running from my dad's belt with everything I owned in a big black garbage bag."

I set down a run of cards.

Dylan laid down a set of aces and ended the game.

He was quiet. I couldn't tell what he was thinking. Was he upset because I'd never told him about my family secrets? I felt a wave of shame wash over me—shame for not telling Dylan all of my secrets, but more shame for being my father's daughter.

I shuffled the cards.

"I wasn't joking when I said I was homeschooled without the books–they never bought one textbook."

I slid the cards across the table so he could cut the deck.

His hand fell over mine. It was warm.

"We had to hide and move all the time because my dad took money from people."

As I dealt the cards, Dylan shook his head.

"Why didn't you tell me about this stuff before?"

"Because I never wanted you to feel sorry for me. I wanted to be like normal people so much that I tricked myself into thinking that what I didn't talk about never happened."

I was beginning to realize that I needed to speak up about our struggles, or my younger siblings might forget that these events ever happened. It was bad enough they couldn't remember when we lived like normal people.

Throughout the day, I start remembering all the things I tried to forget. I shared one event at a time with Dylan as we played the game.

"Momma would say I broke the rule because families should always stick together and have each other's backs."

"It doesn't seem like your dad has your back."

I had to ask him.

"Dylan, do you believe me?"

"Of course. This is just a lot of information to take in."

He sat up straight.

"So, what happened to Jake? Why was he in the hospital?"

"It was only for a few days. Carrie said he got depressed from trying to attend college and support his family with a third-grade education."

"Your dad screwed up your lives by not allowing you guys to go to school."

We played cards and talked for hours while I told Dylan things I never told anyone else. When we got hungry, we sorted through the cupboards, looking for things that wouldn't require cooking. We found canned beans, chips, crackers, and noodles that we could make by heating water with the camp stove on the balcony.

As the shadows fell, Dylan turned our camping lantern on. "Good thing we kept the camping equipment."

We went to bed that night a little colder than usual but hopeful that the power would come on in the morning.

The power wasn't on in the morning, but some streets had been cleared. We drove to Walmart to buy more batteries, instant noodles, and cookies. Very few businesses in town had power. Restaurants were closed, and only one gas station remained open.

We heated water with our camping stove and made noodles. It was nice to eat something warm.

Once again, we played cards until we were sick of looking at them. And I told more stories than I'd ever told anyone. My voice was hoarse from crying for three days and talking for two.

Many of our neighbors had driven south below the storm to stay in hotels where they could take hot showers and stay warm. We couldn't do that because I'd given all of our money to Daddy. Dylan was kind enough not to point out that we could be staying in a warm hotel room if it weren't for me.

At ten thirty that night, we lay shivering in bed, trying to sleep with our clothes on. I had my coat zipped up to my neck.

Dylan got up and looked at the camping thermometer I'd hung on the wall. "Dang! It's only seventeen degrees in here."

"What can we do?"

"Let's get in the car and warm up."

"Walmart's closed by now. Where can we go?"

"I know it scares you, but we need to go to the warming shelter."

"I don't want to—I won't be able to sleep if we go there."

"It's better to stay up all night in a warm place than to freeze to death in our bed."

I knew he was right, so I grabbed my pillow and sleeping bag and followed him to the car. The warm air blowing on my face from the car's heater felt like heaven.

By the time we got to the shelter, it was past eleven. I stayed in the car while Dylan knocked on the door. Through the window, I could see the lights were out so people could sleep. The only visible light was a small green desk lamp. It was far across the room where a man sat writing. Dylan knocked again and even tried to open the door, but it was locked. He pounded on the glass, but the man kept writing as though he heard nothing.

Watching Dylan from the car, my heart filled with love for this kind man who cared for me. He was so earnest. We were about to freeze to death, and he bravely stood in the freezing wind so I could stay in the warm car.

I tapped the horn for him to give up. It was too cold to stand outside knocking on a door that wouldn't open. I held back tears while I watched him walk back to the car.

Once inside, he removed his gloves and held his fingers over the heater vent. I kept a brave face while I silently begged God for help.

As we sat in the car thinking, I remembered the grape juice money. I believed there had to be a way to stay warm. We just had to find it.

Dylan drove to the gas station. It was the only lit building on that side of town.

"If we have to sit in the car all night, we better make sure we have a full tank."

He got out and jumped up and down, trying to stay warm while he waited for the pump to shut off. As soon as it clicked, he spun the cap shut and ran inside.

I glanced around the parking lot and noticed plenty of cars for such a late hour. People crowded the tiny convenience store, making it hard for Dylan to wind his way through the crowd to pay.

I noticed a spring in his step as he returned to the car. Was he more optimistic or just cold?

He slammed the door shut and turned to face me.

"Do you still have the hot water bottle you brought for camping?"

"Yes." I instantly knew what he was thinking.

"They have hot water in there. It'll keep us warm."

We went back, and I pulled out a red hot water bottle and a white fluffy towel from a suitcase. The towel would keep the bottle warm until we got back to the apartment.

With our prize secured, we rushed back into the apartment and took apart the extra bed in the second bedroom.

Placing the mattress and box spring on each side of our bed, we made a canopy by hanging a heavy blanket across the top from one side to the other. It looked like a blanket fort. Then, we gathered every blanket and piece of clothing we could find.

We put on our sweats, stocking caps, and socks as we crawled into bed and pulled our extra blankets and clothing on top of us. We hugged it for dear life as we snuggled around that hot water bottle. That little heat, the covers, and our love for each other kept us cozy until morning.

We woke up warm inside our blanket fort and were thrilled to find blue skies and sunshine waiting outside. We still had no power. How much longer would this trial last? At least we knew how to stay warm for another night if necessary.

Some of the restaurants in town had the power back on, so we went out to find a warm breakfast.

After breakfast, with full stomachs and warm hands, we drove back to the neighborhood. A million icicles continued to sparkle from the trees. Filtered through the sunshine, they looked magical. As I squinted into the light, I was relieved to see a white utility truck pulling onto our street.

28 Don't Stop Believin'

*A bleeding heart
is of no help to anyone
if it bleeds to death.
-Frederick Buechner*

After a week, I stopped crying over Daddy's betrayal, and my pain simmered down to a dull ache in my chest. I needed friends and resources in case any more emergencies came up. I'd always turned to God for comfort, so with the roads cleared and the power back on, I went to church.

The sermon was about forgiveness. Sitting in the pew, surrounded by strangers who knew nothing about my situation, I felt my face burn with shame. Since childhood, I'd been told to "forgive and forget." Whenever I fought with my siblings or argued with my parents, I was taught to take responsibility and smooth things over to keep the peace.

My heart was torn between my love for Momma and my anger toward Daddy. I was used to talking to Momma every day, but I hadn't called for several days, and she was probably wondering why. I was beginning to feel lonely. Dylan was gone all day, and I hadn't made any local friends yet. Perhaps connecting with other people would take my mind off my pain. I decided to call the pastor and volunteer to help with community services.

Dylan's job was to drive along the bayous, making home health visits to those who needed physical therapy. I didn't have any transportation because we only had one car, so I asked the pastor if someone could give me a ride. He said another young wife named Leta lived in the same apartment complex, and he would give us both a ride.

The pastor was a balding man in his mid-fifties with drooping shoulders. When he picked us up, he brought another young woman with him. Her dress was worn, and her matted hair hung down to the middle of her back. When I smiled at her, she quickly looked away. The pastor didn't bother introducing her. I figured he picked her up off the streets, and we were going to help her.

I had hoped to join a ladies' quilting circle or help with the food bank, so it was surprising to discover that there were only four of us at the church that day.

When the Pastor set out boxes of envelopes, Leta looked as confused as I was.

"I thought we were helping with community services?"

"No, we shut that down."

He set a box of flyers on the desk.

When he turned his back, I rolled my eyes at Leta before I spoke.

"I've never heard of a church shutting community services down."

"You ladies are still young, but in time, you'll understand that community services are the biggest drain on the church's finances."

"What about all the Adventist churches that give away food and clothes?"

"They aren't smart enough to phase it out. If you stuff these envelopes, I'll be grateful. And if you run out of anything, I'll be in my office."

With that, he turned and went down a very long hall to the other end of the building while the younger woman followed him. She really looked like she could use some clothes and supplies from the community services. I wondered if he had a stash of supplies and was taking her to get some.

Leta and I got to know each other while we stuffed the envelopes. We were both married and without kids. She was from Los Angeles, but they'd moved to Louisiana for her husband's job as a geologist for some oil company.

After a while, Leta groaned.

"I have plenty of things to do at home, I didn't wake up this morning planning to stuff envelopes–I thought we'd be helping people."

"Me too."

I reached for an empty box.

"We're out of envelopes."

Since Leta was still working on a large stack of envelopes, I ran down the hall to get more.

The office door was almost closed and slightly ajar. The pastor had told us to come to the office if we ran out, so I didn't hesitate to open it wide.

What I saw made me freeze. The pastor's belt and pants were on the floor around his ankles while the girl knelt in front of him.

I screamed.

Then, embarrassed and scared of what he might do to me, I ran down the long hall to the other end of the church, where Leta continued stuffing envelopes.

As I came into the room, she looked up. "Did you hear something?"

The pastor must've dressed fast because I was surprised to turn around and find him standing over my shoulder. Still in shock, I said nothing.

"Are you ladies ready to go?"

I couldn't believe he acted like nothing happened. The young woman, who I later learned was named Bella, slunk into the room behind him. I was afraid to look at her because I didn't know what the pastor might do to all of us. I questioned if it was safe to let him drive me home, but what could I do? We didn't have cell phones, and Dylan wouldn't be back in town for hours. I had no local friends to call for help. The other two women would be riding with us, so I decided this was my best chance to get away from him.

Everyone was silent on the ride home except Leta. She had no idea what had happened and kept rattling on about the loss of community services. I wanted to tell her to shut up—that we had worse problems than no community services—but I counted the pine trees flying past the window instead.

I was relieved when the pastor pulled up in front of my apartment.

As I opened the door to get out, he said, "Thank you for your help. Maybe we can do this again sometime."

I felt my face growing red, but I waited until my feet were firmly on the ground before I replied.

"I don't think so!"

I slammed the door as hard as I could and ran inside.

After I locked the door, I frantically paced back and forth, wailing and trying to process the tight pain in my chest.

Why did I feel so panicked? Then I realized the pastor reminded me of Daddy. They both hid their sins by acting as if nothing had happened. If I needed help, this pastor wouldn't care. He'd never admit the truth, just as Daddy never admitted the truth. In a world where men stood as gatekeepers to the family, church, and possibly God, where could a young woman like me go for help?

I sorted through the garbage to find the church bulletin. It was wadded up and torn, with strawberry jam on the corner, but the number of the head elder was still legible. I didn't know him, but I remembered his son as a nice guy from Walla Walla College. Dialing the number, I took a deep breath before a woman answered.

"Hi, I was visiting your church last week. I'm the one who knew your son."

"Oh, how are you?"

"Fine. I have a stack of church magazines from the northwest conference, would you like them?"

"No thanks, I already have plenty of reading material, and I'm trying to eliminate extra clutter."

"Okay. See you next week."

I tried to keep my voice cheerful even though I felt deflated.

I hung up and paced some more.

Two minutes later, I called her back.

"Hello?

"Have you noticed anything strange about your pastor?"

There was a pause before she answered in a suspenseful tone.

"Tell me where you live, and I'll be right over."

I gave her my address, and she was at my door within minutes.

Jan said the community service ladies had been suspicious of the pastor having an affair, but no one could prove it. He often took Bella into his office and locked the door. Some people even wondered if he'd shut down the community services to give them more privacy.

The pastor had been smug and condescending to the older ladies, but now I had foiled his plans. After weeks of speculation, the ladies would be thrilled to have an eyewitness.

Jan invited us over for dinner, and we soon became friends. Her husband, Ed, was a doctor. They'd spent their lives in the mission field caring for sick people. They listened to our stories and told a few of their own. They had four adult children, and it was obvious they cherished them from their conversations and pictures on their walls. Their home was clean, and I felt relaxed around them.

Ed told us the pastor could be fired if the conference found out what happened. He encouraged us to come to church and stand up against this evil.

"He's already run off half of the congregation." Jan looked like she might cry. She was the motherly kind of woman that I didn't like to see sad, so we agreed to come to church and sit with them in solidarity.

A couple of weeks later, the church ladies asked me to go with them to visit the conference president. We rode in a car for three hours so each of us could tell the president what we'd seen.

When it was my turn, I nervously described what I saw.

The president smiled and leaned closer to me, while he spoke in a Southern drawl.

"Now, darlin', are you sure you wanna make this allegation? It's just gonna be his word against yours."

I was disappointed by his response, but I said yes. It felt good to tell the truth, but it didn't take long to discover he was right. The pastor denied having an affair and called me a liar.

There was an elder at the church who was good friends with the pastor. He and his wife began to glare at me every time I came through the church door. One day, the wife took me aside and told me they didn't want liars in their church. I stood my ground and glared right back.

"Then maybe you need a new pastor."

After that encounter, I rushed into the bathroom to hide in a stall. The ability of Daddy and this pastor to lie and twist the truth while they falsely accused me of lying, left me shaking. It was almost more than I could take. Where was God in all of these lies by supposedly godly men?

Jan's friendship got me through these dark times. She often called me to get a taco or walk through the mall. We spent one weekend in New Orleans with Ed and Jan, even riding in a buggy throughout the French Quarter. After working so hard to have quality time with my parents, I was surprised to discover that people my parents' age could still have fun.

The Southern winter was beautiful, and the job was good, so we agreed to stay in Louisiana for another year.

One day, while I was helping Jan count the church offerings, I confessed one of my deepest fears.

"I hate giving money to the church. It always feels forced, but if I don't, I'm afraid God will punish me by killing me in a car accident."

Jan stopped counting the dollar bills and looked at me with tenderness.

"Oh Cheri, how scary! Jesus doesn't punish people like that. He owns the cattle on a thousand hills. God invented gold and silver. If he wants more, he can always create more. God doesn't need your money—he wants your heart."

I was stunned. Who was this God that Jan was talking about? The God I grew up with was always waiting to punish me—like Daddy with the belt.

In contrast to the lying pastor and angry church members, Jan made me feel heard and loved.

One evening, Dylan came home and said he wanted to get a different car. We wanted to get a personal computer, but it would add to the stack of stuff we took every time we moved.

"Now that we've got our income back, we should go to the dealer and get a small pickup. It'll be easier to haul the computer along with your paintings.

"Daddy says car dealers are crooks."

Dylan's eyes grew large. "You're mad at your father for lying, but you believe what he says about car dealers?"

"I've never had a car that Daddy didn't fix up. Plus, we don't want to pay interest."

"What do you think we should do?"

"I'll ask Daddy if he can get us a pickup. It'll cost less."

And so, at the intersection of "forgive and forget" and our need for a different vehicle, I called Daddy. Neither of us mentioned how he'd betrayed me, but he seemed genuinely glad to talk. He promised to fix a pickup and drive it down to Louisiana if we bought his airfare home.

"Do you think Momma can come with you?"

"I'll ask, but you know how she hates to fly."

"It might be a fun trip and a chance to see places you guys have never been, like the Grand Canyon."

We ended up paying my parents for the truck, covering their gas and hotel bills on the way down, and buying their return tickets. I didn't mind. I was thrilled to see Momma. After the cancer scare, I hoped she could enjoy the trip.

I spent days planning what to do when my parents arrived. There was so much I wanted to share with them. I thought of taking them to the French Quarter in New Orleans, where we enjoyed the coffee and beignets at Cafe du Monde, but my parents didn't drink coffee, and the beignets had eggs in them. The Creole townhouses and iron balconies would probably be lost on Momma, who might get anxious and intimidated by the city crowds.

Instead of going into the city, I made reservations to stay in an antebellum home in the Atchafalaya basin where we could feed baby alligators from the porch. Momma thought that sounded terrifying, so we canceled the bed and breakfast and stayed in our apartment. I was grateful the travel company had provided us with two furnished bedrooms.

It turned out that all Daddy wanted to do was rest. Despite the change in plans, we had a pleasant visit. I managed to talk them into a day trip to St. Francesville, where we explored an antebellum home.

My parents didn't enjoy eating out, so I made Momma's potato salad, and we ate under the live oaks and thirty-foot-high doric columns of the Greenwood Plantation.

Daddy glanced over his shoulder at the Spanish moss hanging from the trees.

"It's a different world here. It's interesting, but it makes me a little uncomfortable."

"We should all be uncomfortable considering how this mansion was built on the backs of enslaved people."

As I listened to Dylan repeat what we'd often discussed while visiting the mansions of Louisiana and Mississippi, I was satisfied to see Daddy nodding his head in approval. At least we agreed about slavery.

Momma seemed to enjoy our visit, but when it came time for her to go home, she was so anxious to get on the plane that I had to prod her into the boarding line. For a moment, I considered keeping her with us, but I knew she'd never be happy without Daddy. It was a relief to see the plane take off with her inside.

For the moment, my breach with Daddy seemed healed. I'd done the Christian thing by choosing to forgive and forget. Dylan and I soon returned to our routines. He went to work, and I hung out with Jan or helped some of the church ladies with their quilting.

The day finally came when all the pastor's secrets became known. He'd applied for a transfer to another state and promised Bella he'd send her a ticket as soon as he got settled. Of course, she never heard from him again. Devastated, she brought her diary to the church elders.

Those who supported the pastor were shocked to read how he'd manipulated Bella into having an affair. Every Wednesday, he made her lie down on the floor of his van and covered her with a tarp while he drove her into his garage. Then, to make sure the neighbors didn't hear two car doors shut, he made her crawl out through the driver's door.

While his wife was at work, they had sex on the bed, then they ate ice cream while he washed the sheets, dried them, and put them back on the bed. They left the house just as they had entered it, both going through the same door with her flat on the floor again and covered with the tarp. It was obvious the pastor had planned every detail to deceive his wife and everyone who knew him. He'd even paid a babysitter to watch Bella's four little children.

The diary revealed that the affair had started before we arrived in Louisiana. The evidence was strong enough to convince the church board. The conference president told the pastor he could come back to Louisiana and stand before a jury of his peers, or he could give up his ministerial license. He chose the latter.

By Thanksgiving of our second year in Louisiana, Jan and Ed invited us to stay with them for the holiday weekend. We were all grateful to have the church crisis resolved. We cooked together and played table games. At night, as I lay next to Dylan in their guest room, I marveled at how these people took the time to care about us.

Dylan and I continued to explore the Gulf Coast. We visited too many antebellum homes to count. The stories were fascinating, and I dreamed of writing novels about some of the plantations. But after two years of living in the South, we craved the cool, mountainous air of our native northwest. Dylan found a job in Washington State, just over the border from Portland, Oregon. We especially liked the area because could drive to see my parents and grandparents within an hour.

We took our furniture out of storage and rented a farmhouse next to the Columbia River. It was autumn, and as I pulled out the grapevine dishes, I remembered the fun we'd had with Jan and Ed and decided to invite my family for Thanksgiving dinner.

29 What About Love

I'm not serving a menu,...
I'm serving my soul.
-Dominique Crenn

Dylan swung a string of colored lights across the front porch and pounded a nail into the trim.

"How does it look?"

He reminded me of an elf the way he balanced precariously on the ladder with a Santa hat draped over one ear.

I walked backward down the driveway until I could get a good look at the roofline.

"It's perfect. It's the prettiest place we've ever lived. I can't wait for everyone to see it."

By everyone, I meant Mara, her husband, and my parents. I'd hoped to gather my entire family around a table, but it wasn't going to happen this year. Abby and her family were living in Wisconsin, and Jake and Carrie wanted to start their own traditions. Despite my disappointment, I was grateful for whoever would show up.

Dylan flipped the lights on and ran to join me in the driveway.

"Maybe it's better to have fewer people this year. It's not so much pressure."

I sighed. "Except it's my parents who bring the pressure."

Our display of colored lights would seem extravagant to Daddy, but everything we owned might seem lavish to people living in a camp trailer.

The first Christmas we were married, I'd started calling Dylan "Mr. Christmas" because he wore a Santa hat to work and insisted on buying a live tree every year. Putting lights on the house was mandatory as far as he was concerned. In contrast, my family had never decorated the outside of a house with colored lights. We didn't have money for lights, and even if we could afford them, we moved so often that they would surely have been left behind or lost in some storage unit that Daddy forgot to pay for. On top of that, I'd been taught that Santa was just a fake god. As I grew older, my parents even stopped having a tree due to concerns that it was pagan.

Between their stark poverty and rigid religious beliefs, I felt the gap widening between myself and my parents. I thought of all the money we'd given them and hoped they could remember how generous we'd been to them.

Before we left Louisiana, Jan had given me advice.

"Don't be giving all your money to your parents. It's not right for kids to support their parents. Parents are supposed to help their kids—not the other way around."

She meant well, and so had Earl. But normal people didn't understand my family situation. People with steady paychecks couldn't relate to the desperation of people always wondering where their next meal might come from.

As much as I'd been tempted to cut Daddy off for lying about me, I was determined that Momma wouldn't have to worry about having money for groceries.

Inside the house, I went to the kitchen and pulled out my wooden recipe box. I searched for Momma's holiday recipes and sighed. Thanksgiving prep would take an entire day since I had to do all the work by myself. It was easier when there were four of us to share the tasks. Back then, one of us would make the pies, another would cut up potatoes, and another would make salads, while the fourth made the gluten steaks. I'd always enjoyed the camaraderie of Momma and my sisters cooking together on a holiday.

Even though I cooked alone, I hummed while I peeled the potatoes. My hands had been doing these tasks since childhood, and my heart felt light in anticipation of seeing Momma and Mara. After I covered the potatoes with water, I set the pan in the fridge and began to make the salads.

Our phone line wasn't connected yet, but there was a pay phone a couple of blocks away. After spending the day baking, prepping, and mopping the floors, I grabbed a roll of quarters and walked down to the phone booth next to the marina.

Momma answered in a cheery voice.

"Hi Momma, the food's ready for tomorrow. I made all your favorite recipes."

Her voice sounded a little strange and far away. She and Daddy were back living on my grandparents' land since Abby and her family had moved to Wisconsin. Perhaps she was guarded because her parents were in the room. They'd been invited too, but my grandparents were getting older and preferred to stay close to home on holidays.

Momma cleared her throat, and I braced myself. Nothing good ever came from my parents clearing their throats.

"Honey, I hope you don't mind, but Daddy and I have decided to go vegan."

"Right now? I mean, you couldn't wait one more day?"

I tried to keep a sweet Christian tone and omit the frustration from my voice.

"You guys can still eat whatever you want, I'm just bringing vegan mashed potatoes."

"Okay, Momma, I just wish you'd told me before. Nearly everything I made has dairy in it."

My heart was heavy when I hung up. As we got ready for bed, I vented to Dylan.

"The whole point of inviting them to our house was so she wouldn't have to go to all that work."

"Don't worry, sweetie. It won't go to waste. The rest of us will enjoy your cooking." He turned out the light and began to snore softly while I stared at the ceiling. The spicy scent of pumpkin pie filled the house, and it irritated me to think my parents wouldn't be eating any of it.

I barely slept that night and got up early to make dinner rolls. Since they weren't going to eat anything else I'd made, I took comfort in thinking my parents might enjoy my homemade bread.

Mara and Kip arrived about the time I was putting the rolls in the oven.

"Can I warm up my vegan steaks?"

"Sure. "I turned to hug her and noticed she was carrying a pumpkin pie.

"Oh, you made pie, too?"

I was surprised she hadn't told me when we spoke on the phone.

She took the foil off the pan of steaks and stuck it in the oven.

"I decided to experiment and make a vegan pie."

The lead feeling in my stomach increased as I realized Momma and Mara had planned an entire alternate menu without telling me.

"If you guys wanted to have a vegan Thanksgiving, why couldn't someone inform the hostess?"

I tried to smile as I spoke, but inside, I felt disrespected.

When our parents arrived, most of the food was soon heated between the microwave and oven. We sat down to eat while my rolls continued to bake.

As soon as Dylan said amen, Mara gave me a puzzled look.

"I don't know why you care if the rest of us go vegan."

"I'm not judging anyone for going vegan—I'm just saying it would've been nice to let me know before I spent an entire day cooking for you."

"Why does it matter? You can eat your food, and we'll eat ours." Daddy spoke as a matter of fact.

"Because I spent the entire day yesterday preparing a meal that none of you will eat." I looked around the table for a response, but even Dylan was busy stuffing his face. I never felt so alone and underappreciated. I remembered how Jan had appreciated my help with dinner.

"Who wants the vegan mashed potatoes?" Mara held up the bowl.

Nobody mentioned missing Jake or Abby and their families, but I brought up a concern.

"I hope everyone realizes it's a big stretch between Jake and Abby, who eat meat, and you guys going vegan. Do you think we'll ever be able to meet in the middle for a family dinner?"

The smoke alarm reminded me to check my rolls, but I jumped up to find them burned. Someone had placed them on the top shelf of the oven.

Tears filled my eyes as I tossed the entire pan in the sink.

"I got up early to make these rolls so I could contribute one thing that you guys might eat."

Daddy handed a bowl of green beans to Kip.

"Oh, come on, Cheri. You're too sensitive. Can someone please pass the vegan steaks?"

I tried to act like it was no big deal, but it was. I was physically free from Daddy's belt, but I wasn't mentally free from his criticism and judgment. It felt like nothing I did was ever good enough.

I managed to hold my head high and get through the meal, but this gathering seemed to mean only one thing to my family. It was all about the food. Not delicious food or comfort food—just vegan food.

I was glad none of our guests were spending the night. They gobbled down their vegan pie and were soon ready for the drive home. I thought of the last Thanksgiving with Jan and Ed—how we'd played games far into the night. Daddy hadn't had time for table games since I was ten.

My family's presence brought pain, but their leaving left a dark void where my fantasies of a cozy family meal had evaporated like the mist along the river.

I smiled and waved goodbye, but I felt like I was going to explode. And it wasn't from eating too much–I'd barely touched my food. As soon as they drove away, I felt like I needed to go for a walk or cut my hair off.

Dylan joined me as I walked along the Columbia River. He remarked how the sunlight filtering through the red and yellow leaves on the trees was so beautiful, but the beauty was lost on me.

"I have no idea how I got through that meal."

We passed another couple walking their beautiful white dog, but I didn't bother to say hello.

I hoped Dylan could understand my pain.

"Do you think I'm too sensitive?"

"The fact that you even ask that is ridiculous. They should be asking themselves why they're so rude."

"But they never do."

"No, and if you ask me, I don't want those people in our house ever again."

"Stop it. You're not helping."

I motioned toward the people with the dog. Perhaps it was Momma's rule about keeping secrets, but I didn't want our new neighbors to hear us arguing.

"Why do you even want to spend time with them?"

"I want a relationship with them."

"They don't even know what a relationship is."

I started to cry, while he began to shout above the roaring of the river.

"No one but your family can make you so miserable."

"That's because I love them. Maybe you don't know what love is," I yelled back.

"Yeah? Well, I love you, but your family is like a noose around our necks, pulling us into the undertow."

I stopped to stare at the river flowing beside us.

Dylan took a few steps in front of me and turned around.

"Look, I won't stand by and watch while they abuse you, so you'll have to choose between your family and me."

"What are you saying? I need you to support me—not abandon me."

"I'm sorry, but no one makes you more miserable than your parents."

Forgetting to keep my voice down, I began to wail.

"I could never live without my family. My family is everything to me! How can you do this to me?"

"I'm not doing it to you–I'm doing it for you."

To make his point, Dylan flung his keys as far as he could.

I watched in alarm as the keys sailed over the rocks and into the river.

I turned back to him.

"You moron! Now we're locked out."

The minute I said it, I felt ashamed. From the look on his face, I could tell he already felt bad.

Too defeated to talk, we trudged back to the house in silence. We sat on the front porch, wondering what to do.

I shivered. The sky was getting dark, and the air was nippy.

Dylan spoke softly.

"Do you know where your keys are?"

"Somewhere in the house."

The people with the dog walked by and waved. This time I waved back with a forced smile, hoping we didn't look like we were locked out.

"How embarrassing," I mumbled under my breath.

"Oh, it's worse than embarrassing—the nearest locksmith is in Longview, at least an hour away."

"And who knows how long they'll take to get here on a holiday."

"Or how much they'll charge."

"By then, it'll be dark."

I shivered.

"Our only option is to break down the back door."

"What? No. It'll cost our deposit."

The words were barely out of my mouth before Dylan jumped up, ran around back, and made a run for the door. I heard a crash, then shuddered as I heard something being ripped apart.

Afraid to look, I got up slowly as Dylan opened the front door with a triumphant smile.

"I busted it open on the first try, and it didn't even break the window."

"What a relief."

I stumbled through the door and into the kitchen to observe the damage for myself.

The entire door frame had come off from the inside.

Dylan went to the back porch, rattled around in his toolbox, and came back with a hammer. Within a minute, he'd nailed the door frame back in place. I marveled that no one could see the difference.

It was harder to find my keys. I rarely used them because Dylan usually did the driving. I searched through cupboards and drawers before remembering they were in the pocket of my purse.

"They've been there for months. I just forgot."

"Didn't anyone ever teach you how to drive?"

His grin was a little flirty, so I swatted him with affection.

"I remember how proud I was to take the keys out of Daddy's hands that day we took the Mustang."

"Perhaps you should use your keys more often."

I thought about all the times I'd passively allowed Daddy or Dylan—and even Momma and Mara–to drive. I usually went along for the ride. I paused and wondered why it mattered to me if my family ate the food I prepared. Why did I want everyone's approval?

Dylan went to the fridge and pulled out a pie. "Do you want cream or vanilla bean ice cream?"

"Both."

I grabbed the hammer and shuffled through a box in the pantry to find a nail.

He licked a blob of whipped cream from his finger.

"What are you doing?"

"I'm hanging the key rack."

I pounded a nail into the stud and hung a moose-shaped piece of wood on it. After stepping back to make sure it was straight, I hung my keys on one antler. It looked like a little piece of Alaska on the wall.

"There. Now we can keep track of the keys."

With two complete pumpkin pies and no one else to eat them, we each took a quarter of a pie and smothered it with whipped cream and vanilla bean ice cream.

Dylan stuffed a fork full of orange and white fluff into his mouth.

"This is the most decadent pumpkin pie I've ever eaten."

I savored the pie while I grabbed a pencil and started to write a poem. When I was finished, I read it to Dylan.

"If anyone ever tries to tell you that Thanksgiving is all about the food, don't you dare believe them, sure, some people will try to make it about the food, but it's really about love, respect, and gratitude. Without those ingredients, you might as well be serving cardboard."

"Bravo." Dylan clapped his hands before grabbing a bottle of sparkling cider from the fridge. Filling the tulip-shaped glasses from our wedding, he made a toast.

"To peaceful holidays—without the family!"

30 My Life

Years of love have been forgot
in the hatred of a minute.
-Edgar Allan Poe

For years, at least once a month, I'd called each of my siblings and my parents, but I was beginning to realize long-distance relationships weren't enough. It was good to have a phone conversation, but it wasn't the same as sitting across the table and looking each other in the eye. I'd always had my family on the other end of the phone line, but now I didn't feel safe to call. Even worse, after the Thanksgiving disaster, I was afraid we'd never have a meal together without fighting over food.

Once again, I was living in a new town where I didn't know anyone. When Dylan left for work each day, I got depressed. When the local care center advertised a part-time activity assistant position,

I applied and was hired immediately. At least it was something to keep me busy.

My first task was planning a Christmas party for the residents. I enjoyed getting paid to bring families together, but my heart ached to think that I'd failed my own.

Two days before Christmas, Dylan came home to find me sorting through the pantry.

"What's up?"

"I'm gathering ingredients for a Christmas feast."

"That seems like a lot of food for two people."

"I'm thinking about taking Christmas dinner to my grandparents' house."

His cheerful expression fell.

"And why are you doing this?"

"I haven't seen my grandparents since we got back. They're getting older, and after years of living two thousand miles away, it seems sad to ignore them on Christmas."

"Do you think this will please your parents?"

"If they don't appreciate it, my grandparents will. Grandma's not a cook, and Grandpa will love whatever I make."

"It makes me nervous."

"Don't worry." I set the flour, salt, and sugar on the counter next to a can of pumpkin. "I'm making everything vegan this time."

I spent the next two days revamping Momma's recipes to create a vegan version of everything I'd made for Thanksgiving. Dylan was right—it was a lot of food. I was glad for his help transporting it to Grandma's on Christmas morning.

After loading three boxes of food and a few presents into the car, we took the ferry over the river, drove around Portland, turned off at Gladstone, and wound our way through the hills and Christmas tree farms to Grandma's house. It was a journey that always made me giddy with anticipation. I always loved giving Grandma her hug.

My grandparents always bolstered my self-worth. They were just as grateful as I'd imagined. Momma seemed satisfied with my cooking, and even Daddy had nothing but good things to say. A heavy weight fell from my shoulders as I once again felt good enough. I'd redeemed myself with my vegan offerings.

I flashed a victory smile toward Dylan and whispered, "See? Forgiving and forgetting is worth it."

When we packed up to go home, I was sorting out the dishes to give my parents and grandparents the leftovers when my cousin Derek came over to talk with me.

Derek and I rarely saw each other, but there was a time when we'd been childhood friends. As the two oldest grandchildren, we'd enjoyed playing and helping Grandma in her garden. I'd always been fond of him, and now he was living on my grandparents' property in a single-wide trailer.

"Hey Cous', that was the best apple pie I've had for years."

His smile lit up his face like it had on my wedding day when he snuck down to my dressing room to hug me. I looked down at the pie plate and noticed one slice left. He was single, and I figured he probably didn't bake much.

"There's one piece left, and you can have it."

"Thank you!"

We made small talk before Dylan reminded me that we didn't want to drive home late on a holiday. I hugged everyone goodbye, and we drove home.

The next day, I was still basking in the afterglow of our peaceful Christmas when Daddy called.

"Do you mind if Momma and I stop by tonight?"

Since things had gone well the day before, I said, "Sure, come on over!"

As soon as I hung up, I rushed to bake some vegan chocolate chip cookies.

We were playing Rook when they arrived and invited them to join us. They seemed to be in a good mood. Momma loved table games. She especially liked Scrabble, which she usually won. Daddy had taught me Rook when I was small enough to sit on his lap while he played with Uncle Joe. For most of my growing-up years, Daddy didn't have time for table games, no matter how much we kids begged him, so this seemed like a special treat.

After a few rounds of cards, Daddy and Momma seemed to be enjoying themselves. When Dylan and I went to the kitchen to get snacks, we were out of earshot, and I could hardly contain my joy.

"Can you pinch me to make sure I'm not dreaming?"

"You're not dreaming."

"For years, I've tried to get Daddy to relax and play games, but he always has too much work to do."

"He surprised me. I've never seen him play games before."

I danced around the kitchen, balancing a tray of chips and hummus in one hand and a plate of chocolate chip cookies in the other.

"This is the happiest day of my life."

After double-checking the sandwiches to be sure everything was vegan, I waltzed back to the dining room with the food.

The minute I entered the room, I knew something was up. It felt like the temperature had dropped twenty degrees.

When I set the food down on the table, Momma barely glanced at it. Dylan picked up the cards and shuffled them before sliding them across the table for Daddy to cut the deck.

When Momma cleared her throat, I waited, suspended between joy and fear, to see what she would say. Whatever it was, I figured Daddy was behind it because Momma hated any sort of confrontation.

"Cheri, I've been meaning to ask you something."

I sucked in a deep breath to listen.

"Why'd you give Derek the leftover pie?"

"What?"

Caught off guard, I wondered why she asked such a question. Wasn't she the one who taught me everything I knew about hospitality? Wasn't I doing as she taught me? I had a feeling there was going to be no right answer.

"He likes apple pie, and it was Christmas."

"It seems strange that out of all the people in the house, you gave Derek that pie."

"But I gave you the rest of the pumpkin pie and most of the leftovers—if you want an apple pie, I'll bake one for you."

Even as I spoke, I knew food couldn't resolve this conflict.

Daddy's face was growing redder by the minute.

"Do you realize what Derek is trying to do to us?"

"He's my cousin—and it was just pie!"

I hated the way my voice shook.

"It was more than pie—Derek's our enemy. He's trying to steal your mother's inheritance."

I vaguely remembered that Daddy had mentioned my cousin wanting to be a caretaker for Grandpa and Grandma, but I usually stayed out of Daddy's disagreements with other people.

"Didn't Jesus tell us to be kind to our enemies?"

"Stop twisting scripture. You know Derek's in a court battle with us. It wasn't appropriate to give him pie."

My hands were going numb from gripping the side of the table.

"Then why did he eat Christmas dinner with us? Why didn't you make him stay away?"

"Because you had to make a big deal out of Christmas dinner and feed everyone, and you know Grandma would never leave one of her grandkids out."

"So now you're blaming me for making dinner? What happened to the Christmas spirit and having peace and goodwill toward all?"

"Oh, come on, don't be so dramatic. Jesus wasn't even born on Christmas."

Determined to stand my ground, I glared at Daddy.

"I don't think I did anything wrong."

He turned to Momma. "I think we should go now."

"But what about our card game? You guys haven't even eaten?"

Tears filled my eyes. I wasn't ready to let go of my beautiful dream of spending time with them, but it was becoming clear they'd come to play mind games rather than table games.

Momma shook her head with tight lips. "I thought you'd at least try to see things from our perspective."

She grabbed her purse and went out the door. I watched them drive off with tears streaming down my face.

In the days that followed, my depression grew worse. Ever since I could remember, I'd worked hard to please my parents and received very little gratitude in return. I was beginning to think my parents didn't love me.

Dylan tried to comfort me.

"Your parents can't enjoy a holiday with anyone. Your mom's obsessed with vegan cooking, and your dad's consumed with taking your cousin to court. Any attempt to celebrate seems a waste of time to them."

I felt angry remembering everything I'd given up just to please my parents. I was tired of being judged for what I ate and wore, and I was sick of Daddy treating me like I wasn't good enough because I went to the movies and listened to rock music. Their condemnation for giving my cousin a slice of pie was the final garnish on a long, repulsive diet of shame served to me by my parents.

The more I thought about it, the more I decided that my parents' religious beliefs were the problem. Daddy had spent most of my childhood running to the woods to avoid bill collectors, but he also believed we had to be perfect and stop sinning before Jesus came. I was tired of preparing for the end of the world. Fears of not being ready still haunted me. And every time my parents judged me, it re-awakened the old nightmares about being judged by God.

And it wasn't just my parents. It felt like God was letting me down, too. Hadn't I tried to be a good person since childhood? Why couldn't God answer my prayers to help us get along?

Trying to sort out my feelings, I turned to writing and wrote a poem. I was tired of people telling me how to spend my money, what to eat and wear, and how to live.

When I finished the poem, I remembered what Mara said when I bought my Kitchen Aid. She was right. We didn't need to justify how we spent our money. She was the most hard-working person in the family, and she wrote poetry, too. If anyone could understand my predicament, it might be her. I decided to give her a call.

Despite our Thanksgiving disagreement, my phone call to Mara started friendly. I asked about her baby, and she asked how Christmas dinner went. She lived hours away, so I wasn't upset that she couldn't make it for Christmas.

Finally, I got up the nerve to share my poem. After I read it, Mara was quiet, which wasn't a good sign. It usually meant she disagreed but was afraid to say so.

"What are you thinking?"

"Honestly? I think it sounds like a selfish poem."

"What?" I was caught off guard by her judgmental tone.

"Add up all the times you used the words I or me."

"Of course, it has personal pronouns—it's a poem about how I feel."

"But rules for healthy eating are for our health."

"Healthy eating is a personal choice, and no one lives or dies because of one holiday meal. That's just control."

She remained silent.

I exhaled. "Well, maybe my poem is a little selfish. It's almost like I have to be selfish after all the things Daddy's done."

"What do you mean?"

"Like when he lied about me to Dylan in Louisiana."

"I asked him about that, and he says he doesn't even remember saying that."

My stomach felt like I'd swallowed lead. If Daddy continued to lie about me to everyone, who would believe me?

"You know it's not enough to waltz over to Grandma's and fix a fancy meal. Maybe you should think about how Daddy feels when you go out of your way to be nice to his enemies."

"What? You weren't even there—and I didn't go out of my way. It was just a piece of pie. Ugh! I can't talk to you, so I'm hanging up." I slammed the receiver down with a bang.

I loved Mara. She was my first playmate and friend, and I felt devastated whenever we disagreed. But whenever Daddy entered our conversation, she seemed less like a friend and more like an extension of him. I wasn't sure which hurt worse—Daddy lying about me or my sister believing his lies. I felt outnumbered and bullied. My only comfort was that Dylan was a witness, and he knew the truth.

A few days later, the phone rang. It was Abby calling from Wisconsin to say she and her family were moving back to the Portland area. They needed to find jobs and a place to rent. I invited them to stay with us until they found a place. I finally had a guest room and guests who needed to use it. Abby and her family were the most precious guests I could imagine. As I hung up the phone, my heart filled with joy to think of seeing my little sister again.

31 Greatest Love of All

*If you are always trying
to be normal, you will never
know how amazing you can be.
-Maya Angelou*

A few days before Abby arrived, I drove into town to stock up on supplies. I wanted to be prepared if Abby's family was going to stay with us.

I was driving home singing with the Christian radio station when a catchy song caught my ear. It was "Jesus Will Still Be There" by Point of Grace.

The song claimed that Jesus would still be there, but I knew better. From childhood, I'd been given a long list of things that would offend God and destroy my salvation. Daddy had warned me about "cheap grace" since I was a child, and in the past, I'd dismissed this song as bad theology.

Perhaps it was my shifting perspective on Daddy's beliefs, but this time, as I listened to the words, I thought about finding money in the grape juice aisle, surviving the ice storm, and Dylan's steadfast love. I realized God had come through for me—even though I wasn't a perfect Christian.

I was so overcome by the idea of Jesus giving me unconditional love that I had to pull off the road because tears were distorting my vision.

"Jesus, are you really there?"

As the song faded and another came on, I turned the radio off and continued to hum it all the way home.

I got a taste of Jesus that day. It was like a quick flash of lightning illuminating my soul. And it was just enough to make me want more.

That night, I put on a movie about Jesus. I watched it every night for a week, and when I finished, I started over again. I noticed how Jesus seemed to love everyone he met unconditionally. I couldn't get enough of this Jesus. The possibility that Jesus could love me like those people in the video filled me with wonder.

As I began to embrace Jesus's unconditional love, I knew Daddy would judge me. He wanted me to share his views on what a Christian should do and be, but I was no longer willing to jump through hoops to get God's or my parents' love. I reasoned that if Jesus would accept me, they could, too.

Grace permeated my thoughts as I prepared the large attic room for Abby's family. If Jesus loved me, surely he loved Abby and her precious family. I was beginning to realize that Jesus loved all of us—from Mara and Kip to Daddy and Momma. I hesitated to think about it, but surely Jesus was there for Jake, too—even though he was no longer a believer.

My goals morphed from trying to be normal and setting a perfect table to simply allowing myself and others to be loved.

By the time Abby and her family arrived, I was so convicted of God's grace that I no longer cared what Daddy thought about what I ate, wore, or what music I listened to. Now that I'd discovered God's unconditional love, I was determined to be myself, and only myself. And I hoped to give that gift to others.

It was fun to have our home filled with children's chatter and laughter. Abby's older boys enjoyed playing table games and watching the children's movies we bought for them. The youngest was a cuddly two-year-old. Each child was full of wonder, and having them in my home seemed to magically wash the pain from my heart.

They arrived in winter when the coastal air was damp and frigid enough to chill us to the bone. Even though we didn't have snow, the white, frosty grass was a reminder to grab some gloves when we went outside.

Despite the cold weather, I noticed that Abby's husband, Diego, kept eating his meals on the front porch. It had been years since he'd been violent to her, and with maturity, he'd grown into a kinder person. I was beginning to like him. He deserved God's grace as much as I did.

One day, Abby and I were eating lunch around the table with the kids when I glanced at the thermometer and noticed it was thirty degrees outside.

"Why is Diego eating on the porch?"

Abby rolled her eyes.

"He started that when Daddy and Momma lived with us. They don't like him eating meat at the table."

I jumped up and marched out the front door.

"Diego, please come inside and eat with your family. It's too cold to eat out here."

He shook his head. "It's okay. I don't want to make you sick with my food."

"That's nonsense. When Dylan and I were on Tour, we ate at the table while other people ate meat all the time, and it never made us sick."

He looked surprised.

"Are you sure?"

"Yes. Please, come eat with your family where you belong."

From then on, Diego ate with us at the table. It felt good to include my brother-in-law, but I still had more lessons to learn.

Daddy and Momma came over to visit and see their grandchildren one Sunday. The rest of us were planning to see the movie Titanic. Dylan and I had already seen it once, and we were eager to share it with the rest of the family.

I decided to take a risk and asked my parents to join us. I was surprised when they came along.

We went to the early matinee. The only person who was not impressed with the movie was our two-year-old nephew, who required exorbitant amounts of candy and frequent walks to the lobby to sustain him.

After the movie, we went back to our house with Daddy and Momma following behind us.

Diego surprised me by offering to help with supper. He wanted to make what some call breakfast burritos. Knowing none of us ate eggs, he asked if I'd make a large batch of scrambled tofu, a vegan substitute for scrambled eggs.

While I mixed up the tofu, Diego made Mexican-style rice, then he opened the fridge and pulled out tortillas and fresh ingredients to make salsa. While Diego chopped tomatoes and cilantro, I squeezed the limes. When we were finished, he showed everyone how to fill the tortillas with scrambled tofu, rice, and vegetables. It was delicious.

As I savored my burrito, I looked around the table, and my heart overflowed with joy to see my family eating together while they discussed the movie and laughed at the antics of my youngest nephew. This was what I'd been craving my entire life. I marveled that it was my brother-in-law who brought us together by preparing this feast. In a magnanimous act of grace, Diego had invited me to my own table.

All evening, I kept my eye on Daddy, bracing for some new conflict, but it was such a joyful gathering that I began to dream of bringing the family together again.

A few days later, while Abby and I were folding laundry, Jake's name came up.

I told her about Thanksgiving and Christmas. She despised conflict and always did her best to stay out of family fights.

"I don't understand. Why can't everybody just get along?"

She set a stack of neatly folded shirts on the table with a sigh. "I haven't seen Jake for a while."

I spread the kids' socks across the table, searching for the mates.

"I've spent too much of my life trying to get Daddy's approval, and I'm afraid I've let you, Jake, and Mara down."

"What do you mean?"

"Jake was the first to speak up about the way we were raised. Remember that Thanksgiving when we lived in Sunnyside? The rest of us talked about him behind his back because he stopped going to church. Momma and Daddy thought he was being bitter."

"I understand it makes Momma sad. She just wants all of us to be saved." Abby set a stack of jeans on the table and began folding underwear.

"Yes, but saved from what? Momma's sadness doesn't cancel Jake's right to think for himself. We should treat him with as much respect as the rest of us."

Abby remained quiet.

"Look, I've done some stupid things like dumping that potted plant over Carrie's head and not standing up for Jake when everyone scapegoated him. No wonder he rarely hangs out with the family."

"I don't think Jake is trying to avoid us, he just gets depressed. I miss him."

Her dark almond-shaped eyes reminded me of a sad puppy. She and Jake were only ten-and-a-half months apart. They'd always been close—closer than any of us.

"It's almost his birthday. Why don't we plan an over-the-hill party for his thirtieth and invite the entire family."

"What a great idea. All the little cousins will have fun playing together."

Abby loaded the laundry basket and carried the clothes upstairs while I made a list of party supplies.

After Diego's dinner, I'd found a new sense of hope for family gatherings. I just knew Jake's party would be a success—if for no other reason than Jake himself was coming. Everyone agreed to show up for Jake's birthday. I knew throwing a party wouldn't make Jake a believer, but such hope might keep the rest of the family on their best behavior. For the first time in years, my entire family would be together. My dream was finally coming true.

32 What's Love Got to Do with It

*The price of anything
is the amount of life
you exchange for it.*
-Henry David Thoreau

By the age of thirty-five, I still had neither tasted an egg nor touched one. I was still following my parents' house rules despite living on my own for fifteen years. The only time I saw Momma break this rule was on her grandchildren's birthdays. A store-bought cake was the closest she ever came to eating an egg. If you were to ask me if this mattered, I'd say worrying about what other people ate was low on my priorities.

When it came to making a birthday cake for Jake on his 30th birthday, the idea to put an egg in the cake wasn't even my idea—it was Carrie's. When I called to plan the party, she had one suggestion.

"It sounds like fun." Her voice lowered as she spoke directly into the phone. "But are you going to put an egg in the cake?"

I cringed at the thought. "I hadn't thought about it." I sighed. "Did you know half of the family has gone vegan?"

"Well, your brother likes to bake from scratch these days. He always complains about your family making cakes without eggs. He hates it when they fall apart."

"I remember Jake serving me cake while I was visiting you guys once. It was an exquisite chocolate layered cake. It looked like it came from a bakery."

She laughed. "Yeah, that's Jake."

I suddenly felt stressed about making a cake for my brother, but I couldn't ask him to make his own cake. How hard was it to crack a couple of eggs?

"Sure, I'll do it for Jake. Why not?"

Carrie sounded relieved. "Thank you. I look forward to seeing everyone."

I was grateful for my sister-in-law. Despite our rocky start when I dumped that potted plant over her head, she'd never held it against me, and we'd become friends. At every family gathering, she did her share of the work. And she was always thoughtful and friendly.

On the morning of Jake's birthday, I got up early to bake the cake. Abby and her family were still living with us. Mara and her baby had arrived with my parents the night before. Kip had to work, so he wasn't there.

I hummed while I set out the ingredients for the cake. My heart was filled with affection for my brother. I hoped he'd be surprised to find the entire family waiting to celebrate him. I wanted to be sure the cake was finished, and the house decorated by the time he arrived.

I opened the fridge and stared at the egg carton. Cracking an egg open felt like a formidable task. Momma had warned me about the dangers of eggs my entire life. She said they contained salmonella and cancer. Just touching one would require a thorough bleaching of my skin and any surfaces it touched.

I turned on the oven and laid a double layer of paper towels across the counter. Next, I studied the cake mix box for clues on how to crack an egg. I'd heard of people leaving shells in a cake. The last thing I wanted was for my brother to find white shells in his chocolate cake. I also wondered if I needed to use all three eggs as the box suggested, or would one egg be enough to hold it together? I decided to use three because I wasn't sure.

Finally, I'd put it off as long as I could, and it was time to crack my first egg. Carefully opening the carton, I cradled the white oval gently in my hand. It felt different than I'd imagined. I thought it would be light, like a Cadbury chocolate egg, but it felt like there was a weight inside that moved around when I turned it.

When Mara entered the kitchen to get her baby a bottle, I was staring at the egg like it was a piece of kryptonite.

"What are you doing?"

"I'm cracking an egg for the cake."

"Why do you have to do that? We've always made our cakes without eggs. Why start now?"

"It's not my choice. It's for Jake. He's not vegan, and he hates cakes that fall apart."

By the look on her face, I could tell she was upset.

"Why does it matter? Every time one of the kids has a birthday, we eat store-bought cakes."

"Not my kid. I made him a homemade banana cake."

"That's fine, but this is Jake's birthday, and he likes eggs.

She started putting her shoes on.

"I'm going for a walk."

"I thought you were feeding the baby."

"I'll do it when you're not in the kitchen." Her voice was curt.

"Honestly, Mara, why is food always such a big deal?"

"My baby has never tasted dairy, let alone an egg."

"He's still a baby. He won't even know what he's missing. You can give him something else while the rest of us have cake."

"Why are you so rude?"

"I'm not trying to be rude. I'm thinking of Jake."

"Well, he's not the only one eating here."

"Mara, I don't understand. When I was at your house, you told me you always use a brand of pancake mix, which has eggs. How is putting an egg in a cake any different?"

She ignored my question. "I'm just thinking about Momma and Daddy. You know they've never had an egg in their house. You're supposed to honor your parents."

"Why does every family dinner have to be about controlling people with food?"

"It's not about control—it's about the health message."

I turned at the sound of Daddy's voice. He'd slipped into the kitchen behind me.

"But it is about control. You guys can eat whatever you want in your own homes. Today isn't about the health message—it's Jake's birthday."

Daddy's voice lowered like he was talking to a child.

"Cheri, doesn't it seem more Christ-like to avoid using eggs if the majority of us don't eat them?"

"I fully expected you to take Mara's side."

I bristled with anger.

"You have seven grandkids, and every time they have a birthday, we all enjoy a store-bought cake. What's the difference between a store-bought cake with eggs and one baked at home?"

"The difference is that you can choose not to put the egg in at home." Mara glared at me.

With Mara and Daddy both standing in my kitchen yelling at me, the entire universe seemed to be spinning.

"You guys ruined Thanksgiving by switching the menu to vegan, and I'm sick of your control games. It's Jake's birthday, and I'm using an egg."

Dylan had entered the kitchen, and Momma watched from the doorway with wide eyes.

Towering over me, Daddy raised his hand and his voice.

"For crying out loud, Cheri, why do you always have to dig up the past?"

Dylan protectively stepped between us, thinking Daddy might hit me, but I was the one who snapped.

Standing as tall as I could, I looked Daddy right in the eye and shouted.

"Get the fuck out of my house! And don't you ever yell at me or raise your hand to me again!"

Daddy's face grew red, then he turned to Momma.

"Get your stuff. We're leaving."

Mara rolled her eyes at me.

"Now look what you've done."

She'd gotten a ride with our parents, and now she had to leave with them, but by the look on her face, she didn't mind.

Momma shook her head slowly, like I was lost forever.

"For Pete's sake, Cheri, Jesus is coming!"

Still angry, I yelled, "Who cares if Jesus is coming? What's the point if we can't treat each other with love and respect?"

I could hear Daddy honking the horn impatiently while Momma and Mara rushed around the house, gathering up their stuff.

That's when I remembered Jake. He'd be coming to his birthday party, and half of the family would be gone. It was all my fault. I had to undo what I'd done.

I ran outside and knelt in the gravel by the driver's door. If there was ever a time to grovel, this was it.

"Daddy, I'm sorry. Please stay for Jake's sake. He's the non-believer. What a terrible witness if we Christians can't get along enough to celebrate his birthday."

Daddy didn't look at me.

"Please, Daddy, you don't have to forgive me. Just stay for Jake. You don't even have to speak to me. Please, just stay for Jake's sake." By now, tears were streaming down my face.

Abby and Dylan stood on the front porch watching while Daddy handed the keys to Mara so she could put her stuff in the trunk. Momma added her bags, and then Mara grabbed the baby and hooked him into the car seat. They slammed both doors for emphasis.

I continued to beg. It was my only hope.

"Momma! Can't you help him see that we need to get along for Jake's sake?"

No one in the car looked at me. Not Momma. Not Mara. And not Daddy, who stared straight out the windshield, started the engine, and drove away.

33 Straight from the Heart

*The paradox of trauma is
that it has both the power
to destroy and the power
to transform and resurrect.
-Peter A. Levine*

I don't know how long I knelt in the driveway, but the sharp pain from pieces of gravel cutting into my knees was nothing compared to the suffocating ache in my chest.

Moisture fell on my arms. Was it raining, or were my tears just soaking everything around me? I was vaguely aware of Dylan gently lifting me by the arm and leading me up the steps and into the house. My legs shook like jelly as he guided me up the stairs, where I collapsed onto the bed.

By the time he brought me a cup of tea and a cool washcloth, my sinuses were plugged, my eyes were red, and my throat was too parched to speak.

Sipping the tea, I placed the cool cloth over my burning eyes.

"I've finally sealed my fate. No one in this family will ever believe I'm a good Christian now."

"Who cares what they think?"

"They'll assume I'm lost—except Jake, but even Jake wouldn't use the F word on Daddy."

Abby stuck her head inside the door. "Are you okay?"

I shrugged my shoulders. "No matter how hard I try, I can't win."

"Give it time. It will eventually blow over."

When she left to feed her hungry baby, Dylan turned to me.

"It's going to be okay."

"I don't know how. Momma says angry words can never be taken back."

"That's her perspective. I've never been so proud of you in my life—you finally stood up for yourself."

I appreciated Dylan's support, but I could barely hear him over the roaring in my ears. None of us had mobile phones and panic was rising in my throat when I realized Jake was on his way to our house. There was no way to let him know that half of the family had left his party before it even got started.

"Jake expects everyone to be here. What am I going to do?"

"You're going downstairs to bake your brother a birthday cake."

"I can't. It wasn't my idea to use eggs in the first place, and I don't even know how to crack one.

"I'll help, and everything will be okay."

There was no bakery in the tiny town we lived in, so I had no choice but to go downstairs. I tried to smile like I was happy as I walked past the wide-eyed stares of my nephews, who'd never seen their Aunt Cheri yell like a maniac before.

Dylan cracked three eggs and mixed the cake in the Kitchen Aid while I beat the frosting with the hand mixer. I ended up emptying an entire container of black food coloring to get it dark enough.

As the aroma of baking chocolate filled the house, I focused on the creative process, and my racing heart began to calm down.

Once the cake was cool, I spread the black mass of icing across it and set a tombstone candle with the number thirty on one side. I wrote, "Happy Birthday, Jake," across the other two-thirds of the cake with neon pink, green, and orange tubes of icing.

It wasn't a fancy bakery cake, but it was a step up from the lemon cake I'd made when he was five. That cake had been a disaster because I'd accidentally caught my hair in the beaters, and Daddy had to cut me free. Tears threatened to undo me at the memory. A lot had happened in twenty-five years, but one thing was still true: I loved my brother.

Jake and Carrie finally arrived, bringing two more nephews and a niece. For a few minutes, I was distracted by admiring their baby girl, but I knew sooner or later I'd need to explain why Daddy and

Momma weren't there. Lowering my voice so the kids wouldn't hear, I took Jake aside.

"Momma, Daddy, and Mara were here, but they left."

I noticed he was clenching his jaw while I told the story.

"Mara was upset because I was putting an egg in the cake, then we got into an argument, and Daddy took her side and yelled at me. When he raised his hand, I snapped and told him to get the fuck out of my house."

Jake's eyebrows raised as he heard me confess that I swore at Daddy. He took the news as well as could be expected, considering a family fight had ruined his birthday party before he arrived.

After listening to our conversation, Carrie threw her hands up in despair.

"I'm sorry. When I asked you to put an egg in the cake, I didn't realize it would be such a big deal."

Jake and Carrie understood, but a dark shadow hung over the house. Jake's party was much quieter than I'd planned.

Jake seemed to enjoy the cake, perhaps because he realized the personal cost for me to make it. He was being kind. A cake from a mix couldn't begin to compare to any cake he had baked. But this party had never been about the cake—it was supposed to be about Jake. I'd planned this celebration to show my only brother how much we all loved him. I was heartsick every time I remembered how I'd failed to pull it off.

The next morning, Jake surprised me by running to the local store and bringing not just a dozen but eighteen eggs into my kitchen.

He smiled in that endearing way he had since he was a little boy and asked if he could use my frying pan. I knew this was a test to see if I would practice the tolerance I preached. I wanted him to feel at home in my kitchen, so I nodded my approval. I hid my nausea while he cracked a bowl of eggs in front of me and made omelets for the entire family. He even made one for me, which I graciously declined, but Dylan was happy to eat it.

After sleeping outside in a tent, the rain had left Jake's family with wet sleeping bags. I volunteered to go to the laundromat with him while our spouses played table games with the kids.

It'd been years since I'd been alone with my brother. I always cherished time alone with my siblings because we could speak uncensored without our parents or spouses present. Such moments allowed us to be fully ourselves and talk about the things we'd been warned not to speak about.

As we sat watching the dryers spin, I started to tell Jake about my church.

"They're very open and friendly."

Jake tossed his head back.

"I hope you're not trying to convert me, Cheri—it won't work. You can't make people believe in something they don't."

My face felt hot. On some level, I supposed I was still trying to convert him.

"Oh, I didn't mean to push—it's just that church has helped me cope with life."

"I'm glad that works for you, but it doesn't help me. My counselor told me that most people who leave controlling religion are in therapy. Many of us are trying to recover from all types of legalism."

"Have you ever tried going to another church—like a different denomination?"

"To be honest, every church I enter leaves me physically ill."

"I understand. Sometimes, when I walk through a church, I feel like the Persuader is stalking me, but I break its spell by breaking the rules. I chew gum and gossip during the sermon to remind myself that I'm free."

"I don't think I'll ever get over the Persuader. That's why I don't spank my kids."

"I'm proud of you."

We sat in silence for a few minutes.

I was still blaming myself and felt the need to apologize.

"Jake, I'm so sorry."

He grimaced. "Look, I appreciate everything you've done, Sis, but I didn't expect much. Every family gathering disappoints me."

The pain on my brother's face was so deep that I ached for him. I questioned how I could have let so much time and distance come between us.

He continued. "Have you ever thought about how much easier life would be if we didn't have to deal with all this crap? I mean, it's always there in the back of my mind."

I nodded. "Nobody but our family fights over an egg in a cake."

"But it's not really about an egg—or even a swear word—is it? It's all about control."

"I hate how we kids have been afraid to talk to each other about stuff for years."

"It's not fair when they ask us to ignore the past."

"But it is the Christian way to forgive and forget."

I winced as soon as I said the word Christian. I knew it would be better to leave religious terms out of my conversation with Jake.

"I disagree. Look at how you always do that and get hurt."

"I'm just trying to be unselfish."

"And that's another thing I hate about Christians. They teach kids to put everybody else first when they need to love themselves. Even Jesus said to love your neighbor as yourself—not better than yourself."

I thought of Mara calling my poem selfish.

"Perhaps you're right."

Jake put his arm around me, then lowered his voice as if Daddy and the Persuader were standing over his shoulder. "My counselor says we'll never be able to live until our parents are dead."

His words hit me like a slap in the face. Tears filled my eyes. I didn't want my parents to die, but I wanted to live.

34 You're the Inspiration

*Your heart knows the way,
run in that direction.*
-Rumi

When Jake left, I could barely crawl out of bed. I didn't even shower for three days. Even though we'd had a good talk, I couldn't shake my depression over yet another failed family gathering.

I could only guess how Jake's visit with Daddy and Momma went. Everything I said and did and cooked would be discussed and rehashed. I knew they considered me a "bad" Christian for swearing. But the truth was my choices—from music to the way I dressed and wore makeup to the books I read and the way I prayed—had aroused their suspicion for years.

I didn't hear from Mara. Whenever I picked up the phone to call her, I remembered what she said about my poem being selfish and set it back down. I sensed those were not really Mara's thoughts as much as they were Daddy's, but I couldn't take the chance on more heartbreak.

I'm not sure how I would've survived without Dylan's love—or Abby's support. When we agreed my sister and her family could live with us, I had no idea that I'd need them as much as they needed a place to land. When Abby and Diego finally found jobs and got an apartment in Portland, our house seemed strangely quiet.

I didn't hear from Jake once he went home. I figured he was lost in his own world again. I couldn't blame him because we hadn't been close for years. The more I thought about it, the more I realized no one in our family seemed close.

Each of my siblings was important to me in a different way. As the sister closest to me, Mara knew what we had survived more than anyone else. She was smart in ways I wasn't, and I relied on her other ways of thinking to help me cope with life.

Abby, who was once my baby sister, had surpassed me in maturity as a loving and wise mother of boys. I couldn't imagine my life without sharing her children since I had none of my own. Each sibling and their children were precious, and I tried to remember every birthday.

Jake was the bravest of all of us, he took a stand to be himself despite criticism from our parents. His parting words were stuck on repeat in my head. I wondered how any of us could live as long as our parents were alive to make us feel fear, shame, and guilt for not being like them.

A month later, Carrie called.

"Can you give me your family's gluten steak recipe?"

"Sure, let me get my recipe box."

As she repeated the list of ingredients back to me, I heard a tremor in her voice.

"What's wrong, Carrie?"

"I'm worried about your brother. He's depressed. I'm trying to make a special dinner to cheer him up."

As I set the phone down, a gnawing ache filled my gut. I wasn't the only one who was hurting. I loved my brother. He deserved the love of his family and the party that Abby and I had planned for him. Why had Daddy thought it more important to refuse forgiveness to a daughter than to celebrate his only son?

Four months went by, and I still hadn't heard from my parents. I stretched my brain, trying to comprehend what happened. How could something as beautiful as a birthday party turn into a family fight?

It was hard to override the religious training that I'd been fed my entire life. I'd been taught that God withheld love from people who used the F-word. In my parents' eyes, I'd committed an unpardonable sin. Maybe I had gone beyond their love this time.

I could still hear Mara's voice echoing in my head.

"You're supposed to honor your parents."

I felt like a sinner shut out of Noah's ark and doomed to die alone for cursing at my father.

But no matter what Daddy and Momma had done or not done, they were my parents, and I desperately wanted them in my life. I wondered if we'd ever be a family again.

The only good thing that came from this separation was that I'd stopped sending my parents money.

I told Dylan, "It might sound selfish, but it is nice to have our paycheck back."

He replied, "That's not selfish—it's how normal people live."

Dylan planned a vacation to cheer me up. We'd often dreamed of visiting Banff and Jasper National Parks in Canada. That summer seemed like a good time. We enjoyed traveling through rugged mountains with blue-green lakes with lots of elk and deer.

Whenever I took a picture, I thought of showing it to Momma. Then I remembered we hadn't spoken for months, and tears blurred my vision, leaving my photographs out of focus.

We saw a large cooler that a grizzly had ripped open as we drove into Banff National Park. Tufts of insulation stuck out of the large plastic chest like orange clown hair. Momma's worst-case scenarios filled my brain when I saw it, and I panicked.

Dylan laughed, but I saw nothing funny about it. If a bear could do that to a cooler, it could do worse to my body. I was terrified to sleep in the tent, so Dylan removed the van seat and propped it against a tree next to the campfire. Then he laid our foam sleeping mats on the van floor. It turned out to be a safe and comfortable bed.

We hiked on some of the most gorgeous trails I'd ever seen, but my heart kept tugging at the distance between myself and my parents. It was a painful distraction—much like a tongue that keeps returning to a broken tooth.

On our last night in the park, we sat on our makeshift sofa by the campfire and discussed the things we'd seen while we roasted vegetarian hotdogs.

Dylan turned his hotdog over the fire and asked, "What was your favorite part of this vacation?"

"The mountains and blue-green lakes. I wish I could share them with Momma—she loves mountains, and she'd love the color of those lakes. What was your favorite thing?"

"Banff Hot Springs."

I thought of the heated pool where the mountains seemed so close I could almost touch them.

"It was surreal to soak in mineral waters with people from all over the world—many speaking in a foreign language." Dylan pulled out a hotdog bun and dressed his sandwich while he spoke. "It was like a family of strangers. We were different, yet everyone belonged."

"I'm glad you can imagine strangers as family, but I still crave my own flesh and blood."

Later, as the shadows closed in, Dylan slid closer to me and opened a bag of marshmallows.

"Why is it so hard to let go of your family?"

My eyes flooded with tears. "My family means everything to me. I understand why Daddy got offended, but I didn't do anything to Momma. Why does she always take his side?"

"You don't know she took his side. Maybe she can't override his anger."

"I've thought about calling to apologize, but I don't want another fight, and I don't think saying fuck can be undone."

Dylan shrugged his shoulders.

"Isn't there a Bible verse that says fathers shouldn't provoke their children to anger?"

He rarely spoke about other people, but after being in the family for ten years, Dylan knew my family well.

I felt a rush of love for this man who sheltered me and allowed me to be myself.

"I finally understand that you weren't being selfish when you asked me to choose between you and my family at the river—you were just trying to protect me."

Keeping his arm around me, he picked up a stick to stir the coals with the other. We watched orange sparks rise and scatter throughout the dark trees above us.

"All I've ever wanted was to sit around a table and share a meal with my family like normal people."

Sliding a marshmallow onto the stick, Dylan held it over the glowing coals.

"What if that never happens? Are you going to spend the rest of your life waiting and crying?"

I thought about what Jake said. I wanted to live while my parents were still alive.

"Maybe we should move. I'm happier when we don't live near my family."

"Where would you like to go?"

"I'm tired of traveling. I want to move somewhere familiar, maybe back to western Washington."

We sat in silence while we contemplated yet another move. The marshmallow turned golden brown. Dylan pulled it from the coals and held it out to me.

"I hate to move away from Momma, but maybe if I live further away, I won't fall into the trap of hoping they'll come over."

"Even when they do, you're often disappointed."

I felt myself reviving at the thought of a new place to explore.

"What do you think? Can you find another job?"

"We won't know until I try, but let's do it!"

With our future up in the air and the grizzlies and my family forgotten for the moment, we joked and played cards by lantern light.

When we finally snuggled into our makeshift bed at the back of the van, I marveled at the freedom I had with Dylan. I was always welcome to speak my mind, to have an opinion, to disagree, to win a game—with no retaliation. The contrast between Dylan and Daddy was like oil and water. I wondered what I'd done to deserve this man.

I thought of all the places we'd been and realized home wasn't a building. Dylan was my family, and wherever we were together, became home.

Two days later, we passed the International Peace Arch at the Canada-United States border. I felt overcome with emotion to be back in northwest Washington—my childhood home.

A familiar shape loomed in the distance. A phone booth stood beside the road like a beacon. The receiver swung below the change box as though someone had called and left it off the hook, just waiting for me to answer.

I thought of all the hours I'd stood on aching feet to hear my parents' voices. I'd endured every kind of weather, from Michigan winters to Louisiana summers and every season in between, to have a relationship with them through a phone line. I'd hoped those long-distance days were over, but now I was planning to move again.

As we approached the phone, my superpowers began to awaken. It was time to use my elephant memory, remind Daddy of the past, and speak the truth in love.

I glanced at Dylan.

"Can you pull over?"

He raised his eyebrow, and I could tell by the set of his jaw that he didn't think this was a wise idea, but he turned the wheel anyway.

Fishing around in the console between the seats, I found twelve quarters—just enough to talk for twelve minutes. I jumped out of the van and stepped into the booth. Once the quarters had clinked into the machine, I punched in the number and held my breath.

It rang several times before I heard Daddy's voice.

"Hello."

I froze. Perhaps this wasn't such a good idea. Then I remembered I had twelve minutes to make my point.

"Hi, Daddy, it's Cheri."

"Oh, hi, I was just thinking about you."

"I'm at a phone booth and don't have much time to talk, but I just called to say I love you.

I paused.

Also, I want to say I'm sorry for telling you to get out of my house. I'm not sure what happened, but when you yelled and raised your hand over me, something in my mind just snapped. It reminded me of all the times you yelled and hit me with the belt when I was a kid."

The silence on the other end increased the tension in my neck. I hoped calling wasn't a mistake.

"Cheri, listen to me."

I braced myself while he stuttered, "I, uh, I'm sorry for every time I ever hit you or yelled at you…"

He paused, and I could tell he was getting all choked up.

"And I promise I'll never do those things again."

My eyes began to water as I whispered, "Thank you, Daddy."

"I wasn't perfect. None of us are, honey, but I'm sorry."

When I got back into the car, Dylan saw my tears.

"Are you ok?"

"Yeah, he apologized for every time he ever hit me."

I was glad Dylan didn't start the car right away. I needed a moment to savor Daddy's words and let them sink in.

"If he's sorry, then it wasn't my fault."

Dylan pounded his fist against the steering wheel. "Of course not."

He slowly turned the key in the ignition and started the car, then looked at me.

"Do you still want to move?"

I narrowed my eyes to the road ahead.

"Yes. I can forgive, but I will never forget."

35 Epilogue-I'm Still Standing

*Freedom is what you do
with what's been done to you.
-Sartre*

"Be careful!" I called as Dylan climbed the ladder to hang a cobalt blue ornament from the ceiling.

"Are you worried about me or your precious ornament!" He teased.

To be safe, I ran to the foot of the ladder to hold it steady. Then, I followed him throughout the room until eighteen blue ornaments of varying hues and shapes hung over the table, shimmering in the afternoon sun.

White linen was soon spread across two long tables set end to end. A large blue vase filled with orange roses nestled in the center among the red, orange, and yellow leaves stolen from the maple down the road.

Dylan set out the plates and stemware while I opened the oven to make sure the vegetarian stuffing and gluten steaks were golden brown. The scent of toasted mushrooms and onions in sour cream gravy filled the house and made my stomach growl.

I loved our home among the Skagit Valley tulip fields. The living room window overlooked Mount Baker. It was close to Whidbey Island, where I grew up, and most importantly, we had a group of church friends who were joining us for dinner.

I was setting out baskets of homemade dinner rolls, cranberry sauce, and candied yams when we heard a knock at the door. Our first guest was Caroline, a woman my parents' age, who sometimes annoyed me with her long lectures, but she had a good heart.

"Happy Friendsgiving!"

She looked over the table. "It all looks so lovely. I hope I don't offend you because I can't eat soy, I'm gluten intolerant, and I'm definitely not a fan of candied yams. I'm afraid you've invited a diehard carnivore to your vegetarian feast."

I searched the table full of my holiday favorites and turned back to her.

"Can you tell me what you'd eat if you could eat anything?"

She smiled. "It's okay, dear. I'm used to vegetarian potlucks. I can always eat potato chips and carrot sticks."

I thought of all the times I'd eaten those same two foods on tour and how they didn't seem special enough for a holiday meal. I wanted to serve something Caroline would enjoy.

"You never know what we might have in the pantry."

"Well, since you asked, I love cheddar cheese, plain potato chips, and sweet pickles."

A quick search revealed that we had none of those items on hand.

I motioned at Dylan, who was greeting more guests, and tossed my head for him to meet me in the kitchen.

"What's up?"

"Can you run to the corner store and get some cheddar, plain potato chips, and sweet pickles?"

Always willing to serve, he grabbed his keys and ran out the door.

The house was soon filled with a couple dozen adults and several children. What started as a young adult fellowship had begun to include people of all ages. We took pride in embracing everyone, no matter what their age.

With so many people, the conversations were lively. Everybody seemed to be having a good time, including Caroline, who nibbled on her pickles and cheese while she told stories to the rest of us.

After the pies were served, I looked around the room, listening to the happy chatter of friends laughing with friends. I marveled that we'd only lived in Mount Vernon for a short time, and these faces around the table had already become dear to me.

I'd read somewhere that friends are the family we choose, but I wasn't sure if the word family was adequate. Families come with judgment and expectations, while friends don't bring so much baggage. I was learning that true friends, whether blood or not, embrace us for who we are and with gratitude for whatever we have to offer.

Long after everyone finished their pie, we sat around telling stories. This was my favorite part. Oh, how I ached to experience moments like this with my family.

The sun had set by the time I got up to clear the table. That's when I overheard Caroline mention my name.

"I'm grateful for Cheri and Dylan hosting this meal. I have no family of my own anymore, and your group is so inclusive that it warms my heart. Thank you for including me."

As our friends said goodnight, one husband turned to me and said, "I believe your greatest gift is hospitality."

I smiled. His wife was an amazing hostess and probably a better cook than me, but it felt good to be validated for my gifts.

Hours later, after everyone had gone home, Dylan helped me rinse and load the dishwasher.

I was basking in the joy of being my authentic self. For the first time in my life, I felt like a normal person. I still missed my family, and I'd never stop dreaming of gathering them around the table, but I couldn't make it happen by myself. For now, I was content to host dinner parties for my friends.

Dylan's voice broke into my thoughts.

"It was nice of Caroline to say it, but do you really think we're so inclusive? It seems when it comes to church, certain people are never included."

Studying his face, I sensed the unspoken angst in his heart. If he weren't married to me, he'd be one of those on the outside—shunned because he was different.

As I snuggled into bed next to him, I was haunted by the pain on his face. It never occurred to me that he wasn't living an authentic life. He paid the bills and didn't steal or cheat. Anybody who knew Dylan would say he was a man of his word. But I wondered, was there more to being authentic? The church we belonged to expected gay people to change or pretend they were straight. How could he be authentic if he had to hide himself?

Dylan was my best family, the person I trusted most in the entire world. He'd always taken care of me and shown me unconditional love. His shelter and belief in me had set me free to be myself. I shuddered to think that the very thing he had given to me, he wasn't able to experience for himself.

There was a new gnawing in the pit of my stomach as I faced a choice I'd never considered before—was I willing to set Dylan free to be himself? What would that even look like?

We'd struggled to speak the truth on this one topic—even between best friends. It seemed too risky. There was another elephant in the room, and this one really scared me.

Acknowledgements

To Dylan,
for believing in me and supporting my writing.

To Mara, Jake, and Abby,
your memories might be different, thank you for indulging me.

To Jeannie Robinson
for your friendship and editing expertise.

To Shelley Curtis Weaver,
for friendship, writing discussions, and revisions.

To my Cousin Cheri Roberts for friendship and helping with editing,

To my Cousin Lucy Lee Roberts Krauss,
for love and encouragement to tell my stories.

To my Cousin Elton Roberts,
for asking what happened next and your loving father energy.

Thank You

Thank you to the
Beta Readers and Kindred Spirits

Wendy Miller Anderson · Cathy Rice Bechtel
Brooke Bigelow · Janet Proudy Brock · Marjory Button
Kathy Hill Clem · Trudy Morgan Cole · Sarah Cooper
Terresa Cornelius · Virginia Davidson · Anna Erickson
Bethel Freidline · Sheila May Garrow · Barbara Hall
Merry Herrman · Michelle Ruehle Lewis
Laura Dalgleish Nelson · Lanetta Lewis-Phelps
Esther Recinos · Sheila Reed · Bronwyn Reid
Margi Dalgleish Roth · Susie Schuetz · Janelle Smiley
Audrey Speer · Brit Stickle · Cindy Tutsch
Veta Wilson · JoAn Witzel · Barbara Womack
Susan Stickle Woods · Cynthia Rempel Zirkwitz

And to you, Dear Reader
Thank you for listening to my stories!

About the Author

Cherilyn Christen Clough has dreamed of writing a book about her family since she was eleven years old. Her inspiration came from the TV shows "The Waltons" and "Little House on the Prairie" because the main characters wrote stories about their family life. It took a while to catch on that her family was not going to be another Waltons. For starters, they moved too many times to count, and that was only the beginning of the differences. When she finally picked up her pen, it was because of her mother's lost dream of being like the Waltons and her own heartache due to family estrangement. She currently lives with her two cats in Portland, Oregon, where she enjoys birding, gardening, baking, and researching her family tree. She is currently writing a historical fiction series about Southern Oregon Pioneers.

Also by
Cherilyn Christen Clough

Religious Narcia: Surviving Narcissism in the Church (2024)
Chasing Eden (2019)
Love Letters 1909 (2014)

Made in United States
Troutdale, OR
07/07/2024

21062255R00235